A YEAR IN NUMBERS

KYLE D. EVANS

For Edwin & Juno

First published in the United Kingdom in 2023 by Allen & Unwin,
an imprint of Atlantic Books Ltd.

Copyright © Kyle D. Evans, 2023

10 9 8 7 6 5 4 3 2 1

A CIP catalogue record for this book is available from the British Library.

Hardback ISBN: 978 1 83895 891 6
E-book ISBN: 978 1 83895 892 3

Illustrations on pages 13, 28, 55, 56, 64, 133, 162, 168, 197, 199, 200,
224-25, 240, 241, 248, 281, 284, 305 by Hana Ayoob.

The picture acknowledgements on page 341 constitute an extension of this
copyright page.

Printed in Great Britain

Allen & Unwin
An imprint of Atlantic Books Ltd
Ormond House
26–27 Boswell Street
London
WC1N 3JZ

www.atlantic-books.co.uk

CONTENTS

INTRODUCTION

Welcome, dear reader. I'm sure you don't need instructions on how to read a book, but if I may make a few recommendations before you begin.

In my day-to-day life as a maths teacher I am constantly barraged by what I call 'nuggets': fascinating little numerical titbits that catch the attention and stick in my mind when I get home and my six-year-old asks me what I learnt at school today. These nuggets may come from students, my fellow teachers or a conversation with a colleague that jogs a memory of something I once knew but was buried in the back of my brain. I have attempted to collect a year's worth of these little gems in loosely connected themed monthly chapters.

This book is intended to be read a little bit per day, perhaps while brushing your teeth or completing another short morning routine. I appreciate, however, that you may find the book just too compelling to read in such tiny chunks and want to speed on ahead. That's fine: there's no real reason it couldn't be read like any other book.

Sometimes the factoids are so exciting and intriguing that I have had to spin them out over several days. The upshot of this is that if you seek out your birthday / anniversary / the day that you met Lee Latchford-Evans from Steps at Fleet Services, there's a small chance that you'll be dumped in the middle of something that's hard to understand in isolation. My apologies, but I'm sure you'll work it all out in the long run (actually, the kind of person who'd skip ahead to a certain day would almost certainly not read the introduction anyway).

Some of the maths is a little complicated, but I promise it's never for the sake of it. In some places where you may be interested in longer explanations, I have expanded in the Further Notes at the back of the book. There's also a glossary in the back in case you forget any word definitions along the way – glossary words are underlined the first time they appear.

I hope you enjoy this numerical trip around the sun as much as I enjoyed putting it together.

JANUARY

BUILDING BLOCKS

1 January

Happy New Year! May this year leave you healthier, wealthier and wiser than the last. Speaking of wealth, I'm afraid to report that **Amazon founder Jeff Bezos has already earned more than you will this year**. Even if you're actually reading this on 1 January. Actually, even if you started reading this entry at midnight on New Year's Day (and honestly, why wouldn't you?) then by the time you've reached the end of this sentence Bezos will have earned more than you will this year.

Bezos' earnings reportedly come in at around 9 billion dollars per month, which equates to about $3500 per second. Some estimates have the figure as low as a measly $2000 per second, but unless I have any billionaires reading my books (give us a tenner?) it's safe to say that Bezos has already earned more than you will this year. In an entirely unrelated point, around 10% of the world's population live in extreme poverty – that is, on less than $2 per day.

2 January

In this chapter we'll lay the foundations for everything that follows, so what better place to start than with 0 and 1? Think of them as the Lennon and McCartney of numbers: in many ways polar opposites, but unarguably the building blocks of everything else that follows. It may therefore be surprising that, much in the same way that the can opener was invented fifty years after canned food, **the numeral for 0 was not seen until thousands of years after that for 1.**

Cultures in Egypt, Mesopotamia and China, among others, all converged upon the familiar single stroke numeral for the number 1 between 3500 and 1500 BC.

Table showing Egyptian numerals, from Kurt Sethe, A History of Mathematical Notations Vol. I *(1928). It includes hieroglyphic, hieratic and demotic numeral symbols. Note the agreement over the numeral for 1 and the shocking lack of zeros anywhere.*

Though there were various symbols for the absence of a number across the years – the Sumerians first opting for a slanted double wedge around 5000 years ago – we would not see an empty circle to indicate zero until around the eighth century AD in China. Britain and Europe used Roman numerals up to around AD 900 – there is no zero whatsoever in this numbering system. That must have made people absolutely 51 6 500.*

3 January

In Vegas, I got into a long argument with the man at the roulette wheel over what I considered to be an odd number.

Steven Wright

There should be nothing clearer in mathematics than the designation of odd and even numbers: even numbers are those that can be shared into two equal piles; odd numbers are all the other ones. But what about zero? Can something that is essentially the absence of a number have the property of oddness or evenness? Well, yes – a pile of no sweets can be shared fairly between two people: none each. Also, zero being even preserves the even, odd, even, odd sequence that all other numbers follow. All of this is essentially a preamble to clear a path for the following revelation: **every single odd number has an 'e' in it**. When spelt in English, at least. Don't believe me? Check a few…

---

* That's LI VI D. But you knew that, right?

4 January

Many cultures have their own superstitions, including lucky and unlucky numbers. **In China, the pronunciation of the number four sounds similar to 'death', meaning that four is considered an unlucky number.*** This means that parking spaces or the floors of buildings will often go straight from 3 to 5, but it has also had a more unexpected practical downside for the superstitious.

For some time, Beijing has implemented a traffic calming measure that means that only certain cars can use inner city streets on certain days. Cars are split into five equal groups by means of the last <u>digit</u> in their car registration (tail) number, as shown in the following table (correct as of 2019):

Monday	0 and 5	Tuesday	1 and 6
Wednesday	2 and 7	Thursday	3 and 8
Friday	4 and 9		

Can you see the potential issue? Chinese drivers actively avoid having a 4 in their tail number, to an extent that is quite marked:

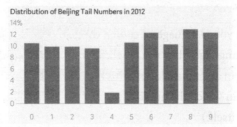

Distribution of Beijing Tail Numbers in 2012

Credit: From Anderson et al., 'Superstitions, Street Traffic and Subjective Well-being', *Journal of Public Economics*, vol. 45 (2016), pp. 1–10.

---

* Conversely, the number 5 in Thai sounds like 'ha', so 555 is a sort of shorthand for laughing, the equivalent to the detestable Western 'lol'.

Fewer drivers choosing tail numbers featuring a 4 means that days when 4-plates are allowed to drive have been measured as significantly less busy in terms of traffic. It's rare to get actual, concrete evidence of how not being superstitious can improve your daily life, but there it is: pick a 4-plate and get to work quicker.

5 January

Here's a neat and entirely non-superstitious feature of the number 4: **if you write out every number in English, 'four' is the only number that has as many letters as the size of the number itself.**

This leads to a quick and fun word game: pick any number and spell it. Count the letters in the spelling and that is your new number. Spell this number, and keep repeating the process until you eventually end up at 4. Try to form the longest chain you can:

Fifteen (seven letters) → Seven (five letters) → Five (four letters) → Four (four letters)
Seventy-seven (twelve letters) → Twelve (six letters) → Six (three letters) → Three (five letters) → Five (four letters) → Four (four letters)

If English isn't your language of choice you can play this game just as well in other languages, but you might end up at more than one final destination, or in an endless loop! (This happens in French, where there isn't a number in which the number of letters in the spelling is the same as the number itself.)

6 January

There are *definitely* two people in London with exactly the same number of hairs on their heads. Around 9 million people live in London, but there are only about 100,000 hairs on a human head, so if you tried to match all the Londoners to a list of hair numbers you would exhaust the list pretty quickly. In fact, any town or city with a population over 100,000 (Gillingham, Woking, St Helens) has two people with exactly the same number of hairs on their head.

You might think this is obvious – all you have to do is find two bald people in London; perhaps Right Said Fred are playing tonight? So how about this instead: there are definitely two people in London with exactly the same number of hairs on their *entire body*. The average body has about 5 million hair follicles, so still less than London's population. This idea is called the *pigeonhole principle*, which essentially says that if you have more pigeons than holes, you either have to put two pigeons in the same hole or a pigeon is going to go homeless.

7 January

Speaking of baldness, how many hairs would you say you'd have to remove from your head to become bald? 10,000 hairs? 50,000? 100,000? Do you think a person could ever become bald by removing a single hair?

Most people's answer to this would be: of course not. Hairs fall out all the time; every time you comb or wash your hair you lose a couple. You'd never come out of the shower and find that your spouse no longer recognizes you due to your sudden baldness.

But there lies a <u>paradox</u> within this. Imagine removing a single hair from your head, and then another, and then another. Of course it logically follows that you will eventually not have a single hair on your head; not even a Rab C. Nesbitt or a Homer Simpson wisp to comb over. So we have to accept the contradiction that **removing a single hair could never make a person bald, but by repeatedly removing a single hair a person can absolutely go from a full head of hair to completely bald**. This is sometimes known as the *bald man paradox*, and the nub of it lies in our rather woolly definition of what 'bald' actually means.

8 January

The letter 'e' is by far the most commonly used in the English language, accounting for over 12% of all letter usage.

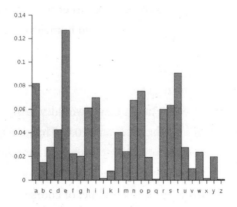

Graph showing the frequency of use of letters in the English language.

'e' is also the most commonly used letter in Spanish, French, German, Italian, Dutch, Swedish, Norwegian, Finnish and Hungarian, but it's pipped by 'a' in Turkish, Icelandic and Slovak and by 'i' in Polish.

9 January

One of the most ubiquitous paradoxes in mathematics – thanks largely to Mark Haddon's excellent novel *The Curious Incident of the Dog in the Night-Time* – is the *Monty Hall problem*, in which the contestant on a game show is offered a choice of three doors, behind which lies a prize they will take home: two of the doors have a goat behind them and one hides a car. Contestants pick a door, but rather than being shown what is behind their chosen door they are shown the goat that lies behind one of the doors they didn't pick. The contestant now faces two closed doors: one of which they have picked, the other they haven't; one hides a goat, the other a car. The question is: should the contestant stick to the door they chose, or switch to the other door?

Most people will not think that it matters whether you stick or twist, since the odds seem 50/50: two doors, one good outcome. For this reason most people tend to stick to their original choice, not wanting to switch and then lose – a bit like the worry of changing your lottery numbers on the week that the jackpot comes in on your old numbers. But **you should always switch!** Yes, it's counter-intuitive and frustrating, but it's correct.

The best way to visualize this is probably to imagine six people who play the game; we'll label them players A–F. Players A and B choose door 1, C and D choose door 2, E and F choose door 3. We'll say that the car is behind door 1, though of course it makes no difference to the rest of our calculations. So, as things stand, players A and B are in a winning position and everyone else is taking a goat home.*

Now, at the next step, half of the players will keep their door and half will change. So A stays at door 1 and wins a car, B switches to another

---

* My students often like the idea of winning the goat, but I fear they would change their minds when they actually had to take it home and put it somewhere.

door and gets goat; C and E stick with their original door and get goat; D and F switch from goat to car. Pulling this together into a table:

Player	Original choice	Stick or switch?	End choice
A	Car	Stick	Car
B	Car	Switch	Goat
C	Goat	Stick	Goat
D	Goat	Switch	Car
E	Goat	Stick	Goat
F	Goat	Switch	Car

The crucial thing now is to look at the outcomes for the stickers or switchers: the stickers get the goat two times out of three, but the switchers get the car two times out of three. It is always better to switch.

The final choice of goat or car is indeed 50/50, but *you're more likely to already have chosen a goat!* So on average you're better to switch, as two times out of three you'll be improving your lot.

You're still not convinced, are you?

10 January

All of the numbers used in the book so far are confined to the world of positive whole numbers (or positive <u>integers</u>), but of course <u>negative numbers</u> are equally valid numbers and their existence helps us to incorporate concepts such as debt into mathematical calculations. The best way to think about negative numbers is to visualize a thermometer with hot and cold temperatures: −8 is less than −3 because −8 °C is colder than −3 °C, for example. This is a concept that most children are taught at the age of 11 or 12, but just because they're taught it doesn't necessarily mean they learn it.

In 2007 in the UK, a National Lottery scratchcard based on negative numbers and temperatures had to be withdrawn from sale due to a large number of players not understanding whether or not they had won. The 'Cool Cash' card required players to scratch off a number – representing a temperature – and if it was lower (or colder, if you will) than the number printed on the card then the player was a winner. Since the card had a winter theme the temperatures involved were usually negative, leading to much confusion. The following marvellous quote was given willingly to the *Manchester Evening News* at the time, though I will protect the identity of the person who gave it:

> *I phoned Camelot and they fobbed me off with some story that –6 is higher, not lower, than –8, but I'm not having it. I think Camelot are giving people the wrong impression – the card doesn't say to look for a colder or warmer temperature, it says to look for a higher or lower number. Six is a lower number than 8. Imagine how many people have been misled.*

11 January

On the subject of chilly temperatures, **the only temperature that's the same in both the Fahrenheit and Celsius/Centigrade scales* is –40 degrees.** The formula for converting from Centigrade to Fahrenheit is to multiply by 1.8 (or $\frac{9}{5}$) and then add 32 (or to use my Dad's shorthand, 'double it and add 30', which is much easier mentally). This means a little <u>equation</u> can be formed and solved:

---

* Celsius and Centigrade are essentially the same thing now, though at one time Celsius ran the other way, so water froze at 100 degrees and boiled at 0 degrees.

$$\tfrac{9}{5}x + 32 = x$$
$$9x + 160 = 5x$$
$$4x = -160$$
$$x = -40$$

So if ever it's −40 degrees, in either scale, and someone asks you what the temperature is, you can proudly respond 'forty under' without having to worry about if they're from the United States, the Bahamas, the Cayman Islands, Liberia, Palau, the Federated States of Micronesia, the Marshall Islands or any other country that primarily uses Fahrenheit. Oh, hang on, that's an exhaustive list. Maybe those countries could just use the scale the rest of the world uses instead?

12 January

Many people's strongest recollection of mathematics lessons in school will be learning or even reciting multiplication tables. They may have stuck for life, or you may have some grey areas around the trickier <u>products</u>, but everyone did them. I personally have worked with several mathematicians who have a secure understanding of the most abstract and esoteric mathematical concepts, but who are unsure whether seven 8s are 52 or 54.*

Speaking of which, the answer to 7×8 seems to have taken on a certain folklore status in the British press and media, largely due to its regular use as a potential banana skin for politicians under questioning. In 1998 the Labour MP Stephen Byers gave the answer of '54' when asked this question in a radio interview on school standards. At the time the British prime minister, Tony Blair, responded that he 'applaud[ed]

---

* Just teasing, I know it's 58… I mean 56!

anything which gets up in lights the issues we are seeking to promote' and that 'it is one of those character-forming events', all of which seems perfectly reasonable. George Osborne had clearly been paying attention though, as by the time the then chancellor was asked the same question by seven-year-old Samuel Raddings on a *Sky News* youth panel event in 2014, he refused to answer, stating that he 'made it a rule in life not to answer a whole load of maths questions', a response indicative of the determination of a certain type of modern politician to put not getting caught out ahead of all else.

That isn't as hard as it gets though – **the hardest product in the standard multiplication tables* is 6 × 8, which should be 48** (I think). In 2013, Caddington Village School in Bedford asked 232 students to complete their times tables on an app, providing more than 60,000 individual answers. The dreaded six 8s was answered correctly by only around one in three students. The most consistently correct response was inevitably 1 × 1 = 1 (though scarily only 90% of the students got it correct – perhaps because the app credited speed of response as well as accuracy). Girls overall answered more slowly but more consistently correctly than boys, perhaps reflecting something we could learn about society as a whole.

---

* It's worth noting that this comes from a British school, where it is standard that students learn their multiplication tables up to 12 × 12. Many countries stop at 10 × 10; some go on to 15 × 15 or even 20 × 20. I have heard from a Sri Lankan friend that they learnt tables 1 to 12 and 14 to 16 – good news for any 13-fearing triskaidekaphobics. The reason for stopping at 12s seems to stem from pre-decimal British currency in which there were 12 pence in a shilling, so mental multiplication with 12s was useful. Given the bizarre current push for the re-introduction of imperial measures in the UK, this could yet become useful once again...

13 January

Some times tables are clearly easier than others, but I think we'd all agree that 2, 5, 10 and 11 are fairly easy numbers to multiply by. Oh, and 526,315,789,473,684,210. I'm serious! **This very special number is incredibly easy to multiply by numbers up to 18.** From this point on I'm going to refer to 526,315,789,473,684,210 as 'the beast', just to save on typing.

Notice that the beast has two of every digit from 1 to 8, as well as a single 0 and 9. If you want to multiply it by any number from 2 to 9, simply 'cut' the beast after the number you're multiplying by, as long as the neighbour on the other side of the cut is smaller than it. This is easier displayed than explained, so bear with me...

Say you wanted to multiply the beast by 7. There are two 7s in the beast; one followed by an 8 and the other followed by a 3. So we cut between the 7 and the 3. From our cut, we read through the beast, returning to the start when we get to the end, and adding a zero to the end as a cherry on top:

$$526{,}315{,}789{,}473{,}684{,}210 \times 7 = 3{,}684{,}210{,}526{,}315{,}789{,}470$$

Similarly, to multiply the beast by 5, the options are to cut between 5 and 2 or 5 and 7. We choose the lower option, which is to cut between 5 and 2, and then read off the rest of the number as before, adding the final zero:

$526,315,789,473,684,210 \times 5 = 2,631,578,947,368,421,050$

If you want to multiply the beast by a number from 11 to 19, look for the second digit from your chosen number but choose the *larger* slice. So if I wanted to multiply the beast by 14, I notice that there are two 4s: one before a 7 and one before a 2. This time we choose the larger cut, so between the 4 and the 7, move the remaining digits and add the zero: $526,315,789,473,684,210 \times 14 = 7,368,421,052,631,578,940$

14 January

If, like many people, you've often struggled with seven 8s, you may find it useful to realize that **the first eight numerals form a coincidental and useful pattern**:

1   2   3   4   5   6   7   8
$1 \quad 2 = 3 \times 4 \quad 5 \quad 6 = 7 \times 8$

These are the only two times this consecutive coincidence will work, and it's very useful – up to a point. I showed a colleague of mine who was initially impressed but came back to me a few days later to check it with me: they'd half-remembered it and wanted to check if it was definitely correct that $1 \times 2 = 34$ and $5 \times 6 = 78$, because that didn't seem right. Always employ common sense too…

15 January

The 9 times table is without doubt the most enjoyable times table, because of the very satisfying embedded rules:

$1 \times 9 = 09$
$2 \times 9 = 18$
$3 \times 9 = 27$
$4 \times 9 = 36$
...

The two digits in the solution always add up to 9, and the first digit increases by 1 as the second digit decreases by 1. Also, the first digit of the answer is 1 less than the number being multiplied by, so if you want to know seven 9s, you know the first digit of your answer must be 1 less than 7, i.e. 6, and the other digit must be whatever makes the <u>sum</u> to 9, that is, 3. So you have your answer: 63.

Unfortunately schoolchildren don't go as far as their 1089 times tables, but if they did they would discover some even more impressive <u>symmetry</u>:

$1 \times 1089 = 1089$
$2 \times 1089 = 2178$
$3 \times 1089 = 3267$
$4 \times 1089 = 4356$
$5 \times 1089 = 5445$
$6 \times 1089 = 6534$
$7 \times 1089 = 7623$
$8 \times 1089 = 8712$

$9 \times 1089 = 9801$

Not only do the digits always add up to 18, but the first two digits rise by 1 every time, while the other two drop by 1 every time. And, like the 9 times table, **each answer's mirror image can be found elsewhere in the list**.

16 January

The fact that the numerals '6' and '9' have <u>rotational symmetry</u> (one is the other upside down) is a narrative device that has often been exploited: it provides a pivotal twist in two award-winning BBC shows – *Line of Duty* and *Numberblocks* – when a fallen '9' on a front door leads to the house number being misread and a consequent case of mistaken identity.*

Without this rotational property it would be impossible to construct a 'cubic calendar'. You'll almost certainly have encountered these – perhaps you even own one?

This is a calendar where each <u>face</u> displays a number, and the order of the two cubes can be swapped when required. There are twelve faces available to us and only ten different digits that need to be displayed, so it should be easy, right? Except each block needs a 1 and a 2, or we couldn't display the 11th or 22nd of the month. We also need a 0 on each block: if there were only a 0 on one block then we could only make six of the nine required dates that involve a 0.

---

* Minor apologies for the spoiler, but it happens literally within the first five minutes of *Line of Duty*, and *Numberblocks* is a five-minute CBBC show for young schoolchildren.

This creates a problem: we require space for thirteen digits with only twelve faces available to us. But since 6 and 9 are never needed at the same time, we can have a 6 on one cube with no need for a 9 on the other. Here's a possible arrangement:

Cube 1:   0   1   2   3   4   5
Cube 2:   0   1   2   6   7   8

17 January

Anyone in the Western world who is familiar with meaningless superstition will be aware of the supposedly unlucky nature of Friday 13th, and if you regularly frequent pub quizzes (or read the footnote on page 12) you may even be aware that the fear of the number 13 is known as *triskaidekaphobia*.

The origin for the superstition over the number 13 may originate from a Norse myth about Loki being the thirteenth guest at a dinner party, or from the thirteen diners present at Jesus's Last Supper. Personally, the thought of thirteen people eating in my house fills me with terror, but for the very rational and non-superstitious reason of having to maintain all that chit-chat and do the washing-up afterwards. Particular fear of Friday 13th may originate from T. W. Lawson's 1907 novel *Friday the Thirteenth*, but it's hard to find any solid evidence of why Fridays in particular should be unlucky.

Italians would find Friday 17th to be an unluckier day than Friday 13th, since 17 is deemed to be a bad omen. This is because the Roman numerals for 17, XVII, can be rearranged as VIXI, meaning 'I have lived.'

18 January

The footballer Paddy Kenny felt the brunt of the Italian fear of the number 17 in 2014 when he was unceremoniously sent home from Leeds United's pre-season tour – and later sacked by the club – for having the audacity to be born on 17 May. Leeds's notoriously hot-headed chairman at the time, Massimo Cellino, was terrified of the number 17 and believed that having any player born on that date would be a bad omen for the club.

Cellino left Leeds United in 2017 (of course). They were promoted to the Premier League three years later under new ownership.

19 January

Every integer (whole number) can be written as a sum of <u>powers</u> of 2 in one unique way. We'll cover powers more in March, but for now you just need to know that the powers of 2 are simply a doubling <u>sequence</u> starting from 1, so: 1, 2, 4, 8, 16, 32, 64, and so on.

For example: $18 = 16 + 2$

$$31 = 16 + 8 + 4 + 2 + 1$$

$$100 = 64 + 32 + 4$$

In fact, when you represent a number in this form you are actually converting it to <u>binary</u>, the counting system of 0s and 1s that computers use.

	64s	32s	16s	8s	4s	2s	1s
18	0	0	1	0	0	1	0
31	0	0	1	1	1	1	1
100	1	1	0	0	1	0	0

So the binary representation of 18 is 10010 (no need to include the zeros to the left of the first 1), and similarly 31 and 100 in binary are 11111 and 1100100 respectively.

20 January

Next time you're in St Gallen, Switzerland, do pop along and check out the huge binary clock at the train station:

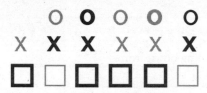

A reminder from yesterday: the rightmost column represents 1, then the column one to the left represents 2, the next column to the left 4, and so on. If there is a symbol in that column then that value is 'on'; if there isn't, it's 'off'. Add up all the 'on' values to convert from binary to decimal.

So the time displayed here in hours, minutes and seconds is (in binary) 1001:11001:101110, and:

$$1001 \rightarrow 8 + 1 = 9$$
$$11001 \rightarrow 16 + 8 + 1 = 25$$
$$101110 \rightarrow 32 + 8 + 4 + 2 = 46$$

So the time pictured is 09:25:46, but by the time you've worked that out you've probably missed your train.

21 January

Utilizing binary equivalents in a clever way reveals that **we can multiply two numbers together by simply halving one and doubling the other.** If your times tables are as weak as a British MP's then this might be the method for you. For example, let's say we wanted to multiply 18 by 35. Put them alongside each other, and halve the smaller number until you get to 1. (If halving means you hit a decimal number, round it down; so, instead of 6.5, write 6.) Every time you halve the smaller number, double the larger number. So we get something like this:

35	18
70	9
140	4 (rounding down from 4.5)
280	2
560	1

Then cross out any rows with an even number in the halving column, and add up the remaining numbers in the doubling column:

~~35~~	~~18~~
70	9
~~140~~	~~4~~
~~280~~	~~2~~
560	1

560 + 70 = 630, which is the correct answer to 18 × 35. We could have doubled and halved the other way round; it takes a little longer but of course leads to the same result:

18	35
36	17
~~72~~	~~8~~
~~144~~	~~4~~
~~288~~	~~2~~
576	1

576 + 36 + 18 = 630. This method is most commonly known as 'Russian peasant multiplication', though it has roots in Ancient Egypt.

22 January

How on earth does Russian peasant multiplication, which we saw yesterday, work? Consider the halving sequence that takes you from 18 down to 1, and at each step consider whether there is a remainder when dividing by 2:

18 (9 lots of 2 with **0** remainder)
9 (4 lots of 2 with **1** remainder)
4 (2 lots of 2 with **0** remainder)
2 (1 lots of 2 with **0** remainder)
1 (0 lots of 2 with **1** remainder)

If you now **read the bold remainders from bottom to top, you will find the binary equivalent of 18: 10010.** This means that 18 can be written as 16 + 2, as we saw earlier. Therefore

$$18 \times 35 = (16 + 2) \times 35 = (16 \times 35) + (2 \times 35) = 560 + 70 = 630$$

which is exactly the calculation that we were led to with the 'Russian peasant' method.

23 January

This 23rd day of the year feels an appropriate time to announce that **any room with 23 people in it has a 50/50 chance of two people sharing a birthday.*** This legitimately mind-bending idea is often referred to as the *birthday problem* and I highly recommend you test it next time you find yourself in a room with 23 people in it (though you may draw strange glances in the greengrocer's queue).

The most commonly guessed (wrong) answer to the question of how many people would be needed before there was a 50/50 chance of two of them sharing a birthday is 182ish, in other words approximately one person for every other day of the year. But with over 180 people in a room the chances that they all have a unique birthday is absolutely minuscule, because there are so many potential pairings between all of the people in the room.

The key to understanding this problem is not to think of the number of people in the room, but rather the number of potential 'meetings' (shared birthdays) that could occur. Imagine one person alone in a room, who is then joined by one more. They shake hands and check whether they have the same birthday; a tiny 1 in 365 chance (ish... damn that pesky leap year). Then another person joins, and crucially there are now *two* people with whom they can check birthdays. When

---

* I enjoy the thought that someone is certainly reading this entry on the birthday paradox on their actual birthday. Happy Birthday to you, if so! And I mean that sincerely.

the fourth person joins that's three more potential checks, and for every person that joins we are adding more potential shared birthdays.

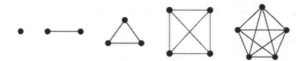

These <u>complete graphs</u> for one through to five people show the potential numbers of meetings: 0, 1, 3, 6, 10. The number of potential meetings is growing quickly, and this is why it takes fewer people than you might expect to reach a common birthday.

To calculate the precise solution to this problem we should consider the <u>probability</u> of *not* finding anyone with the same birthday. When the second person enters the room there is a $\frac{364}{365}$ chance that they have a different birthday to the person already in the room (in other words a probability very close to 1). When the next person enters, there are now only 364 birthdays they could have that wouldn't clash with the others already in the room. So the probability of reaching this point with no birthday clashes is $\frac{364}{365} \times \frac{363}{365}$: still very close to 1. Repeat this process, however, and you'll find that adding the 23rd person tips the probability past 50%.

24 January

A room with 23 people will give you a 50% chance that two people share a birthday, but if you don't fancy those odds, perhaps **wait for a roomful of 40 people: this would garner nearly a 90% chance of a joint birthday**. Fifty people takes you all the way to a 97% chance of success (but by the time you've checked all 50 people, many of them will have lost interest).

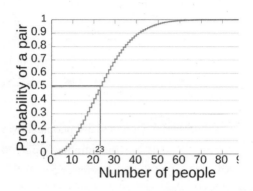

Graph to show the probability of finding a birthday pair for different numbers of people in a room; 23 people gives a 50% chance.

And once you're up to 88 people, you have a better than 50% chance that *three* people are all born on the same day.

25 January

Since a group of 23 people have a 50% chance of sharing a birthday with someone in the group, **every other football match should feature a common birthday somewhere on the field** (11 players on each team, plus the referee).

As an example, let us consider England's two greatest footballing successes: winning the 1966 men's World Cup and the 2021 women's European Championships. In the former game, nobody who started the match shared a birthday, but in the latter there was a birthday pair: England strikers Beth Mead and Ellen White were both born on 9 May.

One could reasonably argue, though, that a football match (or indeed any sporting event) is not a fair situation in which to check the birthday problem, since sportspeople are not equally likely to be born on any day of the year. This is due to what the author Malcolm Gladwell calls the 'Relative Age Effect', which says that people born towards the start of the academic year in their country of birth are more likely to excel at sport. The thinking goes as follows: children born earlier in the academic year will be the largest and strongest in their early years at school, when proportionally the age difference – and hence difference in size, coordination and balance – between the oldest and youngest in the year is greatest. These children are more likely to excel at a young age due to the size/strength imbalance, which makes them more likely to reach elite teams and receive top-level training, thus exacerbating the talent gap in a continuing cycle. The theory is borne out in the English football leagues: a 2021 survey by casino.co.uk found that 58% of players in the top two divisions of English football were born in the first half of the academic year, with just 18% born in the fourth quarter of the year. Manchester United have a staggering five out of every six players born in the first half of the academic year, though whether this is evidence of the Relative Age Effect producing quality players is up for debate.*

26 January

The sum of a list of consecutive powers of 2 will always be 1 less than the next power of 2 (remember that the powers of 2 are simply the 'doubling numbers' starting from 1: 1, 2, 4, 8, etc.). For example, 1 +

---

* I'm writing this rather obvious gag in Spring 2023, so if Manchester United have enjoyed a glorious period of success since then, I will have egg on my face. They haven't though, have they?

2 + 4 = 7, one short of 8. And 1 + 2 + 4 + 8 + 16 = 31, one short of 32. Proving why this happens comes very easily if we work in binary (*base 2*) rather than our usual base 10 counting method.

Here are the powers of 2, written in binary: 1, 10, 100, 1000, and so on. Add these together and you have a long list of 1s: 1111…

Adding another 1 to this number would change all of the 1s to 0s, and require an additional 1 to be added to the far left: 10000…, which is the next power of 2.

So the sum of a list of powers of 2 will always be 1 less than the next power of 2.

27 January

Happy Birthday Charles Lutwidge Dodgson, aka Lewis Carroll! Both a mathematician and writer, Dodgson penned dozens of books, including *A Syllabus of Plane Algebraic Geometry, Symbolic Logic Parts I & II, The Fifth Book of Euclid Treated Algebraically, Alice's Adventures in Wonderland* and, of course, *An Elementary Treatise on Determinants, With Their Application to Simultaneous Linear Equations and Algebraic Equations.*

Legend has it that it was the last of these books that Queen Victoria was sent when she appealed to the author for a copy of some of his other work, having been so charmed by *Alice*. Dodgson always strenuously denied this story, though, so we had better not use it for today's fact. Instead, let's have this: **an avid puzzler, Dodgson also created the 'word ladder' puzzle, still going strong in newspapers to this day**. He called them 'doublets' and here's one that was published in *Vanity Fair* in 1897 – can you get from 'head' to 'tail' in five steps? You can change only one letter per line, and every word you form along the way must be a real word in the English language. The answer is in the Further Notes at the back of the book.

28 January

Here are some more unlucky numbers from other cultures:

- 7 in Japan, because the word for seven sounds like 'torture'
- 26 in India, because many natural disasters and tragedies have occurred on this date (with a large pinch of superstition and numerology thrown in too…)
- 39 in Afghanistan, because it sounds like 'morda-gow', meaning dead cow
- 666 in some Christian cultures, as it's mentioned in the bible as the number of the beast. Ridiculously long names for phobias are always good fun, so here's another: **fear of the number 666 is called Hexakosioihexekontahexaphobia.**

29 January

Here is a beautiful 'complete graph' showing ten <u>vertices</u> or <u>nodes</u>, which might represent the number of potential meetings between ten people. But how many lines, or <u>edges</u>, are required to join all the vertices? Please don't try to count them. The answer is given after the diagram.

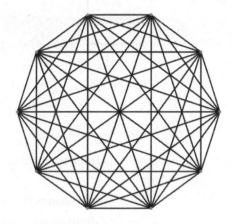

You may observe that the first node has to be joined to 9 others, the next to 8 (because it's already joined to the first) and so on, but there is a more elegant way. Each of the ten nodes is joined to nine others, leading to $10 \times 9 = 90$. However, by counting in this way we are counting each edge twice – once from each direction – so we need to halve this answer to give the correct value of 45. Generally speaking, the number of edges on a complete graph with n nodes can be calculated as $\frac{n(n-1)}{2}$.

30 January

These four symbols are synonymous with the musician Ed Sheeran and, to a lesser extent, mathematics. They can be found on the cover of maths textbooks around the world, but one of these symbols is more controversial than the others.

The division symbol, something like this (÷), can often lead to confusion that you wouldn't necessarily encounter with the other symbols. For example, the following question can give an answer of either 16 or 1, depending on which way the wind is blowing:

$$16 \div 4(2 + 2)$$

Actually I believe the answer is 16, but more importantly it's clearly an ambiguous question, largely due to the lack of certainty over how to apply the division operation. If we were to use a horizontal fraction bar, it becomes much clearer what we are trying to ask:

$$\frac{16}{4(2 + 2)} = 1 \qquad \text{or} \qquad \frac{16}{4}(2 + 2) = 16$$

What many people don't realize is that **the division symbol is literally a fraction bar with a blob to signify some unknown value above and below**, 'blob over blob': ÷

For many this is a life-changing realization to rank alongside first noticing the little arrow on your petrol meter that shows you which side of the car the petrol cap is on, or the first time you're told that the word 'helicopter' is not made up of the parts 'heli' and 'copter', but rather 'helico' meaning to spin, as in 'helix', and 'pter' meaning wing, as in the start of 'pterodactyl'.

31 January

Every two-digit number that ends in 9 is equal to the product of its digits added to the sum of its digits. In other words, multiply the digits and add on both digits. Behold!

$29 = (2 \times 9) + 2 + 9 = 18 + 11$
$59 = (5 \times 9) + 5 + 9 = 45 + 14$
$99 = (9 \times 9) + 9 + 9 = 81 + 18$

It always works! The trick here is to realize that the original number, which looks like $x9$, where x is the digit in the tens column, would more correctly be represented as $10x + 9$. This leads to a digits product of $9x$ and a digits sum of $(x + 9)$. Put this all together and you get:

$9x + (x + 9) = 10x + 9$, as required.

FEBRUARY

ABOUT TIME

1 February

The number of <u>milliseconds</u> in a day is $5^5 \times 4^4 \times 3^3 \times 2^2 \times 1^1$

That's a string of five 5s, four 4s, three 3s and two 2s multiplied together (no need to write the one 1 since multiplying by 1 has no effect anyway).

$5 \times 5 \times 5 \times 5 \times 5 \times 4 \times 4 \times 4 \times 4 \times 3 \times 3 \times 3 \times 2 \times 2$ milliseconds

Let's check that this really does give us the number of milliseconds in a day. Since there are a thousand milliseconds in a second, and $1000 = 5 \times 5 \times 5 \times 4 \times 2$, we cast out these numbers from the original product to convert from milliseconds to seconds:

$5 \times 5 \times 4 \times 4 \times 4 \times 3 \times 3 \times 3 \times 2$ seconds

Sixty seconds in a minute, and $60 = 5 \times 4 \times 3$, so cast these out to convert from seconds to minutes:

$5 \times 4 \times 4 \times 3 \times 3 \times 2$ minutes

Likewise, there are 60 minutes in an hour, and again $60 = 5 \times 4 \times 3$, so finally we have:

$4 \times 3 \times 2$ hours

This is 24 hours, or exactly one day.

2 February

The speed of sound is relatively slow, about 343 metres per second, a phenomenon you may have observed when watching a plane in the sky that seems to be markedly ahead of where the sound is coming from, or at a large sporting event when the crowd can't seem to sing or clap in time with each other (to be fair, lager may also have something to do with this).

Port towns would traditionally have a time signal at the same time every day, allowing ships' captains to correctly set their chronometers and hence calculate longitude and be able to find shortest routes when at sea. In Edinburgh this time signal was given by a daily cannon shot from Edinburgh Castle – the so-called 'One o'clock gun' – a tradition that remains to this day. The trouble is, Edinburgh Castle is some distance from the ports at Leith and Newhaven, so captains had to be given a chart which told them how many seconds to adjust their clocks by; for some areas it would be up to ten seconds past 1 o'clock when the cannon was heard.

3 February

Happy 34th day of the year! Can you find four numbers that sum to 34 in this square? You might be able to do it in more than one way.

16	3	2	13
5	10	11	8
9	6	7	12
4	15	14	1

The image on the left is a *magic square* taken from *Melancholia I*, a 1514 engraving by the German artist Albrecht Dürer. It contains a startling number of geometrically pleasing sums to 34, including the rows, columns, diagonals and all of the selections below, plus many others. How many did you spot?

4 February

It is a long-established norm that the time on the face of analogue clocks in shops or advertisements is set to 10:10, with the minute and hour hands apparently forming a 'smiley face'. You might also recognize these hand positions as the 'ten and two' positions that your driving instructor taught you to keep your hands in. The origin of the practice of setting clock hands to 10:10 is hard to trace, but my favourite unverifiable (almost certainly false) rumour is that it's to honour the guy who invented the clock, who died at ten minutes past ten. Whatever the reason for it, **setting clocks to 10:10 seems to have a genuine positive effect on people**. A 2017 research paper* found that 'watches set at 10:10 showed a significant positive effect on the emotion of the observer and the intention to buy', so don't expect to see the trend going away any time soon.

A friend once told me that every clock in one of my favourite films, Stanley Kubrick's *The Shining*, was set to 10:10 to add to the general sense of eeriness in the Overlook Hotel. Of course I instantly went back to check… and it's false. As is the rumour that all the clocks in *Joker* are set to 11:11, and that all the clocks in *Pulp Fiction* are set to 4:20. Sorry!

5 February

Cleopatra lived closer in time to the release of the iPhone than to the building of the pyramids. The great Pyramids of Giza were built around 2500 BC, while Cleopatra, the last active Pharaoh of Ancient Egypt, was born in 69 BC and died in 30 BC. So it's even likely that

---

* Karim, Lützenkirchen, Khedr and Khalil, 'Why Is 10 Past 10 the Default Setting for Clocks and Watches in Advertisements? A Psychological Experiment', *Frontiers in Psychology*, vol. 8 (2017).

Cleopatra's life will turn out to be closer in time to humans reaching Mars than to the building of the pyramids.

6 February

A fact for the 37th day of the year: **any three-digit <u>multiple</u> of 37 remains <u>divisible</u> by 37 when the digits are rearranged in a cyclical manner.** For example:

814 ÷ 37 = 22
481 ÷ 37 = 13   (moving the 4 so that it's before the 8)
148 ÷ 37 = 4   (moving the 1 so that it's before the 4)

A party trick for your next social gathering, perhaps. Also note that any number that can be written in the form ababab* is divisible by 37. For example, 767,676 = 37 × 20,748.

7 February

'I'll be there in a jiffy!' This rather old-fashioned English term for a short period of time dates to the 1700s, but more recently **a jiffy has been formally defined as the length of time required for light to travel a centimetre.** However, to some physicists, it's a vastly shorter time period: the time light takes to travel a distance of one femtometre, which is a millionth of a millionth of a millimetre. Since this is all a bit of fun, and the scientist would never use the term without some contextual backing, it doesn't matter too much. And since scientists

---

* Also the name of Birmingham's top tribute to the Swedish Eurovision legends.

disagree on the length of a jiffy by a <u>factor</u> of billions, I think it's safe to use a 'jiffy' to describe any time length you wish.

8 February

The word 'fortnight' is derived from the old English *fēowertīene niht*, quite literally meaning 'fourteen nights'. In France the term for a fortnight is 'quinze jours', literally meaning... fifteen days. The etymology of this apparent error seems to stem from a classic 'fencepost' problem. Imagine counting the days for a fortnight from midday on a Monday to midday on a Monday two weeks away. The exact time interval you've counted is fourteen days, but there are fifteen weekdays in the period if you include both Mondays.

9 February

For the fortieth day of the year, a spelling-based number fact: **forty is the only number which, when spelt in English, has all of its letters fall in alphabetical order**. There is seemingly no reasonable explanation for why forty does not contain a letter 'u', yet four and fourteen do. The current spelling has been going strong since the sixteenth century, but before that it was an absolute bunfight for what came after thirty-nine, with all of the following and more up for contention: féowertig, fowwerrtig, feortig, fuerti, vourty, fourthy and, eventually, forty.

10 February

Here are some more word-based number curios:

- 'One' is the only number with its letters in perfect reverse-alphabetical order.*
- Spell out all the numbers in English, starting from 'one', and you won't use the letter 'a' until you get to 'one thousand'.
- Spell out all the names of the cards in a standard deck – 'two' to 'ten', plus 'jack', 'queen', 'king' and 'ace' – and you'll find 4 three-letter words, 5 four-letter words and 4 five-letter words, totalling 52 letters: the same number of cards in a pack.

11 February

Surprising historical overlaps are plentiful if you're prepared to look for them. For example, woolly mammoths still roamed the earth when the great Pyramids of Giza were being built. Recent discoveries have dated the most recent mammoths to Wrangel Island in the Arctic Ocean at around 4000 years ago, roughly 2000 BC, but certainly more recent than 2500 BC. Here's another one: **France sent its last man to the guillotine the same year that** *Star Wars* **was released**. Found guilty of murder, rape and torture, Hamida Djandoubi was executed by guillotine in a Marseilles prison in September 1977.

---

* Side note: edam is the only cheese that is made backwards.

12 February

President Joe Biden was born closer to Abraham Lincoln's presidency than his own. Lincoln, the 16th US president, was shot while attending a play in 1865, 77 years before Biden's birth in 1942; 79 years later, in January 2021, Biden was inaugurated as the 46th and oldest US president.

13 February

Some celebrities are so well known, and live for so long, that newspapers and other news outlets keep obituaries on file so that they can quickly go to press when news of their death breaks. It's a sad but inevitable precaution for public figures of a certain level of renown. I would personally think of it as the highest compliment to know that my obituary is on file somewhere (in fact I might write my own and keep it in the bottom drawer).

The actor **Elizabeth Taylor, though not living to an especially noteworthy age of 79, nonetheless managed the impressive feat of outliving the writer of her own obituary**. The author of Taylor's *New York Times* obituary was one Mel Gussow, who died six years before she did.

14 February

Happy Valentine's Day! Two numbers are 'amicable' if the factors of one number, excluding the number itself, add up to the other (<u>factors</u> of a number are the whole numbers that divide into it equally, so the factors of 6 are 1, 2, 3 and 6). For example, **220 and 284 form an amicable pair**:

Factors of 220: 1, 2, 4, 5, 10, 11, 20, 22, 44, 55, 110, which sum to 284
Factors of 284: 1, 2, 4, 71, 142, which sum to 220

Because of this, 220 and 284 take on a special resonance in the mathematical community and are sometimes paired together on locket keyrings or other such novelty items (yes, the world of mathematical knick-knacks exists). Interestingly, partners born on the 220th and 284th days of the year – that's 7/8 August and 10/11 October, depending on whether you are born in a leap year – have statistically exactly the same chance of staying married for life as any other couple.

15 February

How big is a <u>million</u> and how big is a <u>billion</u>? People regularly confuse these two quantities, but even though they sound very similar, the latter is of course a thousand times bigger than the former. It probably isn't ideal to confuse two quantities where one is a thousand times bigger than the other. Oh, you wanted one flake in your ice cream? I've accidentally given you a thousand, but who's counting?

A useful and oft-cited way to appreciate the difference between a million and a billion is by considering a million seconds (about 12 days) versus a billion seconds (about 32 years). **So if someone gave you a pound every second, you'd be a millionaire by next week, but a billionaire in 30 years' time.** It makes you wonder whether anyone needs to own a billion pounds, doesn't it?

16 February

If a million seconds is about 12 days, then a million minutes should be sixty times longer. Sixty lots of twelve is around 720 days, so just under two years (a million minutes is almost exactly the gestation period of an elephant, if you're interested).

How about a million hours? Well, that would be about 60 times longer again, so around 120 years. Actually, all that approximating means we've lost a bit of accuracy along the way: a million hours is actually closer to 114 years. This has a special significance: **a million hours is more or less the limit of the human lifespan.** Only around 100 people have ever lived beyond this magical benchmark, though of course more and more people will do so as the earth's population increases and humans are able to live healthier lives.

The oldest person ever recorded was Jeanne Calment, who died in 1997 at the grand age of 122½ in a tragic bungee jumping accident (most of this sentence is true).*

17 February

A million hours may represent the approximate limit of a human life, but I intend to live much longer. In fact I'm never going to die, and I have some solid evidence for this.

You're probably aware that the population of Earth has exploded in the last century or so, thanks largely to vastly improved healthcare.

---

* Fantastically, there is a fairly large consensus that Calment was actually an imposter who died at a 'normally' old age and was secretly replaced by her daughter, somewhat like a wrestling tag team swapping out a tired competitor for a fresh replacement mid-fight. Whether she will be dug up and have her leg cut open to count the rings and clarify her true age is unclear at time of writing.

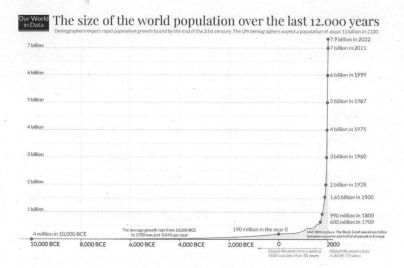

The size of the world population over the last 12,000 years

Demographers expect rapid population growth to end by the end of the 21st century. The UN demographers expect a population of about 11 billion in 2100.

- 7.9 billion in 2022
- 7 billion in 2011
- 6 billion in 1999
- 5 billion in 1987
- 4 billion in 1975
- 3 billion in 1960
- 2 billion in 1928
- 1.65 billion in 1900
- 990 million in 1800
- 600 million in 1700

4 million in 10,000 BCE

The average growth rate from 10,000 BCE to 1700 was just 0.04% per year

190 million in the year 0

Mid 14th century: The Black Death pandemic killed between a quarter and half of all people in Europe.

10,000 BCE   8,000 BCE   6,000 BCE   4,000 BCE   2,000 BCE   0   2000

Global life expectancy before 1800 was less than 30 years

Global life expectancy in 2019: 73 years

Based on estimates by the History Database of the Global Environment (HYDE) and the United Nations. You can download the annual data from ourworldindata.org.

The few humans currently alive who have surpassed a million hours – remember that's just over 114 years – were born into a world of under 2 billion people and will die in a world of 8 billion. This astonishing growth – which we are reaching the end of, by the way – means that a surprisingly large proportion of everyone who has ever lived is currently alive. There is an online theory that re-emerges every few years that argues there are *more* people alive than dead, i.e. more people currently alive than have ever lived in the history of the world, but this isn't quite right.

It's incredibly hard to calculate how many people have ever lived, since for most of human history there was no <u>data</u> collection. I suppose one could argue that avoiding death by animal attack or incurable disease may have been a more pressing requirement than collecting accurate population data. Also, infant mortality was so high in the Middle Ages that some estimates have life expectancy for this period at 10–12 years, which will certainly dampen enthusiasm to fill out a ten-yearly census.

The Population Reference Bureau estimates that about 107 billion people have ever lived, which means **the current world population of 8 billion makes up over 7% of everyone who has ever lived.** Still quite impressive if you ask me. This also means that, since more than 5% of people have not experienced death, immortality cannot be ruled out at the 5% significance level.* So there's hope for all of us…

18 February

While we're talking time, here's a neat coincidence: **one calendar year is incredibly close to ten-pi million seconds**. (Pi, or π, is a number slightly larger than 3.14 with many mathematical applications. More about it coming in August.)

To find the number of seconds in a year, we must multiply 365 by 24 (this gives the number of hours in a year), then multiply by 60 (to give the number of minutes in a year), and then finally multiply by 60 one more time:

$$365 \times 24 \times 60 \times 60 = 31{,}536{,}000$$

Ten-pi million seconds would be 31,415,927 to the nearest second, which as an estimate falls around 120,000 seconds short, or roughly one day off.

---

* I first saw this observation in John Allen Paulos's excellent book *Innumeracy*, which I strongly recommend.

19 February

Establishing that ten-pi million seconds is about a year could be expressed in a different way: **pi seconds is about a nano-century.** At this stage you might need a refresher on the accepted prefixes for very small numbers:

deci	d	tenth
centi	c	hundredth
milli	m	thousandth
micro	μ	millionth
nano	n	billionth
pico	p	trillionth
femto	f	quadrillionth
atto	a	quintillionth
zepto	z	sextillionth
yocto	y	septillionth

(If you can remember anything beyond 'nano' then give yourself a pat on the back.)

So a centimetre is a hundredth of a metre, and a millimetre is a thousandth of a metre, though you may think of it as a tenth of a centimetre, which of course is the same.

To find the length of a nano-century, we must find the length of a century in seconds and divide it by a billion. Yesterday we saw that a calendar year was 31,536,000 seconds, so a century is 3,153,600,000 seconds, or very close to pi billion. Divide by a billion and of course you have something very close to pi.

When the physicist and TV presenter Julius Sumner Miller was asked how long he would speak at a public event, he would often answer: 'About a micro-century'. I'll let you do the maths on that one.

20 February

Today is a special day for the Cummins family of Clintwood, Virginia, as it is the birth date of five siblings: Catherine, Carol, Charles, Claudia and Cecilia Cummins* were all born on 20 February, but in different years.

This is verified by Guinness World Records as the only occasion that a family has produced five non-twins with the same birthday, with odds of a staggering 17.7 billion to one. Which is… not *quite* correct.

One in 17.7 billion would be the probability of five children having the same birth date, and you would find this probability with the following calculation:

$$1 \times \frac{1}{365} \times \frac{1}{365} \times \frac{1}{365} \times \frac{1}{365}$$

In other words, the first child can have any birth date, but the following four must have the same birth date as the first, each of which is a one in 365 chance. However, we must take into consideration the fact that there are two other Cummins siblings: Cheryl and Jim (I'm joking of course: it's Christopher).

Would it be just as interesting if a different arrangement of the seven children shared a birthday? Of course it would, so we should take this into account. It turns out there are 21 different ways that you could select five siblings out of seven, so our one in 17.7 billion is

---

* I would make a pithy joke about all the forenames beginning with a 'C' here, but since my own siblings are named Katie, Klaire(!) and Keith, I will stay quiet.

too small by at least a factor of 21. We could also include the possible cases of six or more siblings sharing a birthday (of course these are phenomenally unlikely, but we should include them too since they'd be just as newsworthy). The actual probability of five or more siblings out of seven sharing a birthday is more like one in 850 million, although almost certainly more likely than this given that the parents, Carolyn and... wait for it... Ralph, almost surely would have been aiming for roughly 20 February once they had hit that date a few times already.

21 February

Several siblings sharing a birthday is of course very rare, but as we have seen already, unlikely events become almost certain given enough trials. Here are a couple of notable examples:

Happy birthday to you... and you... and you too: Couple's three children born on the same date.

The chances of ending up with the same dilemma as Jennifer and Driss Allali is an astonishing 48 million to one.... after their latest child, Sami, was born on October 7. He shares the same birth date as brother Adam, three, and sister Najla, five.

Credit: *Daily Mail*, 13 October 2010

Family with four children who all have SAME birthday: Couple welcome son on January 12 beating odds of more than 133,000 to one.

Emily Scrugham and Peter Dunn, from Cumbria, call it a lucky coincidence. New baby Ryan shares his birthday with his five-year-old brother Sam, and his two-year-old twin sisters Brooke and Nicole.

Credit: *Daily Mail*, 16 January 2014

22 February

Yesterday we saw some huge familial coincidences, reported in the same British newspaper a few years apart. Hang on though...
Allali family: three children born on the same date; 48 million to one;
Scrugham–Dunn family: four children born on the same date; 133,000 to one.

How can having three children born on the same day be less likely than four children born on the same day? In truth, both of the situations above are identical if we assume the Scrugham–Dunn twins were born on the same day, but still, how can the probabilities be different?

The actual probability we're looking for here, once again, is:

$$1 \times \frac{1}{365} \times \frac{1}{365}$$

This is because the first child sets the date that two more must follow, and each following child has a one in 365 chance of being born on that date. This probability turns out to be around 1 in 133,000, so the second article is correct (even though the headline is a little disingenuous in not mentioning the twins...).

The first article made the classic mistake of instead calculating $\frac{1}{365}$ $\times \frac{1}{365} \times \frac{1}{365}$, which is the probability of three children in a row being born on some *particular* date; say, the parents' wedding anniversary, or Christmas Day. This would be remarkable, but there's nothing remarkable about 13 October. (It is the date that the first ever Paddington Bear book was published, but the article says nothing about this having any particular meaning for the Allali family, so we shall have to assume otherwise.)

23 February

Gwenny Blanckaert and Marino Vaneeno, from Belgium, have eleven children,* all named with different permutations of the letters A, E, L, X. There are only 24 possible names that could be made with these letters: there are four possible positions for the A, but once this is placed there are only three possible positions for the E, then two for the L and then the X goes in the final remaining place: $4 \times 3 \times 2 \times 1 = 24$.

Here is a list of all 24 possible names, with the ages of the children given where appropriate (at time of writing):

AELX	AEXL	ALEX (13)	ALXE (6 months)
AXEL (12)	AXLE	EALX	EAXL
ELAX (1)	ELXA	EXAL	EXLA (5)
LAEX	LAXE	LEAX (4)	LEXA (10)
LXAE	LXEA	XAEL (9)	XALE (2)
XEAL (8)	XELA (11)	XLAE	XLEA

They're apparently planning their 12th: my money's on Laex, especially if they're Rachel Stevens fans. Of course some of these letter arrangements don't make legible names; you couldn't really have a child called Xlae. Oh, hang on, that might be the name of one of Elon Musk's children.

---

* It's quite important to point out this is at time of writing in Spring 2023…

24 February

Three of the first five US presidents all died on the same day of the year: 4 July. Can you guess which three? Here they are in chronological order, to remind you:

George Washington, John Adams, Thomas Jefferson, James Madison and James Monroe.*

Even if you've never heard this fact before – or if you had but couldn't quite remember which presidents were involved – you should probably have guessed that Monroe would be one of the five, and you'd be correct. The presidents in question were Adams, Jefferson and Monroe.

Why is it that you should probably have guessed Monroe? Well I told you that it was *three of the first five* who died on 4 July. If Monroe were not one of them then I would have written 'three of the first four', or even 'all of the first three', as this would have made my fact sound even more impressive. This is similar to the way that a sport pundit might make a team's form seem particularly bad by saying they've lost 'eight of their last ten matches', rather than, say, 'nine of their last fifteen matches'.† You always want to draw the line at a defeat to emphasize your point, in the same way that I drew the line after Monroe's death ('three US presidents in total died on 4 July' sounds somewhat underwhelming, but is just as factually correct).

---

* That's the limit of my knowledge of US presidents because that's as far as *Hamilton* goes.
† Supporting the team I do I am quite accustomed to such a situation.

25 February

The incredible lifespans of modern humans – and the ability of men to sire children until very late in life – means that some families can span centuries in just a few generations. Perhaps the most remarkable of these occurrences is that **the tenth president of the United States, John Tyler, who was born in 1790, has a living grandson at the time of writing in 2023**. Yes, not a great-grandson, a *grandson*. In fact, until very recently he had two surviving grandchildren: at the time of writing Harrison Ruffin Tyler is 94; Lyon Gardiner Tyler Jr died in 2020 at the age of 95.

John Tyler had 15 children, including Lyon Gardiner Tyler Sr, born in 1853 when his father was in his sixties. Lyon in turn had five children, including Lyon Jr and Harrison who were both born in the 1920s, when their father was in his seventies.

26 February

The word 'hundred' doesn't really mean 100. In fact 120 is now sometimes known as a 'long hundred' or, even better, 'twelfty', and this is the number that would have been called a 'hundred' in Germanic languages before the fifteenth century. It appears the word just got stuck to the wrong thing and we all got used to it, in the same way that September, October, November and December aren't the seventh, eighth, ninth and tenth months any more, or how the band 5ive now has three (or 3ree) members.

27 February

You will have noticed that I've used a calendar year of exactly 365 days a few times already, rather than an actual solar year – the time it takes the earth to orbit the sun – which is about 365.25 days.

The first 365-day calendar was created in the year we now call 46 BC by Julius Caesar, and was named the Julian calendar. It could just as easily have been called the Caesarean calendar, though this name might call to mind the style of childbirth (possibly named after Caesar) or even the salad (definitely not named after *that* Caesar). Because a solar year is about 365.25 days, the Julian calendar added a day every fourth year to bring the calendar year in line with the solar year. More accurately, however, a solar year is actually more like 365.242199 days.

Even though the difference from 365.25 is relatively tiny, it does account for three days every 400 years. **In 1852, Pope Gregory XIII altered the calendar so that any year divisible by 100 but not 400 would *not* be a leap year. Hence the Gregorian calendar was born.** Here's a handy guide to help you decide if a year is a leap year.

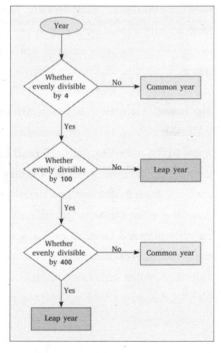

28 February

The modern Gregorian calendar is based on the ancient Roman calendar. This also had 12 months but, marvellously, **only the first ten months had names.** The two months at the end of the year were basically down-time where not much really happened; the government and military weren't active so everyone just chilled and got cracking again in the new year. I'm sure many people today would be in favour of going back to something similar.

The original ten months began with Martius, named after Mars, the god of war, as this was the month that military campaigns would resume. Next up was Aprilis, possibly stemming from the Latin *aperire*, meaning 'to open', in reference to the opening of buds in the springtime. Maius and Junius followed, named after the goddesses Maia and Juno. At this point the naming committee got bored and resorted to the numerical positions of the remaining months to give their names: Quintilis, Sextilis, September, October, November and December.

Eventually, Januarius (named after Janus, Roman god of beginnings and transitions) and Februarius (probably from Februa, an ancient festival dedicated to ritual springtime cleaning and washing) were added to the end of the year, giving all 12 months proper names. When Caesar reformed the calendar by lining it up with the solar year and adding leap years, the last two months of the year were moved to the front, buggering up the whole numerical naming system and giving us the calendar we now recognize. Caesar's death presented the perfect opportunity to do something about the misnamed later months, but instead they just renamed Quintilis as July in his honour, and later Sextilis as August after Emperor Augustus.

BONUS! 29 February

Because the Gregorian adjustment is still not quite perfect, and there is long-term slowdown in the earth's rotation, occasionally it is necessary to add a leap-second to a year. Leap-seconds are always added on 30 June or 31 December, and this is decided around six months in advance by the International Earth Rotation and Reference Systems Service (what a place to work!)

The most recent leap-second was added at midnight at the end of 2016. This means that 31 December 2016 had a 23:59:60 before the clock ticked over to 00:00:00 on 1 January 2017. I still fondly remember counting down the last few seconds of 2016: 'Ten, nine, eight, seven, six, five, four, three, two, one, one, Happy New Year!'

Still, if you think it's weird to live through a second twice, **spare a thought for the people of Samoa and Tokelau who once skipped an entire day**. In order to align with their main trade partners Australia and New Zealand, the two countries decided to move to the other side of the International Date Line (fortunately the line was able to move around them, rather than the islands having to pick themselves up and move 100 km to the east). This meant that they instantaneously jumped 24 hours forward and swapped from being the last to see the sun rise to being the first. This gives us a nice trivia question: What happened in Samoa on 30 December 2011? The answer… absolutely nothing.

MARCH

POWER UP

1 March

Happy 60th day of the year! **The Sumerians developed a base 60 <u>sexagesimal</u> counting system more than 5000 years ago, using multiples of 10 and 6**. A number system based on the number 60 has the huge benefit of the high divisibility of the number: 60 is divisible by 1, 2, 3, 4, 5, 6, 10, 12, 15, 20, 30 and 60.

For this reason the division of time into parts of 60 (60 minutes in an hour, 60 seconds in a minute) and also angles into parts of 60 (360 degrees in a full turn, 60 minutes in a degree, 60 seconds in a minute) have remained resistant to decimalization. There *is* a <u>decimal</u> version of the angle measure called the *gradian*, where 100 gradians make up a right angle and 400 a full turn. But honestly the less said about gradians the better. Just don't do it.

2 March

In fact 60 is known as a highly <u>composite number</u>, because it's the smallest number to have twelve factors (that's twelve different times tables that would land on 60: 1, 2, 3, 4, 5, 6, 10, 12, 15, 20, 30 and 60).

The sequence of highly composite numbers is the list of numbers that 'break the record' for having more factors than any smaller integer.

The first few highly composite numbers are as follows:

Number	First to have...	Factors
1	1	1
2	2	1, 2
4	3	1, 2, 4
6	4	1, 2, 3, 6
12	6	1, 2, 3, 4, 6, 12
24	8	1, 2, 3, 4, 6, 8, 12, 24
36	9	1, 2, 3, 4, 6, 9, 12, 18, 36

It's worth noting that the first number to have five factors is 16 (1, 2, 4, 8, 16), but because this is larger than a number with six factors (12), 16 is *not* a highly composite number. **The only numbers to have an odd number of factors are square numbers** – more about those very soon...

3 March

<u>Square numbers</u> are those that can be made with a square arrangement of dots: 1, 4, 9, 16 and so on:

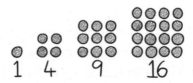

Because each square is, by nature, as long as it is wide, the formula for the nth square number is simply n multiplied by n, or n^2. Triangle numbers are those that can be made with a triangular arrangement of dots: 1, 3, 6, 10 and so on:

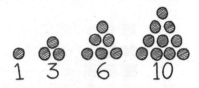

To find the formula for <u>triangle numbers</u>, arrange two of the same triangles together to make a rectangle:

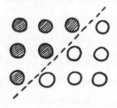

Here I've used the **third** triangle number, 6, and two of these triangles can be arranged appropriately to make a **3** × 4 rectangle. If I did the same with two of any triangle number, I would always end up with a rectangle that has the height of the triangle I'm working with, but is one unit wider. Expressing this algebraically: for the nth triangle number, I'd have ended up with an $n \times (n + 1)$ rectangle, so the formula for triangle numbers is $\frac{1}{2} n(n + 1)$, because the triangle in question makes up half of the rectangle.

4 March

Two consecutive triangle numbers go together to make a square number. Here's the visual proof:

And here's the algebraic proof:

First triangle number: $\frac{1}{2}n(n+1)$

Second triangle number: $\frac{1}{2}(n+1)(n+2)$ (replacing the n above with

$$n+1)$$

Sum of triangle numbers: $\frac{1}{2}n(n+1) + \frac{1}{2}(n+1)(n+2)$

$$= \frac{1}{2}(n+1)(n+n+2)$$

$$= \frac{1}{2}(n+1)(2n+2)$$

$$= (n+1)(n+1)$$

$$= (n+1)^2, \text{ which is a square of side length}$$

$$n+1$$

5 March

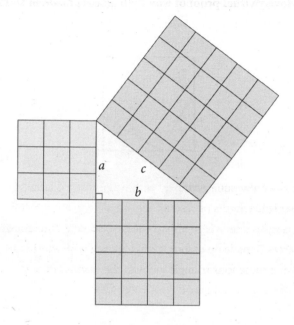

I doubt you were able to look at this image without your brain shouting '$a^2 + b^2 = c^2$!' or 'Pythagoras!' – it is one of the most memorable names in mathematics, along with the famous result for right-angled triangles: the square of the hypotenuse (the longest side) is the sum of the squares of the two shorter sides. The image above is showing that $3^2 + 4^2 = 5^2$ (9 + 16 = 25). 3, 4, 5 is therefore known as a 'Pythagorean triple', and **3, 4, 5 is the only Pythagorean triple made up of three consecutive numbers.**

6 March

Here's a lovely visual proof of why Pythagoras's *theorem* works:

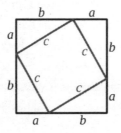

Imagine a wonky square drawn within another square. The smaller square has side lengths of c, so an <u>area</u> of c^2, whereas the larger square has side lengths of $a + b$, so an area of $(a + b)^2$. The difference between the two areas is made up of four triangles, each with width a and height b. So adding these four triangle areas to the wonky square area will be equal to the large square area:

$$c^2 + 4(\tfrac{1}{2}ab) = (a + b)^2 \qquad \text{Expand the brackets:}$$
$$c^2 + 2ab = a^2 + 2ab + b^2 \qquad \text{Subtract } 2ab \text{ from both sides:}$$
$$c^2 = a^2 + b^2$$

7 March

At the time of writing, today marks *Equal Pay Day*, the day to which the (<u>median</u>) average woman would have to work to reach the amount the average man earned in the previous year. In other words, **the average woman has to work for over 14 months to earn what a man earns in a calendar year**.

The issue is nuanced and complicated: I have worked in an establishment where women in teaching roles were actually paid more on average than men (because more women were in senior management) but for the entire workplace women were paid less on average. This was because the lowest paid roles, such as cleaning, were disproportionately held by women. There is a wider societal issue to unpack there, and it is also quite clear that, in many areas of work, women are being paid less than men for doing exactly the same work. Observing Equal Pay Day reminds us of this ongoing inequality, and every year that the date recedes closer to 1 January can only be a positive thing.

8 March

3, 4, 5 is the best-known Pythagorean triple – that is, a <u>set</u> of three numbers where the squares of the first two add up to the square of the third – but there are infinitely many Pythagorean triples, such as 5, 12, 13 and 7, 24, 25. Here's a recipe for making your own:

Choose any two integers: call them p and q, where p is the larger number.

Let $a = p^2 - q^2$
$\quad b = 2pq$
$\quad c = p^2 + q^2$

Now you should find you have an arrangement of numbers that form a Pythagorean triple. For example, if you let p and q be 3 and 2 respectively, we find $a = 5$, $b = 12$ and $c = 13$.

A Pythagorean triple can be made with three even numbers; simply double the values in any existing triple. So, instead of 3, 4, 5, you'd have

6, 8, 10 (36 + 64 = 100). But **you'll never find a Pythagorean triple with three odd numbers**. This is because an odd number squared always stays odd, and an odd plus an odd is always even. So if the two short smaller values in a Pythagorean triple are odd, the third number must be even.

9 March

If you add together a consecutive run of odd numbers, you'll get a square number. Here's a lovely visualization of that:

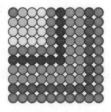

The legendary Greek mathematician and 'father of geometry' Euclid used this fact to prove that there are infinitely many primitive Pythagorean triples – that is, excluding ones like 6, 8, 10 that are simply a multiple of a previously found triple. From the image above it can be seen that the difference between two consecutive square numbers is always odd (e.g. $5^2 – 4^2 = 9$); not only that, but any odd number can be constructed as the difference between two squares:

$2^2 – 1^2 = 3$

$3^2 – 2^2 = 5$

$4^2 – 3^2 = 7$

$5^2 – 4^2 = 9$

This list could be continued indefinitely to include every single odd number on the right-hand side. Since the list of all odd numbers will include all the odd square numbers along the way, there will be infinitely many unique situations where the difference between two square numbers is also a square, and each of these provides a new Pythagorean triple. The first instance of a Pythagorean triple in our list is the bottom line, $5^2 - 4^2 = 9$, which is equivalent to the 3, 4, 5 triple we saw earlier. The list will generate infinitely many unique triples, whenever there's a square number on the right-hand side.

10 March

Here's another neat yet completely unrelated discovery from the ancient Greek mathematician Euclid: **an algorithm for finding the <u>highest common factor</u> of two numbers** (that's the largest number that would divide into both with no remainder). It goes like this:

- Subtract the smaller number from the larger.
- Replace the larger number with the answer from this subtraction.
- Continue to subtract the smaller number from the larger until you hit zero – when you do, you have the highest common factor.

For example, say we wanted to find the highest common factor of 90 and 144:

$$144 - 90 = 54 \quad \text{(swap the 144 for 54)}$$
$$90 - 54 = 36 \quad \text{(swap the 90 for 36)}$$
$$54 - 36 = 18 \quad \text{(swap the 54 for 18)}$$
$$36 - 18 = 18 \quad \text{(swap the 36 for 18)}$$
$$18 - 18 = 0$$

So 18 is the highest common factor of 90 and 144, that is, the largest times table that would have both 90 and 144 in it.

11 March

Pythagoras and Hannibal Lecter had quite different opinions on fava beans. Pythagoras lived around 570–495 BC and, like many prominent Greeks of the era, he was a philosopher as well as a mathematician. Details of his life are shrouded in mystery and hagiography – some even doubt that a single person called 'Pythagoras' existed at all – but the nearest thing we have to a fact is that he moved to Croton in Italy and started somewhat of a cult. Here are just a selection of bizarre facts that have been attributed to Pythagoras:

- He had a golden thigh.
- He was repulsed by fava beans and forbade his followers from eating them or having anything to do with them. One legend says his death came when the Pythagoreans were being chased by an opposing group and Pythagoras refused to run to his escape through a fava bean field, choosing death instead.
- He persuaded a bear towards pacifism.
- The river Kosas once greeted him by name (I heard this is also an upcoming Google feature).

12 March

Adding one metre can give you way more than a metre to work with.
Excuse me? How can that be? Consider 10 metres of bunting, pegged
on to the floor at both ends. Now consider the bunting being replaced
by an 11 m stretch instead, so that there is some slack to work with.

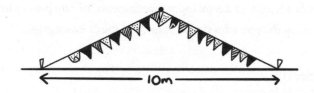

How high would the bunting be in the middle? Could a dog walk under
it? A child? Could *you* walk under it? Maybe it depends how tall you
are, or if you crouch down? The key here is that when the bunting
is stretched to its peak height, it essentially forms two right-angled
triangles, each of which has 5.5 m of bunting covering a 5 m length.
That's when Pythagoras comes knocking...

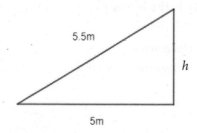

Since Pythagoras says the square of the length plus the square of the height will give the square of the hypotenuse, we can find the square of the height by working backwards:

$$5.5^2 - 5^2 = h^2$$
$$5.25 = h^2$$

This gives a height of 2.3 m, more than enough for any person to walk under (even the guy who stands in front of me at every gig).

13 March

If you like Pythagorean triples then you're going to love Pythagorean quadruples: sets of four numbers where the sum of the square of the first three terms makes the square of the fourth:

$(1, 2, 2, 3)$: $\qquad 1^2 + 2^2 + 2^2 = 3^2$
$(2, 3, 6, 7)$: $\qquad 2^2 + 3^2 + 6^2 = 7^2$

If the first three numbers represent the dimensions of a cuboid, then the fourth number is the length of the diagonal between furthest corners.

And if those Pythagorean quadruples got your blood pumping, behold the beautiful happenstance of this cubic quadruple:

$$3^3 + 4^3 + 5^3 = 6^3$$

14 March

Hold on to your hats… it gets better:

$$3^2 + 4^2 = 5^2$$
$$10^2 + 11^2 + 12^2 = 13^2 + 14^2$$
$$21^2 + 22^2 + 23^2 + 24^2 = 25^2 + 26^2 + 27^2$$

You can make your own similar fact like so: pick any odd square number; say 81. Note that 81 can be written as the sum of two consecutive numbers, $(40 + 41)$ and its root, 9, can also be written as two consecutive numbers $(4 + 5)$. Pair the first number from the first bracket with the second from the second bracket, and vice versa. So 40 with 5 and 41 with 4. The sum of the squares of the five numbers up to 40 will equal the sum of the squares of the four numbers starting from 41: $36^2 + 37^2 + 38^2 + 39^2 + 40^2 = 41^2 + 42^2 + 43^2 + 44^2$

15 March

No square number will ever end in a 2, 3, 7 or 8. Consider:

$$0^2 = 0 \quad 5^2 = 25$$
$$1^2 = 1 \quad 6^2 = 36$$
$$2^2 = 4 \quad 7^2 = 49$$
$$3^2 = 9 \quad 8^2 = 64$$
$$4^2 = 16 \quad 9^2 = 81$$

Notice that none of these square numbers end in 2, 3, 7 or 8. Now suppose you wanted to square a larger number, say 37^2. Whatever your chosen method to calculate this, it will involve performing 30×30, two lots of 30×7 and 7×7. The only contribution to the units digit of the answer will come from the square of the units digit in the question: $7^2 = 49$, so the answer to 37^2 will definitely end in a 9 (and indeed it does: $37^2 = 1369$). If you ever see a supposed square number that ends in a 2, 3, 7 or 8, something has gone wrong.*

16 March

Rational numbers are those that can be written as a <u>ratio</u> of whole numbers: the clue is in the name! A rational number is any number that can be written as a fraction, i.e. a ratio of one value to another. So 0.5 is rational because $0.5 = \frac{1}{2}$, as is 0.125 (because it's equal to $\frac{1}{8}$).

Any recurring decimal can also be written as a fraction and is therefore rational. So $0.\dot{3}$ is rational because it's equal to $\frac{1}{3}$, as is $0.\dot{1}4285\dot{7}$, which is equal to $\frac{1}{7}$. Here's a method for converting a recurring decimal to a fraction; say, for example, you want to convert 0.272727… to a fraction:

Let $x = 0.272727…$
Then $10x = 2.727272…$
And $100x = 27.272727…$

Notice that the decimal part in x and $100x$ are the same. This means that if we subtract one from the other, there will be no decimal part remaining:

$100x - x = 27.272727… - 0.272727…$
     $99x = 27$
       $x = \frac{27}{99}$, which simplifies to $\frac{3}{11}$

---

*   Or perhaps you're working in base other than 10…

17 March

If I were counting all of my daughter's friends who were less than 1 m tall, what is the largest height that I might include? 0.9 m? 0.99 m? 0.999999 m? Around this point you might be thinking 0.9̇ m, but be careful – **0.9̇ is literally the same number as 1.** That will feel odd at first, but upon careful consideration it's really the only possibility.

If 0.9̇ and 1 are not the same, then what's the difference between them? If there was some small, measurable difference between the two values then one of them could not be 0.9̇ – by definition this is infinitesimally close to 1, to the point that no discernible gap could ever be found. We could also use an algebraic approach to prove the same point:

Let $\quad x = 0.999999\ldots$
Then $\quad 10x = 9.999999\ldots$
$$10x - x = 9.999999\ldots - 0.999999\ldots$$
$$9x = 9$$
$$x = 1$$

I'm ashamed to admit I once engaged in a very long argument about this point on social media, with a man who shunned the mathematics of Leibniz, Cantor and Cauchy and had devised his own system (this should have been a red flag, admittedly). He believed that there was a definite difference between 0.9̇ and 1, and that his new system proved it to be so. There was a bit of back and forth, but eventually he saw my way of thinking. I'm kidding! Of course he didn't – have you never been on social media?

18 March

Hippasus was drowned for first discovering irrational numbers (possibly...). Hippasus was a member of the previously described Pythagorean brotherhood, and he had doubts about some of the fundamental tenets of Pythagoreanism. For example, Pythagoras and his followers believed that whole numbers were sacred, and that everything in mathematics, or life in general, can be described using whole numbers and the ratios between them, that is, the rational numbers: from the music that we play and listen to, to the movement of the stars in the night sky. But Hippasus wondered how we might express the distance from corner to corner of a unit square:

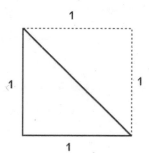

Clearly the diagonal length needs to be somewhere between 1 and 2, so let's apply the Pythagorean theorem and a bit of trial and error: perhaps the diagonal is 1.5? If so then, according to the Pythagorean theorem, $1^2 + 1^2 = 1.5^2$, but this isn't right: $1.5^2 = 2.25$, which is too big. Essentially we're looking for a number that squares to make 2 (the square root of 2), so let's try some more:

$1.4^2 = 1.96$ too low!

$1.45^2 = 2.1025$ too high!

$1.42^2 = 2.0164$ still too high!

$1.41^2 = 1.9881$ too low!

$1.415^2 = 2.002225$ too high!

This feels very tiresome, and it will never bear fruit anyway: $\sqrt{2}$ is *irrational*, it cannot be written as a fraction; if you try to write it as a decimal it will go on forever without terminating or repeating. Actually it starts like this: 1.41421356237…

Whether Hippasus was actually drowned for discovering irrational numbers, or for some other transgression, or even at all, is hard to say for sure. But it's more likely than his leader having a golden thigh.

19 March

If square numbers are the numbers of dots that could be put together in two dimensions to make a square, then <u>cube numbers</u> are the number of dots that could be put together in three dimensions to make a cube. Here are the first ten.

$1^3 = 1 \times 1 \times 1 = 1$ $6^3 = 216$

$2^3 = 2 \times 2 \times 2 = 8$ $7^3 = 343$

$3^3 = 3 \times 3 \times 3 = 27$ $8^3 = 512$

$4^3 = 4 \times 4 \times 4 = 64$ $9^3 = 729$

$5^3 = 5 \times 5 \times 5 = 125$ $10^3 = 1000$

Notice that **every one of the first ten cube numbers ends with a different digit**. Each of the digits from 0 to 9 features exactly once in the units place.

20 March

Happy International Day of Happiness! It's the 79th day of the year, and 79 is considered a 'happy' number. Here's why. Starting with any positive whole number, replace the number with the sum of the squares of its digits (even if it's just a one-digit number) and keep repeating the process. **If the number chain ends at 1, the original number is called a 'happy' number**.

79
$\rightarrow 7^2 + 9^2 = 49 + 81 = 130$
$\rightarrow 1^2 + 3^2 + 0^2 = 1 + 9 = 10$
$\rightarrow 1^2 + 0^2 = 1$

If a number's chain ends up looping in a cycle that does not include 1, it is a sad number 😢.

21 March

A couple of days ago we saw that every cube number ends in a different digit:

$1^3 = 1$	$6^3 = 216$
$2^3 = 8$	$7^3 = 343$
$3^3 = 27$	$8^3 = 512$
$4^3 = 64$	$9^3 = 729$
$5^3 = 125$	$10^3 = 1000$

There are some other fortuitous and useful connections:

- The <u>cubes</u> of 1, 4, 5, 6, 9 and 0 all end in the number itself: 1^3 ends in 1, 4^3 ends in 4, etc.
- 2 and 8, which are *complements* to 10 (sum to 10), have their last digits 'swap over' when cubed: 2^3 ends in an 8, and 8^3 ends in a 2.
- The same can be said for 3 and 7: 3^3 ends in a 7, and 7^3 ends in a 3.

All of this can be put together to form a neat trick, as follows. Ask someone to use a calculator to cube a two-digit number, but to tell you the result only. So they might tell you their cube number is 103,823. With enough practice, you can quickly tell them the number that they cubed.

Here's how it works: 103,823 ends in a 3, so the number that was cubed must end in a 7. We know that only numbers ending in a 7, when cubed, will end in a 3.

For the next step, we observe that cubing a multiple of 10 simply results in the same list as we had above, but scaled up by a factor of 1000:

$10^3 = 1000$ $60^3 = 216,000$
$20^3 = 8000$ $70^3 = 343,000$
$30^3 = 27,000$ $80^3 = 512,000$
$40^3 = 64,000$ $90^3 = 729,000$
$50^3 = 125,000$ $100^3 = 1,000,000$

We can now see that our target cube number, 103,823, is somewhere between 40^3 and 50^3. We already ascertained that it ends in a 7, so it must be true that $47^3 = 103,823$, and indeed it is.

22 March

The sum of the first *n* cube numbers always gives a square number.

Not only that but it always gives the square of the *n*th triangle number (1, 3, 6, etc).

$1^3 = 1$	and	$1^2 = 1$
$2^3 + 1^3 = 8 + 1 = 9$	and	$3^2 = 9$
$3^3 + 2^3 + 1^3 = 27 + 8 + 1 = 36$	and	$6^2 = 36$

23 March

How would you go about working out 3.5^2 without a calculator? Most methods – whether columns, 'box' method or something else – probably boil down to doing three and a half lots of three and a half. So $3.5 + 3.5 + 3.5 + 1.75 = 12.25$. But that's not particularly elegant. Here's something neat:

- 3.5 is halfway between 3 and 4, so multiply those numbers together: $3 \times 4 = 12$.
- Plop a 0.25 on the end: 12.25.

This always works! For example, $5.5^2 = 30.25$, because 5.5 is halfway between 5 and 6. A little bit of algebra can help us to see why this works:

$$(n + 0.5)^2 = n^2 + n + 0.25 = n(n + 1) + 0.25$$

24 March

The fifth power of a digit always ends with the digit itself:

$1^5 = 1$	$6^5 = 7776$
$2^5 = 32$	$7^5 = 16,807$
$3^5 = 243$	$8^5 = 32,768$
$4^5 = 1024$	$9^5 = 59,049$
$5^5 = 3125$	$10^5 = 100,000$

The list of fifth powers is certainly harder to memorize than the list of cube numbers, but if you can manage it then the trick for finding fifth roots is a cinch. Here's a fifth power that I prepared earlier: 1,934,917,632.

Firstly, break it into chunks of five, starting from the right-hand side: 19349 17632

The first chunk of five is going to give us the number in the tens place, and the second chunk of five will give us the units digit. The second chunk of five ends in 2, so we can immediately say that the fifth root we're looking for also ends in 2.

Finally we look at the first chunk: 19,349 falls between 7^5 and 8^5, so in a similar way to the cube roots trick we know that the fifth root we're looking for lies between 70 and 80. Therefore the fifth root of 1,934,917,632 must be 72.

This feature of the units digit being unaffected by raising to a power is true for fifth powers, ninth powers, thirteenth powers, seventeenth powers and any other number in that pattern. But I wouldn't recommend learning your seventeenth powers off by heart – not only is it very difficult but it has limited appeal as a party trick ('Think of a 34-digit number and I'll tell you its seventeenth root', said no one ever.)

25 March

Powers of numbers can grow very quickly indeed, but there is a sequence of numbers that grows even more rapidly. Imagine you have three tasks that you have to complete every morning – walk the dog, put on make-up, brush your teeth – but to keep things interesting you decide to do them in a different order every day. Would there be enough orderings to keep you going for a full week?

Dog, Make-up, Teeth
Dog, Teeth, Make-up
Make-up, Dog, Teeth
Make-up, Teeth, Dog
Teeth, Dog, Make-up
Teeth, Make-up, Dog

There are three options for what you could do first, but once that activity is used up there are only two options for what comes second, and then the final activity is determined by the first two. This means there are $3 \times 2 \times 1 = 6$ possible orderings; not quite enough to get through a whole week.

This operation of calculating the possible number of orderings is called the <u>factorial</u> operation, and its notation is an exclamation mark. It involves multiplying an integer by every smaller integer until you get to 1:

$$5! = 5 \times 4 \times 3 \times 2 \times 1 = 120$$
$$10! = 10 \times 9 \times \ldots \times 2 \times 1 = 3,628,800$$
$$15! = 15 \times 14 \times \ldots \times 2 \times 1 = 1,307,674,368,000$$

As you can see, **factorial numbers grow outrageously fast**: 5! is about the population of a tiny school or moderate-sized business; 10! is about the population of Uruguay, 15! is over a <u>trillion</u> – more people than have ever lived and likely ever will.

26 March

There are 52! orders that a pack of cards could be shuffled into – that is, $52 \times 51 \times 50 \times \ldots \times 2 \times 1$. This is a frighteningly large number. It's larger, for example, than the number of grains of sand on all the beaches and all the deserts on Earth. Actually, it's much bigger than that.

Imagine instead that each and every grain of sand on Earth is replaced by a universe of planets (and stars) as big as our own universe, but with one difference: every single planet in each universe is populated to a similar extent as Earth – that's 7 billion people on each planet. Each person on each of these planets shuffles a deck of cards once per second for their entire life. They'll have to be good at it though, as they'll need to meet a partner and procreate while doing so, and pass on the deck of cards to their offspring when they die. **When this has continued for around 10 million years, the total number of shuffles will be somewhere around 52!.*** If you want to do something unique today, simply shuffle a deck of cards: the chances are, no one in the history of the earth will ever have reached the particular arrangement that you end up with.

---

* My rough calculations if you're interested: 10^{18} grains of sand on Earth, 10^{25} planets, 7 $\times 10^9$ people on each planet, 3×10^7 seconds in a year, 10^6 years. 52! is about 10^{68}.

27 March

Two exclamation signs after a number either mean you're *really* excited about it or you're performing a *double factorial*. A double factorial involves multiplying by all the smaller integers that have the same parity – that is the same odd- or even-ness. So, for example,

$8!! = 8 \times 6 \times 4 \times 2 = 384$
$7!! = 7 \times 5 \times 3 \times 1 = 105$

It's worth noting that 8!! and 7!! between them are made up of all the numbers from 1 to 8 once and once only, so it must be true that $8!! \times 7!! = 8!$ More generally, $n!!(n-1)!! = n!$

One application of the double factorial is finding the number of possible pairings in a group. Say you had six students in your class: Anil, Beatrice, Che, Destiny, Edwin and Fionn (it's amazing how that always happens in these problems, isn't it?). Every day you want to pair up the students so that at least one pair is different from previous days. How many such pairings are there?

First let's pair up A with B and see what else we can do:

AB, CD, EF
AB, CE, DF
AB, CF, DE...

When A and B are paired, there are three people that C can be paired with, and then the last pair is set as there are only two people left over. More generally, once the first person is paired up one of **five** ways, there are then **three** ways that the next pair can be made, and **one** way that the third pair can be made. So there are $5 \times 3 \times 1$ ways that the class can be paired up. If you don't believe me, they're listed below. Generally, the number of pairings for any even number n is $(n - 1)!!$:

AB, CD, EF	AC, BD, EF	AD, BC, EF	AE, BC, DF	AF, BC, DE
AB, CE, DF	AC, BE, DF	AD, BE, CF	AE, BD, CF	AF, BD, CE
AB, CF, DE	AC, BF, DE	AD, BF, CE	AE, BF, CD	AF, BE, CD

By the way, the mathematical meaning of putting an exclamation mark on either side of a number, but with the first one upended – ¡8! – is to shout it in Spanish.

28 March

Powers and <u>logarithms</u> go hand in hand, where a logarithm is essentially the opposite of a power. For example, $10^2 = 100$ and $10^3 = 1000$, so if we are working in base 10 we would say that:

$$\log(100) = 2 \qquad \log(1000) = 3$$

Essentially, a logarithm in base 10 is the power that ten would need to be raised to to find the number in question. For powers of 10, the logarithm in base 10 is simply a count of all the zeros in the number:

$$\log(1,000,000) = 6 \qquad \log(10^{12}) = 12 \qquad \log(1) = 0$$

To take the logarithm of a large number in base 10, you can do a lot worse than just counting the number of digits. This will give you a pretty good approximation, especially for very large numbers. To give an example, the world's population at the time I'm writing this is 7,983,538,901. The logarithm of this 10-digit number is 9.902.

29 March

Mathematicians love a shortcut, and that's why we use multiplication as shorthand for lots of addition:

$3 + 3 + 3 + 3 + 3 = 15$	Boring and time-consuming
$5 \times 3 = 15$	Better

The same goes for multiplying:

$3 \times 3 \times 3 \times 3 \times 3 = 243$	Tedious and runs the risk of writing too few/many 3s
$3^5 = 243$	Much better!

Now if we want to write *really* big numbers we might find it useful to use a 'tower of powers', for example:

$$3^{2^2} = 3^4 = 81$$
$$3^{2^{2^2}} = 3^{16} = 43,046,721$$

Power towers are useful for writing very large numbers in a small space, but they do have a downside: with the convention that each <u>index</u> should be written smaller than the previous one, it does eventually become quite hard to read what's going on with the indices. And if you're using 2s, it does make the base look like it's having a little nap and catching some zzzzzzzs.

To get around this we might introduce another symbol, an 'up arrow' being shorthand for a power tower. **'Knuth's up-arrow notation', named after Donald Knuth, allows us to write preposterously large numbers with ease.** For example:

$2\uparrow3$ means the same as $2 \times 2 \times 2 = 8$, i.e. a string of three 2s, multiplied. This is known as 'exponentiation'.

$2\uparrow\uparrow3$ means the same as $2^{2^2} = 16$, i.e. a string of three 2s in a power tower.* This is known as 'repeated exponentiation' and it has no other widely accepted shorthand.

$2\uparrow\uparrow4$, therefore, is a string of four 2s in a power tower, which is $2^{16} = 65,536$. This all seems fairly reasonable until you realize that $2\uparrow\uparrow5$ will be $2^{65,536}$, which would be nearly 20,000 digits long if written out.†

30 March

We'll end the month with the largest number in the book, and **probably the largest number you'll ever come across**.

$3\uparrow\uparrow3$ is a 'triple stack' of 3s in a power tower: $3^{3^3} = 3^{27} = 7,625,597,484,987$

This is about 7 trillion: pretty big, but it fits on one line of a book at least. Let's add an arrow:

$3\uparrow\uparrow\uparrow3$ is a stack of 3s in a power tower 7,625,597,484,987 levels high. In other words, start with 3 and keep raising to the power of 3 until you have done it over 7 trillion times. Staggeringly huge. Almost offensively large.

---

* Or a 'sleepy two', as only I call it.
† Unfortunately the publisher still says this is an unacceptable way to hit my word count.

3↑↑↑↑3 is 3↑↑↑(3↑↑↑3), which is a power tower of 3s as high as 3↑↑↑3, which was already too large to really write down or conceptualize. However, *Graham's number*, for that is what we are moving towards, is still nowhere near the horizon. To reach Graham's number, you would need to repeat the process I have begun *another 63 times!* There really is no point in trying to understand the size of this number: it's like trying to imagine the fifth dimension, let alone the fourth. But here are three facts about Graham's number:

1) It is larger than the number of atoms in the observable universe.
2) It has an actual mathematical use, albeit as an upper bound for a fairly complicated problem in an area of mathematics known as *Ramsey theory.*
3) It ends in a 7.

31 March

Happy Birthday René Descartes! The legendary philosopher and mathematician was born on this day in 1596 in the town of Descartes – what are the chances?!* Probably best known for his snappy catchphrase '*Cogito, ergo sum*' ('I think, therefore I am'), **Descartes also founded the coordinate system** of x for units across and y for units up that is so fundamental to modern mathematics. It's named after him: the *cartesian* system.

It feels surprising that mathematicians had done just fine for thousands of years doing incredibly advanced mathematics without access to the coordinate system that nine- or ten-year-olds are now taught in schools, but this is the clumpy way in which mathematics often moves.

---

* Yes, yes: his birthplace of La Haye-en-Touraine was later named Descartes in his honour.

APRIL

HARDER, BETTER, FASTER, STRONGER

1 April

Here's the perfect mind-bending trick for April Fools' Day. Look carefully at the image below. You'll see two triangles, each 13 squares long and 5 squares high, and each made up of the same four constituent shapes. The only trouble is… one of them has a hole in it.

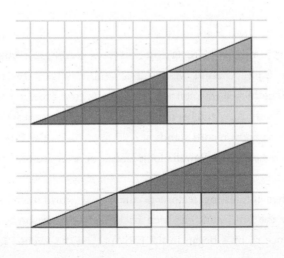

Now, either it is completely possible to rearrange the parts of the shape to make a larger whole (which would certainly be good news in terms of solving world hunger; we just make a giant triangle of rice and move the parts around) or some jiggery-pokery is going on. Of course it's the latter, but where? Keep reading for a couple of months and all will be revealed...

2 April

Ashrita Furman has broken over 600 world records in his lifetime, and at time of writing holds more than 500. The records he has broken include longest hike with a bike balanced on chin, longest distance cycled with a milk bottle balanced on head, and fastest mile travelled on a pogo stick while juggling. This means he holds the world record for the most world records broken (over 600) and the world record for the number of world records for most world records broken (one).

3 April

The long jump world record is longer than the pole vault world record is high. Armand 'Mondo' Duplantis has taken the pole vault to new lengths (or heights) in recent years, first breaking the world record in early 2020 and beating his own record five times in the years since. His current record stands at 6.22 m at time of writing, but this is nowhere near Mike Powell's long jump world record of 8.95 m from 1991.

Another interesting feature of these two world records is how regularly the pole vault has been broken in comparison to the long jump: since records began in the early part of the twentieth century, the pole vault world record has been extended 77 times; the long jump record has increased just 18 times. A large part of the reason for this is Bob Beamon's remarkable 'leap of the century' of 8.9 m in 1968, with which he increased the world record by over half a metre. This jump has only been surpassed once in more than fifty years since.

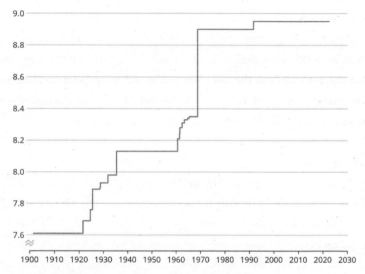

Progression of the long jump world record. Can you spot the 'leap of the century'?

4 April

The highest ever score achieved in a professional snooker match is 178. It's well known that the maximum break in snooker is 147, achieved by potting all fifteen reds (worth 1 point each) followed each time by blacks (worth 7 points each), and then each coloured ball from yellow through to black (2 points through to 7 points respectively), without missing a shot along the way. Breaks of 147 have become increasingly common since Steve Davis achieved the feat in competition for the first time in 1982, with Ronnie O'Sullivan recording the fastest ever 147 break in 1997, clocking in at 5 minutes and 8 seconds – the same length as an episode of *Peppa Pig*. For context, Cliff Thorburn made the first ever 147 break in the World Championship in 1983, and it took over 30 minutes to complete.

But if your partner makes some fouls before you start potting balls, a higher score than 147 can be achieved. Jimmy Robertson beat Lee Walker 178–6 in the final frame of their Scottish Open match in December 2021, with Walker handing Robertson 44 points' worth of fouls.

5 April

There have been 34 instances of men running the 100 m in 9.77 seconds or faster, and 21 of those times were set by athletes who have at some point in their career been banned for using performance-enhancing drugs. Nine of the remaining times, including the fastest three, were set by the legendary Usain Bolt. Thank goodness for the brilliant recent performances of Fred Kerley and Trayvon Bromell, without whom it would seem there are only two ways to win: cheat or be Bolt.

Athlete	Times at 9.77 s or under	Fastest time (s)
Usain Bolt	9	9.58
~~Tyson Gay~~	4	~~9.69~~
~~Yohan Blake~~	4	~~9.69~~
~~Asafa Powell~~	6	~~9.72~~
~~Justin Gatlin~~	5	~~9.74~~

~~Christian Coleman~~	~~1~~	~~9.76~~
Trayvon Bromell	2	9.76
Fred Kerley	2	9.76
~~Ferdinand Omanyala~~	~~1~~	~~9.77~~

6 April

The Albanian runner Luiza Gega has grounds to claim the title of the world's most versatile athlete, holding (at the time of writing) her country's national records in the 800 m, 1500 m, 3000 m, 5000 m, 10 km, 20 km, half-marathon and marathon, as well as the 2000 m and 3000 m steeplechase events. In other words, **no one in Albania's history could ever have beaten Luiza Gega over two or more laps of the track, with or without hurdles.** (Admittedly you don't really see a half-marathon or marathon run on an athletics track – it would take more than 100 laps to run a marathon and the number of athletes being lapped would be head-spinningly confusing. But if there ever *was* a marathon run on a track, she would probably win that too.)

7 April

Have you ever watched a televised marathon and wondered how long you could keep pace with the leading field? I know this is something that often crosses my mind. 'That doesn't look too bad, I could do that,' I'll utter while eating digestive biscuits in my boxer shorts. Not keeping pace for the entire race, of course, but keeping up for a couple of miles couldn't be too bad, could it? Or just for five minutes?

A marathon is 26.2 miles, or 42.2 km, which could be broken down into an incredibly dull 422 shuttle runs up and down a 100 m track.

The holy grail of distance running is the 2-hour marathon, which the legendary Eliud Kipchoge could potentially run in the coming years.*
Dividing 2 hours into 422 parts gives just over 17 seconds: incredibly, **you would need to run repeated 17-second 100 m bursts to keep up with Kipchoge for any given distance**. Even a three-hour marathon – a feat I personally know some people to have achieved – requires running 422 consecutive 25-second 100 m bursts.

8 April

If you live in a country where imperial measures are still widely used, it is often useful to be able to convert speeds between metres per second, often used for scientific purposes, and the more common everyday unit of miles per hour.

Say you were travelling at 30 miles per hour in your car and wanted to know what that is in metres per second. You might know that a mile is around 1600 metres, and an hour of course is $60 \times 60 = 3600$ seconds. 1600 metres in 3600 seconds is (very!) roughly half a metre per second, so 30 mph would be about 15 m/s (in truth it's 13.4 m/s). **Halving takes you roughly from mph to m/s, doubling from m/s to mph**.

This is all very well, but on the spot I can rarely remember which way round is halving and which way round is doubling. In these situations I picture Usain Bolt running the 100 m in under 10 seconds. (I still vividly remember watching him do this on screen through a department store window in Aberdeen in 2008. I locked eyes with a stranger who was doing the same thing as me and we stared agog at Bolt running 9.72 seconds seemingly without trying. No words were needed.)

---

* In fact he *has* broken the 2-hour barrier, but with a rotating team of pacemakers, rendering the time invalid for the history books.

If sprinters can run 100 m in 10 seconds, or 10 m/s, is that 5 mph or 20 mph? Well clearly it's not 5 mph – this is the painfully slow crawling speed that drivers are asked to use on gravel driveways. So 20 mph seems far more reasonable: I believe Usain Bolt could keep up with my car on small residential roads, but probably not when I'm driving around on regular 30 mph roads (that's anywhere with street lights – don't forget your highway code!). So m/s to mph must be doubling, and the other way halving.

9 April

Michael Phelps is the most decorated Olympian of all time, streets ahead of his closest rival with 28 medals achieved between 2004 and 2016, 23 of them gold. Many have commented on Phelps's seemingly God-given physique for swimming, with a huge torso and giant 2 m armspan (7 cm more than his height, in defiance of Da Vinci's *Vitruvian Man*).

It has also been discovered that Phelps creates around only half of the lactic acid that other athletes tend to, giving him a quicker recovery time and better ability to compete in several races within a short time period. Few would suggest that this biological quirk should have excluded Phelps from competing at the top level, but there is a precedent for this that causes a difficult double standard: the South African multi-Olympic champion runner Caster Semenya was ordered in 2019 to take medication to reduce her unusually high testosterone levels. It seems that the world of sport sometimes celebrates biological differences while at other times punishing them.

10 April

An entire basketball court could fit into the 18-yard box of a football (or soccer) pitch, so an average basketball game consists of around 20,000 people watching just one penalty area on a football pitch. In terms of the highest spectator to pitch size ratio, you'd have to go some to beat the 2020 'Match for Africa' between Roger Federer and Rafa Nadal, in which over 50,000 people peered down at a 24 m × 11 m tennis court. Federer won, though few people in attendance would have been able to tell that.

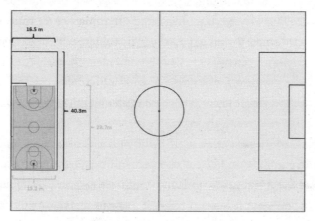

NBA Basketball Court Inside 18-Yard Box

11 April

A tennis match can be won in just 24 strokes for a woman, or 36 for a man. To achieve this feat you would need to win each of your own four-point service games with just one hit of the ball, and require your opponent to hit the net or miss the court entirely with each of their own serves.

Winning a set of tennis without losing a single point is known as a 'golden set', and it has only happened once in the main draw of a tennis Major: in the third round of the 2012 Wimbledon Championships, when Yaroslava Shvedova defeated Sara Errani without losing a single point in the first set.

12 April

The make-up of the world's population will look very different by as early as 2070. As I write this, India is inching towards overtaking China as the world's most populous country – in fact, by the time you read this it has probably happened.

Countries with a fertility rate of over 2.1 children per woman – known as the 'replacement rate' – are expanding the fastest, especially combined with relatively recent improvements in healthcare and medicine, which mean that more children live to adulthood and more adults live to old age. India is one such country, as is Nigeria. Africa is by far the most rapidly growing continent in terms of population, and most experts predict that **Nigeria – currently the world's seventh most populous country – will overtake the USA and leap into third on the world population leaderboard by 2050**.

The high replacement rate in many African countries means that the majority of countries on that continent have a median age of less than 20. The median age is the age that would be in the middle if you stood the entire country's population in age order, which means half the population are below that age. Niger has the world's lowest median age: just 14.8 years at time of writing. Japan's ageing population is well documented, and the country's median age of 48.6 is bested only by that of the wealthy principality of Monaco, with a median age of a whopping 55.4.

13 April

Europe, excluding Russia, makes up just 4% of the land on Earth. The six largest countries on Earth – Russia, Canada, China, Brazil, the United States and Australia – when added to Antarctica, between them cover half of the land on Earth.

Kazakhstan – much-maligned by many due to Sacha Baron Cohen's *Borat* character – is the world's largest landlocked country and isn't much smaller than the whole of Western Europe.

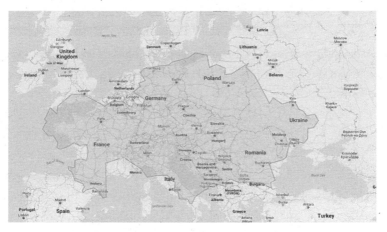

Kazakhstan superimposed over Western Europe.

14 April

The independent city-state of Monaco covers less than a square mile, but has a population of nearly 40,000, making it **the most densely populated country in the world**. To give some context, the combined area of Britain and Ireland is about 125,000 square miles. If people were packed on to these islands as tightly as they were in Monaco, about 6.5 billion people would fit. That's not far off the world's population, if they all squeezed in carefully.

15 April

Happy Birthday Leonhard Euler! The phenomenally talented and influential mathematician was born on this day in 1707, and you'll see his name crop up repeatedly through the rest of this book. For example, he discovered the following fact: **Every solid with flat faces* has two more faces and vertices combined than it has edges**. Take a cube, for example:

From dice games we know without counting that there are six faces. There are eight vertices, or corners (four at the top and four at the bottom) and twelve edges (four for the square at the top, four for the square at the bottom and four that join these faces). The number of faces and vertices combined is $6 + 8 = 14$, which is 2 more than the number of edges, 12.

---

* Strictly what we're talking about here are *polyhedra* – 3D shapes where every face is a polygon.

Let's check the simpler *tetrahedron* (triangle-based pyramid):

This has four faces, four vertices and six edges, so it fits the pattern: 4 + 4 = 6 + 2. This is *Euler's polyhedron formula* and it will work for any shape except for those with curved faces, such as a <u>cylinder</u>.

16 April

Euler's formula states that in any polyhedron (solids with flat faces) the following formula holds: $F + V = E + 2$, where F, V and E are the number of faces, vertices and edges respectively. Here's a way of showing why it works. Imagine looking top-down at a tetrahedron; it would look a bit like this:

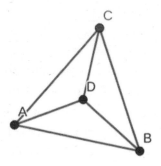

A, B, C and D are the vertices, with D being the <u>vertex</u> that is 'off the ground' and closest to you (though it's hard to tell that in 2D). All of the faces can be seen except the base. Because this is a 2D map of a 3D object, we have to use our imagination a little bit and say that the entire white area outside the triangle represents the base. We can then see from the picture that there are four faces (the three regions that are smaller triangles, plus the outside), four vertices (the dots) and six edges (the lines). So the number of faces and vertices is $4 + 4 = 8$, which is 2 more than the number of edges, 6, and Euler's formula holds ($4 + 4 = 6 + 2$). Now imagine removing the edge AC:

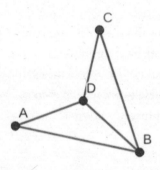

We've removed one face when we removed one edge, but faces and edges are on opposite sides of the equation $F + V = E + 2$, so the relationship still holds: $3 + 4 = 5 + 2$. Remove edge CB and the same happens again:

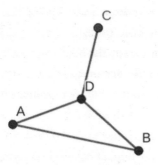

Now there are only 2 faces, still 4 vertices and only 4 edges, so we have $2 + 4 = 4 + 2$, and the formula still holds. Finally, imagine we remove the 'hanging edge' between D and C, and the vertex C with it. This will leave the number of faces unchanged, but reduce the number of vertices and edges both by 1. Again, vertices and edges are on opposite sides of the equation $F + V = E + 2$, so the relationship still holds. Keep removing edges in these two ways and eventually you'll end up with a lonely single point in space:

Ah, bless. Cue violin. That's one face (the whole space around the point), one vertex (the point) and no edges (no lines). In other words, even this fits the formula because there are two more faces and vertices combined (2) than there are edges (0). Because any polyhedron can be drawn as a <u>graph</u> in this way, and edges can always be gradually moved without disrupting the formula, the formula will always hold.

17 April

There are only five polyhedra in which every face is a regular polygon and the same number of faces meet at each vertex. These are known as the *platonic solids*; two of them we've come across already, the other three are a little more complicated.

Tetrahedron   Cube   Octahedron   Dodecahedron   Icosahedron

4 triangles   6 squares   8 triangles   12 pentagons   20 triangles

The platonic solids make great dice: the cube of course is the classic six-sided dice, and nerds will recognize the icosahedron as a twenty-sided 'D20' as popularized by the game Dungeons & Dragons. Plato associated each platonic solid (yes, that's where they got the name from, not because they're all just strictly good friends) with one of the classical elements: the cube being Earth, the octahedron air, the icosahedron water and the tetrahedron fire. Yes, there are five solids and four elements, but don't let facts get in the way of some good old mystical nonsense; Aristotle later decided that the fifth solid, the dodecahedron, represented the 'aether'. And why not.

18 April

There are definitely only five platonic solids, and here's why. In any solid you must have at least three faces meeting at any vertex; it's literally the definition of a corner. Try imagining two faces meeting at a corner and you'll quickly see that it doesn't make sense. We also need all the internal angles of the shapes that meet at a vertex to add up to less than 360° – if angles at a vertex add up to less than 360° then the faces can 'fold inwards' to meet each other and potentially form a 3D solid, whereas if angles at a vertex add up to exactly 360° they would create a 2D surface rather than a 3D solid. For example, the internal angles of an <u>equilateral triangle</u> are all 60°, so it's possible to have either three, four or five such triangles meeting at a point on a 3D solid. If you had six triangles meeting at a point that's 6 × 60° = 360°, which means we'll end up tiling a flat surface as in the picture below, rather than creating a 3D solid.

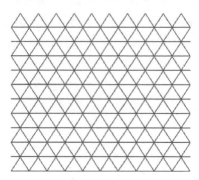

The internal angles of a cube are all 90°, so it's only possible to have three of these meeting at a point without tipping past 360°. Internal angles on a pentagon are 108°, so again we could have three of these meeting at a corner, but no more without tipping past 360°. Internal angles on a hexagon are 120°, but even three of these meeting at a point makes 360°, which means we could not have hexagons or beyond as the faces on a polyhedron. Bringing all of this together gives only five possibilities, each one corresponding to one of the platonic solids:

Three triangles meet at each vertex: tetrahedron
Four triangles meet at each vertex: octahedron
Five triangles meet at each vertex: icosahedron
Three squares meet at each vertex: cube
Three pentagons meet at each vertex: dodecahedron

19 April

Any map can be coloured with at most four colours, so that no two neighbouring countries share the same colour. It's fairly simple to construct a map that requires four colours, such as the one below, but no map could be constructed that would require five colours.

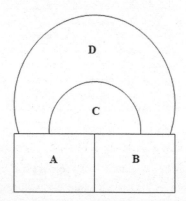

This result, known as the four-colour <u>theorem</u>, though easy to explain to a child, proved fiendishly difficult to prove. The eventual proof in 1976 by Kenneth Appel and Wolfgang Haken was extremely controversial, making great use of computers to manually check thousands of map configurations. Of course it's impossible to check every possible map, but Appel and Haken were able to reduce the infinite set of maps down to a finite but still enormous set, and then use computers to work through the checking of these maps. Many considered this to be a less than satisfactory mathematical approach; it is undoubtedly frustrating that such a beautifully simple idea requires such a complicated and technical proof.

20 April

The inaugural 2022 Laguiole AOP* cheese festival in France invited dairies to compete for the stretchiest cheese, with a scissor lift being utilized to make it possible to vertically stretch the cheese to its full gooey potential. **An outrageously ripe Aligot de l'Aubrac won the day with a stretch of more than 5 metres**. I showed the video of this seminal feat to my dad, whose reaction was: 'Give me a mild Cheddar any day.'

---

* AOP: *appellation d'origine protégée* (protected designation of origin).

21 April

Here's a fun game I like to play in my head on my cycle commute to work: start with any number, and carry out one of the following operations:

- If the number is even, halve it.
- If the number is odd, triple it and add 1.

Starting from 9 would give a chain that looks something like this:

$9 \rightarrow 28 \rightarrow 14 \rightarrow 7 \rightarrow 22 \rightarrow 11 \rightarrow 34 \rightarrow 17 \rightarrow 52 \rightarrow 26 \rightarrow 13 \rightarrow 40 \rightarrow 20 \rightarrow 10 \rightarrow 5 \rightarrow 16 \rightarrow 8 \rightarrow 4 \rightarrow 2 \rightarrow 1$

At this point the sequence just keeps endlessly cycling through 4, 2 and 1, and no starting number has yet been found that doesn't reach this eventual end, though **it has yet to be proved that every number will get to 1 using this process** (and of course it's hard to check them all...). This is known as the Collatz conjecture.

These numbers are often referred to as *hailstone* numbers, because they bounce up and down in a similar way to the formation of hailstones in the atmosphere. On this 111th day of the year, do spare a thought for 27, whose hailstone path takes an outrageous 111 steps to finally settle into the 4, 2, 1 loop.

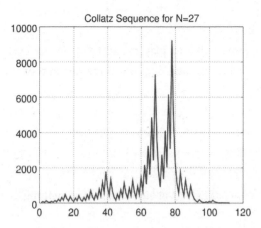

*Collatz path starting from 27 and reaching up
into the 9000s before finally settling.*

22 April

The longest-standing world record in athletics belongs to the Czech middle-distance runner Jarmila Kratochvílová, who set an 800 m time of 1:53.28 on 26 July 1983. Paul Young was riding high in the charts, Cabbage Patch Kids were the hot new toy and the first Super Mario Bros. arcade game was released, but **in all the time since 1983, no woman has run two laps of an athletics track faster than Kratochvílová**.

As you might have guessed, there have been repeated allegations of performance-enhancing drug use against Kratochvílová's achievement, leading to the International Association of Athletics Federations (IAAF) suggesting that all records before 2005 should be reset owing to the impossibility of truly checking the legitimacy of older records. This controversial step, if taken, would reset world records from illustrious names such as Florence Griffith Joyner, Hicham El Guerrouj and Paula Radcliffe.

23 April

It's very nerve-wracking to write about world records that could be broken between the time of a book's printing and publication, but here are some records that I'm confident will not be broken any time soon:

- Most VHS tapes sold: *The Lion King* is the best-selling VHS tape of all time, shifting 32 million copies in the US alone.
- Most bicycles eaten: Michel Lotito, aka 'Mr Eats it All', ate 18 bicycles. Guinness World Records have publicly stated that they will not accept challenges to this record.
- Longest javelin throw: Uwe Hohn threw a javelin 104.8 m in 1984. To throw a javelin this far in an athletics stadium is actively dangerous; as a result of some of the monstrous throws in the eighties, the weight and shape of the javelin was adjusted to assure shorter throws.
- Most holes-in-one in a round of golf: 11, by former Supreme Leader of North Korea Kim Jong-Il on his first and only round in 1994.

24 April

Hans Heyer is the only driver in the history of Formula 1 motor racing to earn a DNQ, DNF and DSQ in the same race. I appreciate you may not be down with the F1 lingo, so here you go:

DNQ: Did not qualify. This means the driver was essentially too slow in qualifying practice to be given a place in the race proper.

DNF: Did not finish. The driver started the race but had a crash or engine failure and didn't finish.

DSQ: Disqualified. The driver was forced to stop mid-race for breaking a rule: insufficient use of mirrors; not wearing seat belt; dropping litter out of the window. (I am not a big F1 fan – you might be able to tell.)

It was Heyer's first-ever race in Formula 1 at the 1977 German Grand Prix. He hadn't quite done well enough in qualifying to bag a space among the 24 starting cars, but he was fast enough to be third reserve. The two reserves ahead of him pulled out because of car engine issues between qualifying and the race, so Heyer would be in the race if just one car pulled out.

Alas, they did not. But when the race was delayed because of a failure with the starting lights, in the ensuing commotion Heyer saw an opportunity and sneaked on to the track at the back of the starting cars. He might have got away with it too, if it weren't for his pesky gearbox giving out after nine laps and earning him a DNF. Up to this point no one had even noticed that Heyer was racing, but when officials realized what he'd been up to he was promptly disqualified and given a five-race ban. As it happened, Heyer never raced in F1 again, but his legacy is secured forever.

25 April

Max Park is without doubt the greatest Rubik's cube solver of all time, holding the speed records for the 3×3×3, 4×4×4, 5×5×5, 6×6×6 and 7×7×7 cubes. The last of these records to fall was the 3×3×3 in 2023, which Max completed in 3.13 seconds (about as long as it takes to read the words between these brackets). I strongly recommend watching the video of this on YouTube – preferably on 0.5x speed. With half the hands it takes him twice as long: his one-handed record is a frankly ridiculous 6.2 seconds.

Max is an inspirational figure; at the age of two he was diagnosed with severe autism and his parents were told that he may need lifelong care. His mother encouraged him to try the Rubik's cube to aid with his motor skills – less developed because of his autism – and the rest, as they say, is history. The brilliant Netflix documentary *The Speed Cubers* is an essential watch for anyone wanting to find out more about Max or competitive cubing. My record is 1 minute 45 seconds for the 3×3×3, if you're interested.

26 April

As a teacher of mathematics (outside the USA) I probably work in one of the most low-risk jobs in the world in terms of personal injury or death, but what is the world's most dangerous job? There is some differing opinion on this matter, but the US-based Occupational Safety and Health Administration (OSHA) rates fishing and hunting work as the most hazardous occupation, with a fatal injury rate of 132.1 workers per 100,000.

However, one might argue that the top job of all – US president – is in fact far more dangerous, with eight presidents out of 46 dying in office. That's a relative rate of 17,391 per 100,000, meaning that **being president is around 130 times more dangerous than hunting.** It could be worse though: out of over 260 popes there have only ever been five papal renunciations, with every other pope dying while in post, resulting in a staggering death rate of over 98%. Yikes!

27 April

If I told you that **the world record for continuously playing a video game is 138 hours and 40 seconds**, you would probably not be all that impressed. Sitting down on your backside staring into a screen for nearly six days straight, while surely very unhealthy to one's mental state, is just about imaginable. I've certainly taught students whose mental presence in lessons has given off the air of someone who'd been wired into *Call of Duty* for days on end.

The record in question, however, belongs to Carrie Swidecki, who in 2015 played the arcade classic *Just Dance* for the best part of a week without breaks. If you're unfamiliar with the game, it involves copying high-energy dance moves to popular songs by placing your feet on the correct part of the floor at the right time. It's about as far from the sedentary ideal of the online gamer as it's possible to get. All hail Carrie!

28 April

The Covid-19 lockdowns of 2020 and 2021 were a horrible time for many of us, robbing us of the social interaction outside of the house that we all thrive on. There were some positives, however: perhaps you took on a new hobby, learnt a language or became a prominent member of the Handforth Parish Council.

One dubious advantage of the lockdowns in the USA was that immensely quieter roads led to multiple record-breaking *cannonball runs* – that is, the quickest cross-country drive from New York City to Los Angeles. **The current record for the 2906-mile cross-country trip (that's 4677 km) is a quite absurd 25 hours and 39 minutes**, set by Arne Toman and Doug Tabbutt with an average driving speed of 112 mph. They took just five fuel stops and hit a peak speed of 175 mph in a car with a reshaped front grille and fake badge to make it resemble a police vehicle.

If you're wondering how any of this can possibly be legal and why Toman and Tabbutt are minor celebrities rather than being in jail, the answer is fairly simple: it's America.

29 April

Here's an altogether more innocent and less dangerous world record inspired by Covid-19: the record for putting on multiple surgical masks. We all got fairly good at putting masks on at that time, perhaps even wearing two masks at once to be on the safe side, but none of us can claim to be as competent or as virus-aware as one **George Peel, who managed to don ten surgical masks in just 7.35 seconds**. This one is well worth a google.

30 April

Happy Birthday Carl Friedrich Gauss! The German mathematician, born 1777, was one of the most influential mathematicians in history and made several huge contributions to the advancement of the field.

An anecdote is often told of a lazy (or possibly inspired) teacher who asked the class that included the young Gauss to add up all the numbers from 1 to 100, hoping to buy themselves a few precious minutes. A precocious youth, Gauss almost immediately returned the correct answer of 5050, by pairing the numbers from either end of the list and noting that this results in 50 pairs that each add up to 101:

$1 + 2 + 3 + ... + 98 + 99 + 100 = (1 + 100) + (2 + 99) + (3 + 98) + ... = 50 \times 101$

Because the '101' is formed by adding the smallest and largest numbers in the sequence, and the '50' by counting the pairs of numbers in the list, this process can actually be adjusted to add together any *arithmetic sequence* – that's any sequence with common gaps between the numbers.

Say you wanted to add together all the numbers in the traditional 5 times table, from 5 to 60. It would be quite laborious to do this, until you realize the table can be written as six pairs of numbers that all add up to 65: $6 \times 65 = 390$, the correct answer.

$5 + 10 + 15 + 20 + 25 + 30 + 35 + 40 + 45 + 50 + 55 + 60$
$= (5 + 60) + (10 + 55) + (15 + 50) + (20 + 45) + (25 + 40) + (30 + 35)$
$= 65 + 65 + 65 + 65 + 65 + 65$
$= 390$

MAY

MEASURE FOR MEASURE

1 May

The names of standard 'A' paper sizes come from the number of folds of an enormous piece of A0 paper that result in those dimensions. So A1 is a piece of A0 paper folded once, A2 is a piece of A0 paper folded twice, and so on. The dimensions for A0 are 849 × 1189 mm – this is charmingly known as 'Grandmother' size – chosen to give an area of one square metre (you can check that if you like). Then the other paper sizes follow by halving. It's curious and somewhat reassuring that, after all this time, we still stick to this halving sequence of paper sizes.

If you use a photocopier a lot in your daily work (or just for fun) you may have noticed that doubling a print size from A5 to A4, or A4 to A3, is called a '141%' enlargement. Where does that very particular percentage come from?

Let's say your garden, overnight, magically doubled its length and width (never mind what the neighbours say). You would find yourself with *four times* as much garden, not twice as much, since scaling up both the length and the width by a factor of 2 scales up the area by a factor of 4. Likewise, if your garden tripled in length and width, you'd find yourself with nine times as much garden, and so on.

When you move from A4 to A3, though, the *area* doubles, not the length:

Length scale factor	Area scale factor
×2	×4
×3	×9
×$\sqrt{2}$	×2

The area scale factor is always the square of the length scale factor, so the length scale factor when a paper size is doubled must be $\sqrt{2}$, or 1.41 approximately, hence the 141% enlargement. (And we must say *approximately* 1.41, because we know from March that $\sqrt{2}$ is an irrational number: Hippasus was drowned for suggesting as much (possibly).)

2 May

Say you were starting from scratch and wanted to invent a paper size that maintained the aspect ratio (that is, the ratio between its length and width) when folded in half. You could show this in the following diagram, where the original paper size has length a and width b, and the new paper size has width half of a ($a/2$):

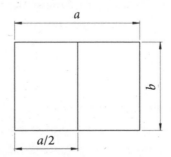

Now we need the ratio between a and b to be the same as the ratio between b and half of a:

$$\frac{a}{b} = \frac{b}{a/2}$$

$$\frac{a}{b} = \frac{2b}{a}$$

$$a^2 = 2b^2$$

$$\frac{a^2}{b^2} = 2$$

$$\frac{a}{b} = \sqrt{2}$$

It turns out that $\sqrt{2}$ is the *only* value that maintains aspect ratio at every step. This aspect ratio is known as the 'Lichtenberg' ratio, as the idea was first noted in 1786 by the German scientist and philosopher Georg Christoph Lichtenberg.

3 May

Happy 123rd day of the year! Take any number, preferably a quite long number, and write down the number of its even digits, odd digits and total number of digits, in that order. Put the three numbers together to form a new number. Then keep repeating those steps. For example,

2,718,281,828,459,045 → 10,616 → 325 → 123

You'll always end up at 123. Try it yourself…

4 May

Happy Star Wars Day! May the fourth be with you! By the time Alec Guinness was approached to play the part of Obi-Wan Kenobi in the original *Star Wars* movie he was already an established Hollywood heavyweight and was not entirely sold on the idea of playing a samurai space wizard, reportedly describing the role to friends as 'fairy-tale rubbish'. He turned down the original offer of $150,000 to play the role, instead requesting this fee be doubled and, crucially, that he receive 2% of the film's gross intake. George Lucas upped this to 2.25% as a goodwill gesture, and the rest is history: **Alec Guinness earned nearly $100 million from the *Star Wars* deal by the time of his death in 2000**.

5 May

Square metres are not the same as metres squared. What? OK, let's slow this down a bit. Imagine a piece of turf that is 1 m long and 1 m wide. Its area is 1 m^2, because $1 \times 1 = 1$. It doesn't matter if you say 'metres squared' or 'square metres', because it's the same either way.

But imagine instead a garden that is a 10 m × 10 m square. The area of this garden is $10 \times 10 = 100$ m^2, which we might be tempted to pronounce as 'one hundred metres squared', but this can be terribly misleading. It implies a square that's 100 m long and 100 m wide, which is drastically larger than the actual garden! If we say 'one hundred square metres', it's clear that we're talking about an area that's 100 times as large as the original 1 m × 1 m square, which is correct. The dimensions of the garden could be 10 m × 10 m, or 5 m × 20 m, or even 100 m × 1 m; they're all 100 m^2, or 'one hundred square metres'.

It's a very easy mistake to make. At one point during the Russia–Ukraine war, Ukraine's president Volodymyr Zelensky announced that the country had regained about 6000 square kilometres of territory. One's brain can't help but imagine an enormous square that's 6000 km by 6000 km, but that would be larger than the whole of Ukraine! Whereas 6000 square kilometres is more like a square that's 77 km × 77 km, about the size of Lincolnshire.

Here's a humorous Amazon review that falls for the same error...

6 May

Proxima Centauri, our next closest star after the Sun, is 4.25 light-years away; our Sun is 8 light-minutes away. If, like me, your brain simply cannot comprehend the sheer number of zeros required to understand the length of a light-year in metres, here's a handy way to remember: **a light-year is 95 followed by (9 + 5) zeros:** 9,500,000,000,000,000 m. To change that to kilometres, of course, just remove three zeros: 9,500,000,000,000 km. To switch it to miles, just swap round the 5 and the 9: 5,900,000,000,000 miles.

7 May

Even though it has the word 'year' in its name, **a light-year is a measure of distance, not time**: it is quite literally the distance that light will travel in a year. Many people have confused it for a measure of time though, and surely will continue to do so: a cursory check through lyrics archive genius.com reveals that oddly popular rapper Logic, pre-Polyphonic Spree psych rockers Tripping Daisy and LSMK (no idea) had all 'waited a light-year' at some point in their lyrical careers. Unless they have developed a new way of waiting for a distance, I am sceptical.

8 May

We've established that light can travel about 9.5 <u>quadrillion</u> metres in a year, and back in February we saw that there are about ten-pi (10π) million seconds in a year. Also notice that 9.5 is close to 3π. Now see what happens when we divide the length of a light-year in metres by the number of seconds in a year, to give the speed of light:

9,500,000,000,000,000 / 31,400,000 ≈ 300,000,000 m/s

That's 300 million metres per second, or 300,000 km per second. The speed of sound is 343 metres per second, so **light travels roughly a million times faster than sound**.* Fans of imperial measurements may enjoy the fact that, since there are about three feet to a metre, light travels a foot per nanosecond (that's about one thousand million feet per second) whereas sound travels a foot per millisecond (that's about a thousand feet per second).

---

* Do you notice how the word 'roughly' is doing quite a lot of work in this chapter?

9 May

You may have heard that it's impossible to fold a piece of paper more than seven or eight times. This challenge has become a piece of folklore passed down through generations of schoolchildren as a boredom buster in slower lessons, but what most schoolchildren probably don't do is work out the underlying maths. It isn't all that complicated: let's start with a piece of A4 paper, which measures 210 × 297 mm* and is 0.1 mm thick. Now, every time you fold the paper the height or width will alternately halve, but crucially the thickness always doubles. Let's track that:

Fold	Length (mm)	Width (mm)	Thickness (mm)
0	297	210	0.1
1	148.5	210	0.2
2	148.5	105	0.4
3	74.25	105	0.8
4	74.25	52.5	1.6
5	37.125	52.5	3.2
6	37.125	26.25	6.4
7	18.5625	26.25	12.8
8	18.5625	13.125	25.6

On the eighth fold we encounter a problem: if this fold were possible we would have made a piece of paper that is thicker than it is long or wide. But that is clearly impossible; **a piece of A4 cannot be folded more than seven times**.

---

* 297/210 ≈ $\sqrt{2}$; thanks, Mr Lichtenberg!

10 May

From reading yesterday's entry on paper folding and the supposed seven-fold limit, you may well be thinking that if an A4 piece of paper was half as thin as regulation paper then you'd be able to make an eighth fold – and indeed you'd be correct. Standard paper sizes tend to keep the thickness within a reasonable proportion of the length and width so that the paper actually has some tangible use, but with thin enough paper – or a long enough piece of paper – more folds are possible.

Britney Gallivan – when she was a junior in high school (that's age 16 for my British friends) – established a formula for folding paper repeatedly in just one direction, and it looks like this:

$$L = \frac{\pi T}{6} (2^n + 4)(2^n - 1)$$

Here T is the paper thickness, n is the intended number of folds and L is the required paper length (remember that width is irrelevant as this formula involves repeated folding in one direction). Gallivan wanted to fold a piece of toilet paper twelve times, and by creating a roll more than a kilometre long she was able to do exactly that.

11 May

The beard-second is a unit of measurement that is both light-hearted and light-inspired: in the same way that the light-year measures the distance that light can travel in a year, **the beard-second measures the distance that a beard can grow in a second**. Whereas a light-year is phenomenally large, the beard-second is pathetically small: it is either 5 or 10 nanometres, depending on whom you ask (that's 5 or 10 billionths of a metre).

Or if, like me, you are a forty-year-old man whose facial hair is routinely less impressive than his teenage students, then the beard-second will be smaller still.

12 May

Happy Birthday Florence Nightingale! Nightingale is remembered by most as the 'Lady with the Lamp', a pioneering nurse who founded modern nursing and did more than any other single person to advance standards of health and cleanliness in hospitals.

What fewer people know is that Nightingale was also a pioneer of data visualization and introduced an advanced version of a pie chart known as a 'coxcomb' diagram in the 1850s, when pie charts themselves

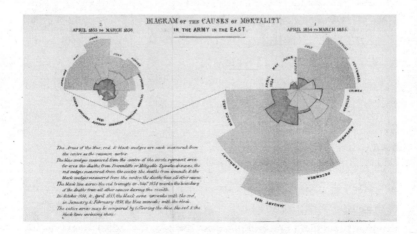

Nightingale's original coxcomb diagram was ingenious and well ahead of its time, showing the death rates from both disease and wounds across two years, each split into 12 months.

were barely even a thing. If you've seen the opening of the film *Inception*, when the characters have barely discovered that they're in a dream when they realize they're actually in a dream-within-a-dream, you'll appreciate how impressive this is.

13 May

You may well have heard the legendary story of the person who invented chess, and how they asked for their payment in grains of rice (or wheat, depending on where you read it): one grain on the first square, two grains on the second, four on the next, and so on until the board is full. It's unclear whether or not this ever actually happened or was constructed purely as an analogy to highlight the nature of <u>exponential growth</u>, but either way the results are startling.

The 32nd square, i.e. halfway through the board, would contain somewhere around 100,000 to 150,000 kg of rice: enough to make a cube of 1 kg rice bags that is 50 bags wide, 50 bags long and 50 bags high. This is an enormous amount of rice, but not unimaginable; you could fit it on the stage at a reasonably large concert venue.

However, **double this quantity of rice another 32 times and you will not be able to find enough rice in the world to satisfy the quantity you require for the 64th square**. To cover the board you'd need more than 300 billion tonnes of rice: there has probably not been enough rice produced in the history of the earth. The American inventor and futurist Ray Kurzweil coined the phrase 'the second half of the chessboard' to describe the point, especially in economics, where exponential growth gets completely out of hand.

14 May

A fantastically fortuitous fluke occurs when you carry out the same chessboard calculation but using British pennies instead of grains of rice (or indeed any coin that is 1 mm thick). The 64th square contains 2^{63} pennies, which is 9.22×10^{18} pennies high, or roughly 9 with eighteen zeros after it. That's the height of the stack in millimetres, since each coin is 1 mm thick, but working in millimetres is a little clunky, so let's convert that figure:

millimetres:	9.22×10^{18} mm	9 with eighteen zeros	9 quintillion mm
metres:	9.22×10^{15} m	9 with fifteen zeros	9 quadrillion m
kilometres:	9.22×10^{12} km	9 with twelve zeros	9 trillion km

Give yourself a pat on the back if you recognized 9-and-a-bit trillion kilometres: it is very nearly a light-year (9.46 trillion km, to be more precise): the distance light would travel in one year. **If you did the chessboard–rice problem with pennies instead of rice, it would take a stack of pennies a light-year high to satisfy the 64th square**.

15 May

The tenth power of 2 (1024) is very close to the third power of 10 (1000), and this fortuitous aligning of easy-to-work-with numbers can make rough mental conversions of large numbers easier.

For example, earlier we wanted to know how many grains of rice, or pennies, would be on the 64th square of the chessboard if you started with the sequence 1, 2, 4, 8, … This would involve taking the first grain or penny, and doubling it 63 times, so we need to know the value of 2^{63}.

Imagine you needed to do this in your head – or you just wanted to do it in your head for an enjoyable challenge. 2^{63} is a string of sixty-three 2s multiplied together, which can be written as:

$$2^{63} = 2^{10} \times 2^{10} \times 2^{10} \times 2^{10} \times 2^{10} \times 2^{10} \times 2^{3}$$

But each group of ten 2s multiplied together (2^{10}) can be swapped (roughly!) for three 10s multiplied together (10^{3}). Using the 'approximately equal to' sign, $\approx$, we can say:

$$2^{63} \approx 10^{3} \times 10^{3} \times 10^{3} \times 10^{3} \times 10^{3} \times 10^{3} \times 2^{3}$$
$$2^{63} \approx 10^{18} \times 2^{3}$$
$$2^{63} \approx 8 \times 10^{18}$$

The actual number of pennies was 9.22×10^{18}, so we were a quintillion or so under due to all the times we used 1000 instead of 1024, but only off by about 15%, which isn't too bad for a mental calculation.

16 May

A 'New York second' is a humorous measurement for the shortest length of time in the known universe. It is defined as **the length of time between a traffic light turning green and the yellow cab behind you honking its horn**.

17 May

The surface area of a <u>sphere</u> is four times the area of the circle at its centre. This fact leads to a fun game to play before you eat a tangerine or satsuma (whatever the difference is). Before you peel it, draw four circles around it on a piece of paper. When you remove the peel and lay it flat it should perfectly fit the four circles – more or less…

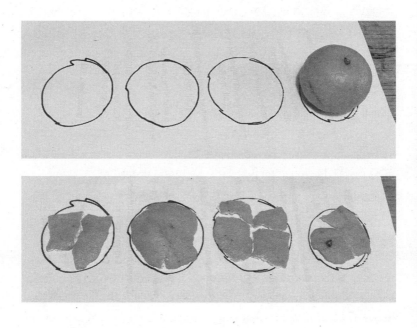

18 May

If a sphere sits perfectly inside a top-and-bottomless cylinder of the same height, the sphere and the cylinder have the same surface area. Imagine a stubby can of soup that is exactly as wide as it is high; a ball inside the can would have the same surface area as the label on the can.

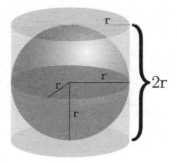

A sphere's surface area is $4\pi r^2$, and the area of the 'label' of the can is its height multiplied by the <u>circumference</u> of the inner circle, which is $2r \times 2\pi r = 4\pi r^2$.

A neat consequence of this fact is that **a spherical loaf of bread, cut into slices of equal thickness, would offer the same amount of crust on every slice**. The perfect solution for families, like mine, where everyone fights over who gets the endpiece.*

---

* What do you call the endpiece of a loaf of bread? The 'crust' seems popular, but that's the name for the whole exterior, surely? I've heard it called the 'heel', but in my family growing up it was always the 'nobby'. I'm absolutely willing to accept that this is very weird. Even if there's no consensus on the name, I'm sure we can all agree that it's the best slice in the loaf.

19 May

Why are coins circular and not square? It may have something to do with aesthetics and minimizing use of materials, but there are other practical reasons. Imagine sliding a square coin into a vending machine – it would not be able to roll once inside the chute, because when a square rolls (or makes a clunky attempt to roll), its height changes because the distance measured from corner to corner is longer than the distance along an edge. The same is true of a pentagon, hexagon or any other polygon, so none of these shapes could roll neatly within a chute of a certain height or width. The only shape that can do this is a circle, right?

Well, not quite. There are other *shapes of constant width*, most notably the *Reuleaux triangle*:

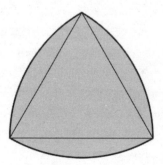

The Reuleaux triangle is formed by starting with an equilateral triangle and then 'rounding off' each edge by drawing a circular arc between two vertices, with the compass point at the furthest vertex. This means that every point on any edge is the same constant distance from the opposite corner; **the Reuleaux triangle can 'roll' along a surface and**

its height above that surface remains constant. More complicated shapes of constant width can be made with a similar approach, such as the 'equilateral curve heptagon' or 'Reuleaux heptagon' shape of British 20p and 50p coins, or the 'Reuleaux hendecagon' shape of the Canadian loonie (that's 11 sides).

20 May

A gömböc is a strange mathematical object: the first known homogenous object with one stable and one unstable equilibrium point. In human speak, that means that **however you place a gömböc on a flat surface, it will always self-right itself to the same position**. This will sound familiar to anyone who ever played with a 'weeble' or similar self-righting toy as a child; the difference is that the gömböc is made of one single homogenous material and does not need to be weighted at the bottom.

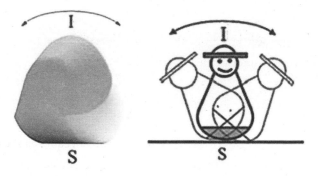

The marked 'S' is the 'stable equilibrium point' that the gömböc will always return to, and the 'I' is the 'unstable equilibrium point': that is, a point that the solid could theoretically be balanced upon, but even if you managed it, the tiniest disturbance would send it toppling to settle on the stable equilibrium point. The shape of the gömböc is remarkably similar to that of many tortoise shells; those tortoises can self-right themselves if upended with little use of their legs.

21 May

In my day job as an A-level maths teacher I'm always keen to see results improve year on year, but I've noticed that my students who also study physics tend to do better than those who don't:

2022 Non-physicists
Sitters: 10
Passers: 4
Pass rate: 40%

2022 Physicists
Sitters: 90
Passers: 76
Pass rate: 84.4%

We had a big push after these results and were delighted to see results for both groups improve the following year:

2023 Non-physicists
Sitters: 30
Passers: 15
Pass rate: 50%

2023 Physicists
Sitters: 70
Passers: 60
Pass rate: 85.7%

Of course I'd like to see the non-physicists doing as well as their physics-studying peers, but I was pleased to see both groups heading in the right direction. In fact I was so pleased that I decided to collate the information and make a poster to show off our success in 2023:

2022 results: 80/100 passers, 80% pass rate
2023 results: 75/100 passers, 75% pass rate

Hang on... the results for physicists and non-physicists improved in 2023, but overall results got worse. What on earth? This statistical phenomenon is known as *Simpson's paradox* and it's a true head-scratcher. Generally it can happen when there is a large discrepancy between the sizes of two merged subgroups (above there were vastly more physicists than non-physicists) and it serves as a warning not to trust too much in percentages without seeing the underlying raw figures.*

---

* Please note this data was completely fabricated to make my point; please do not use it to judge results at my place of work.

22 May

When researching some of the population statistics in this book I had cause to look up the countries of the world sorted by population, and an internet search threw up the following table from the website worldometers.info. See if you can work out what's gone wrong in this list of the world's most populous countries (I've just shown the first ten…).

1	Honduras	9,904,607
2	United Arab Emirates	9,890,402
3	Djibouti	988,000
4	Saint Barthélemy	9,877
5	Seychelles	98,347
6	Antigua and Barbuda	97,929
7	Vietnam	97,338,579
8	Hungary	9,660,351
9	Tajikistan	9,537,645
10	Belarus	9,449,323

Either Djibouti and the Seychelles are more dominant global superpowers than I had realized, or something has gone wrong with the way that table has been sorted. What do these countries all have in common? Their populations all start with a '9' – that's right, the populations have been sorted as if they are words, like you might sort the books on your bookshelf by author name. Honduras wins out because the first two digits of its population (at time of measuring) are both 9s. It doesn't matter that the Caribbean island of Saint Barthélemy has fewer inhabitants than the town you grew up in; it starts with '987' so it flies up the list. This is an easy mistake to make, but it's not ideal that this table was for a long time the number 1 Google hit when searching for 'countries sorted by population'.

23 May

What yesterday's website of wrongly sorted populations does offer us is an easy opportunity to count how many countries of the world have populations that start with each number from 1–9:

Leading digit	Frequency	Percentage of all country populations
1	68	29.1
2	37	15.8
3	30	12.8
4	21	9.0
5	27	11.5
6	18	7.7
7	8	3.4
8	14	6.0
9	11	4.7

The largest proportion is for countries whose population has a leading digit of 1, followed by 2, and then the numbers generally descend, albeit with a little bit of wobbling further down the list. This behaviour tallies strongly with what *Benford's law* predicts – namely, that **in many real-life data sets, around 30% of leading digits will be a 1, with fewer leading 2s, even fewer leading 3s, and so on.** Here's my country data (in black) plotted as a bar chart against what Benford's law would predict (in grey):

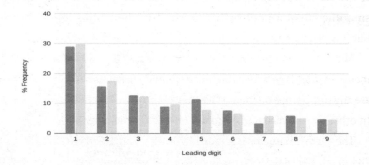

Not a bad fit. Benford's law is often used in criminal trials when investigating fraud: if people deceitfully invent data, they will tend to create numbers with an even spread of all leading digits, whereas true data should follow Benford's law.

To appreciate why this phenomenon occurs I usually use the example of house numbers. Some people live on very small streets with fewer than ten houses, but every street has a house number 1, so 1 is already off to a head start. If your street gets just beyond ten houses that's also good news for leading digits of 1, since house numbers 11, 12, 13, etc. all contribute. If your street just nudges past one hundred houses this is even better news for leading 1s, as the houses from numbers 100–199 all contribute leading 1s. For every length of street there will be at least as many leading 1s as leading 2s, but almost always more – the exact same argument can be used to show that there will be more leading 2s than 3s, more leading 3s than 4s, and so on.

24 May

If the earth was scaled down to the size of a pool ball, it would be smoother than a pool ball. You may have heard this legend before, but it is pleasing to run the numbers and see that it actually checks out.

The World Pool-Billiard Association states that a pool ball is 2.25 inches in <u>diameter</u>, with a tolerance of 0.005 inches either way, so if there are any tiny bumps on the surface they must be within these error bounds. In other words, variation of up to 1/450 of the diameter is allowable.

The earth's diameter is about 12,700 km, and 1/450 of this is around 28 km – more than twice the height of Everest (about 9 km) or the depth of the Mariana Trench (about 10 km). It does appear to be true that if the earth was drained of water, it would be smoother than a pool ball.

25 May

You might have heard that **the deepest ocean on Earth is deeper than the tallest mountain is high**. What's perhaps less well known is just how much difference there is in the accessibility of the two locations.

Challenger Deep, the deepest part of the Mariana Trench, has been visited by just thirteen individuals, whereas over 4000 people have scaled Everest. The photographer Nirmal Purja took this astonishing picture of a queue to scale the peak of Everest, a sight which made the prospect feel suddenly more attractive to millions of Brits.

To put this into perspective, the number of people who have successfully climbed Everest outnumbers those who have swum the English Channel by a ratio of more than 2 to 1 (over 4000 compared with around 1800).

26 May

The official narrowest width of the English Channel is 21 miles, or 34 km (successive Fibonacci numbers – more of this next month). However, if you fancy taking on the Herculean task of swimming across the Channel you must be prepared to swim much further than that: because of the changing tides, you will spend a large amount of time practically going backwards.

Gertrude Ederle, the first woman to cross the Channel, is thought to have swum around 34 miles – more than 150% of the direct shortest distance – due to rough conditions. Jackie Cobell's slowest ever crossing (29 hours!) in 2010 was more like 65 miles because she was swept brutally off course. Here is the path that my friend Anna Ploszajski took when she completed a crossing in 2018.

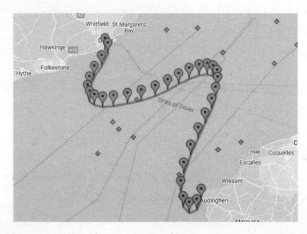

27 May

The New York local television network WKBW-TV developed a method of describing the severity of a snowstorm called the 'Jimmy Griffin Snow Index'. In 1985 the mayor of Buffalo, NY, one James D. Griffin, was given the nickname 'six-pack Jimmy' when he suggested that residents grab a six-pack of beer to wait out an incoming snowstorm. **The index is measured in cans of beer, with approximately one can for every 4 inches (10 cm) of snow**. So a foot of snow is about a three-can storm.

28 May

Multiplying a two-digit number by 11 can be done very easily in your head: simply insert the sum of the two digits between the digits themselves. So $24 \times 11 = 264$, because 6 is the sum of 2 and 4; $36 \times 11 = 396$, because 9 is the sum of 3 and 6.

Occasionally a small amount of carrying will be required: when calculating 58×11 we have a sum of digits that is 13, leading to 5(13)8, which clearly doesn't look right. Just carry the '1' from the '13' and add it to the '5' on its left, to give 638.

11 is a very short 'repunit', that is, a repeated unit. Squaring repunits tends to lead to a pretty pattern:

$$11^2 = 121$$
$$111^2 = 12321$$
$$1111^2 = 1234321$$
$$11111^2 = 123454321$$

and so on.

29 May

One *mickey* is the smallest distance it's possible to move a computer mouse pointing device (the name comes from the Disney character). The sensitivity of a mouse is usually specified in mickeys per inch, with most typical computer devices having resolutions of 500 mickeys per inch (that's about 16 mickeys per mm).

30 May

Some unit conversion rhymes:

> *Two and a quarter pounds of jam, weighs about a kilogram.*
> *A litre of water's a pint and three-quarters.*
> *A metre measures three foot three, it's longer than a yard, you see.*

It's good to know rhymes for these things, but it's also important to employ common sense.

I once read an article on a news website that referenced a suspension bridge that was '230 m long (75 ft)'. Can you see the error here? 230 m is more than half of the distance around an athletics track, or about the length of Wembley Stadium, whereas 75 ft is the length of 12 or 13 men lying end to end. In fact 230 m is more like 700 ft: the article writer divided by 3 instead of multiplying by 3.

31 May

Here is a method for drawing an ellipse; no pair of compasses is required, just a couple of pins or nails, a piece of string and a pencil.

Set the two pins apart, tie your string in a loop and run it around the pins. Now use the pencil to push the string as far as it will flex in every direction. By the time you've drawn all the way around the two pins you will have a perfect ellipse. The positions of the two pins are known as the *foci* (plural of focus*) of the ellipse.

---

* In mathematics, a set of points that satisfy a given condition is called a locus, and its plural is 'loci'. As we've seen, the plural of focus is 'foci'. There's a flower called a crocus, and its plural is… 'crocuses'. Look, I don't make the rules.

JUNE

GOING FOR GOLD

1 June

This chapter will contain several *sequences*: a sequence is simply a pattern of numbers where, at any point, the next number in the sequence is clearly defined. Any of the times tables from the January chapter are sequences, as is the following: 1, 4, 11, 16, 24, 29, 33, …

What's the rule here though? It seems that the sequence always increases, but in chaotic and unpredictable steps. This is known as *Aronson's sequence*, first written about by Douglas Hofstadter and credited to one Jeffrey Aronson. The sequence simply describes the positions of the letter 't' in this sequence: 'T is the first, fourth, eleventh, sixteenth, . . . letter in this sentence'.

Let's see that again, but with the ts clearly marked: 'T is the first, fourth, eleventh, sixteenth…' We can see that the letter t is in positions 1, 4, 11, 16, 24, 29 and 33 in the sentence. What would come next though? This is a self-referential sequence, meaning that the sentence gives birth to the sequence, which in turn extends the sentence. The next number in the sequence after sixteen is 24, so the next word in the sequence would be 'twenty-four', and we continue ad infinitum:

'**T** is the first, fourth, eleventh, sixteenth, twenty-fourth, …'

1, 4, 11, 16, 24, 29, 33, 35, 39, 45, …

2 June

Here's another curious self-describing sequence; the *Kolakoski sequence*, which, like Pete Tong's career, is made up entirely of 1s and 2s:

1, 2, 2, 1, 1, 2, 1, 2, 2, 1, 2, 2, 1, 1, 2, . . .

The 1s and 2s come either in pairs or individually: in other words, in ones or twos. It starts with **one** 1, then **two** 2s, then **two** 1s, then **one** 2, then **one** 1, and so on. List the bold numbers as a sequence and you get the following:

1, 2, 2, 1, 1, 2, 1, 2, 2, 1, 2, 2, 1, 1, 2, . . .

That's right, it's the same sequence. The numbers in the sequence describe the length of number groups, and in turn the length of number groups describe the terms in the sequence.

3 June

Imagine you are writing a 'rhythm' made up of single claps (S) and double claps (D), and you are investigating the number of different ways to write out a rhythm of certain lengths. For example, if you wanted a three-clap rhythm, you could either count single-single-single, or a single either side of a double (because single-double sounds different to double-single).

It's interesting to collate all the possible ways of making rhythms of different lengths:

Length 1: S (1 way)
Length 2: SS or D (2 ways)
Length 3: SSS or DS or SD (3 ways)

It looks like the number of ways is simply the rhythm length, 1, 2, 3. But never assume; it makes a fool of both of us:

Length 4: SSSS or DSS or SDS or SSD or DD (5 ways)
Length 5: SSSSS or DSSS or SDSS or SSDS or SSSD or DDS or DSD or SDD (8 ways)

At this point it gets quite hard to list all the options without missing any, but there is a systematic way to make sure you don't. Next we're going to enumerate all of the six-clap rhythms; we can do this without missing any by taking all of the existing four-clap rhythms with a 'D' appended to their end, and combining these with all of the existing five-clap rhythms with an 'S' appended to their end.

Length 6: (SSSSSS or DSSSS or SDSSS or SSDSS or SSSDS or DDSS or DSDS or SDDS) or (SSSSD or DSSD or SDSD or SSDD or DDD) (13 ways)

There are 13 ways, which we can see has come from the sum of the previous 8 ways (for five claps) and 5 ways (for four claps). It then becomes clear that, if we are interested only in the number of ways, rather than listing them all, the sequence will go something like this: 1, 2, 3, 5, 8, 13, 21, 34, 55, 89. If we add an extra 1 at the front to represent the number of ways of making a no-clap rhythm (there is one way of doing nothing – you just do nothing) then we reach the following sequence, well known as the <u>Fibonacci sequence</u>, **in which each term is found by adding the previous two:**

1, 1, 2, 3, 5, 8, 13, 21, 34, 55, 89, …

4 June

Probably the most famous sequence in all of mathematics is the *Fibonacci sequence*, named after the Italian mathematician Leonardo of Pisa (also known as Fibonacci), although the sequence of numbers was known in India at least a thousand years before Fibonacci introduced the idea to the West in his 1202 book *Liber Abaci*. In fact, the way that the sequence was formed in yesterday's entry – by counting the number of 'rhythms' that can be made up of single claps and double claps – is almost exactly how the sequence was originally discovered in India, via the context of Sanskrit poetry.

Fibonacci was never actually called by that name during his lifetime, rather it was given to him by mathematicians studying his work hundreds of years later. The name simply means 'son of Bonacci', so if you're reading this book hundreds of years from now and it says 'Son of Dave' on the front cover, don't be too surprised.

Fibonacci's angle to create the sequence was to start with a pair of baby rabbits and to ascertain how many rabbit pairs would exist at the end of a year if applying the following (unrealistic, as all rabbit owners will attest to) rules:

- Every month a pair of baby rabbits grow into adult rabbits
- Every month a pair of adult rabbits give birth to a new pair of baby rabbits
- That's it!

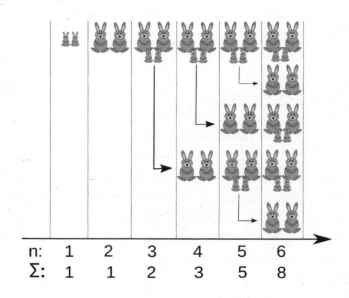

n: 1	2	3	4	5	6
Σ: 1	1	2	3	5	8

At the end of a year you will have the 12th Fibonacci number of pairs of rabbits, which is 55: 1, 1, 2, 3, 5, 8, 13, 21, 34, **55**.

5 June

There are many fascinating features of the Fibonacci sequence, perhaps the most fundamental of which is the ratio of one term to the previous. Let's have a look at these ratios:

$$\frac{1}{1} = 1$$

$$\frac{2}{1} = 2$$

$$\frac{3}{2} = 1.5$$

$$\frac{5}{3} = 1.666...$$

$$\frac{8}{5} = 1.6$$

$$\frac{13}{8} = 1.625$$

The value of this ratio is oscillating – that is, jumping up then down repeatedly – and it also seems to be converging upon some value around 1.6-ish. It turns out that the magic number is 1.61803398875…, the decimal part of which never repeats itself or terminates. **This number is known as the <u>golden ratio</u>**, and it has many uses and applications in mathematics and in nature.

6 June

Yesterday we saw that dividing a Fibonacci number by the previous Fibonacci number converges on the golden ratio; less well known is that **any additive sequence has the feature that the ratio of consecutive**

terms converges on the golden ratio. So if you didn't start with a pair of 1s, but rather the last two years that your favourite football team won a trophy, and then formed subsequent terms by adding the two previous, you would still find the golden ratio soon enough. For example: 1976, 2010,* 3986, 5996, 9982, 15,978, …

$$\frac{2010}{1976} = 1.017206$$

$$\frac{2010}{1976} = 1.017206$$

$$\frac{3986}{2010} = 1.983085$$

$$\frac{5996}{3986} = 1.504264$$

$$\frac{9982}{5996} = 1.664777$$

$$\frac{15,978}{9982} = 1.600681$$

---

* 1976 FA Cup and 2010 Johnstone's Paint Trophy, since you ask. Don't knock it.

7 June

The golden ratio has many numerical and physical properties and crops up in more places than Samuel L Jackson. Consider a rectangle that is divided in the following way:

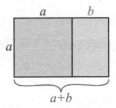

But (adopting sexy Dervla Kirwan Marks & Spencer advert voice...) this is not just any rectangle, this is a rectangle where removing the square on the left would leave you with a smaller rectangle that is (mathematically) *similar* to the original whole rectangle. The ratio of b to a is the same as the ratio of a to $a + b$. The ratio required to make this work is the golden ratio, 1.61803398875..., but to keep things simpler we usually use the Greek letter <u>phi</u> to describe this ratio: φ.

8 June

Which of these rectangles do you find the most pleasing to the eye? You can pick only one! In the 1860s the German physicist Gustav Fechner tested the hypothesis that there is something inherently appealing about the golden ratio by offering people a choice of ten rectangles and asking them to choose their favourite. Whether or not there was an eleventh option – 'I don't find rectangles either appealing or unappealing, I simply accept them for what they are' – is unclear. In the test, 76% of people chose either the golden rectangle or the one either side of it.

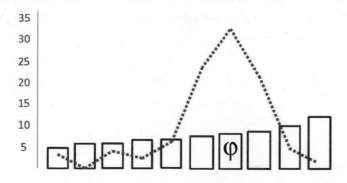

Does this show a significant trend towards the desirability of phi, or could the test have been more rigorous? Several sceptics over the years have become very upset about the supposed appeal of the golden ratio, with the mathematician George Markowsky finding far weaker results in 1992 when subjects were offered a greater number of rectangles that were not sorted into order of ratio.

However you feel about the golden ratio though, it certainly isn't causing any harm and it has many neat features. It isn't the answer to the ultimate question of life, the universe and everything, but it's pretty cool. And no, I don't think any rectangle is inherently more beautiful than any other rectangle.

9 June

Here's something fun to do next time you find yourself with a piece of squared paper (I appreciate this is not all that often for anyone above the age of 16, but I promise it's worth it).

Start by drawing a couple of 1×1 squares next to each other. Then draw a 2×2 square that borders the two 1×1 squares. Next you'll be able to draw a 3×3 square that borders the 2×2 square and one of the 1×1 squares. Continue the process and you'll end up with something like this:

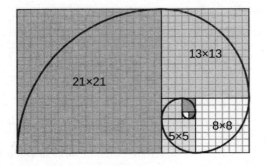

Note how the square lengths follow the established pattern of Fibonacci numbers. Drawing a quarter-circle arc in each box will give you what's known as a *Fibonacci spiral*, which is a close approximation to a *golden spiral*: a logarithmic spiral with a continual growth factor of φ.

One of the neatest features of a logarithmic spiral is that they are equiangular, meaning that any line drawn straight out from the centre will repeatedly meet the spiral at the same angle.

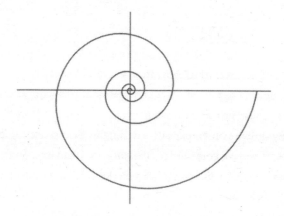

Birds of prey have been observed to approach their quarry in the approximate shape of a logarithmic spiral – doing so means that they can keep their side-mounted eye on their prey at all times.

10 June

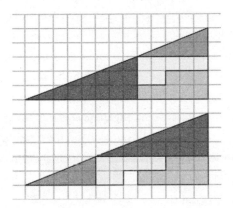

This feels like an apt time to return to the 'missing square illusion' that we saw on April Fools' Day – a triangle that can have its parts rearranged to leave an empty square. It is utterly baffling at first, and you may wish to give yourself an extra moment to think about it before reading on. . . First let's remind ourselves of the Fibonacci sequence: 1, 1, 2, 3, 5, 8, 13, 21, . . .

Now note the dimensions of the whole triangle: 13 × 5; 13 and 5 are semi-consecutive Fibonacci numbers (i.e. skipping the 8 in between). The larger constituent triangle has dimensions of 8 × 3 (skipping the 5) and the smaller triangle has dimensions of 5 × 2 (skipping the 3). The ratios of semi-consecutive Fibonacci numbers also converge pleasingly:

$$\frac{3}{1} = 3$$

$$\frac{5}{2} = 2.5 \ (*)$$

$$\frac{8}{3} = 2.666... \ (*)$$

$$\frac{13}{5} = 2.6 \; (*)$$

$$\frac{21}{8} = 2.625$$

These ratios converge to 2.618..., which just happens to be $\varphi + 1$. But the important thing in terms of our triangle is that the <u>gradients</u> of the slopes created by the two small triangles and the larger triangle are the <u>reciprocals</u> of the starred values above, which come out as 0.4, 0.375 and 0.384615...

The human eye finds it incredibly hard to differentiate between these similar slopes, so our brains make the assumption that they are the same. In fact, neither of the larger 'triangles' in the diagrams of the missing square illusion is actually a triangle – one of them 'bows outwards' on what looks like the longest edge, the other 'bows inwards'.

11 June

Speaking of gradients, which of these roads would you rather cycle up?

If you drive on British roads you'll have seen much more of the right-hand type of sign, since road signs for gradient have gradually transitioned from the ratio style to the percentage style.

In the left-hand style, the ratio represents the steepness of the road as a ratio of the vertical change to the horizontal change. So 1:5 means one unit of vertical change for every five units of horizontal change. The only trouble with this is that a higher number means less danger: 1:10 means one unit down for every ten units across; 1:100 would be a barely perceptible gradient. This is probably why the percentage style is much more common now – in this style, the percentage represents the vertical change as a percentage of the horizontal change. So 20% means 20 units down for every 100 across, equivalent to 1 in 5. (To answer the question from earlier: the two slopes shown above are in fact equally steep, so take your pick.)

The steepest street in Britain – and possibly* the world – is Ffordd Pen Llech in North Wales, with a maximum gradient of 37.5%. That's 3:8 in old money. Does that sound steeper or less steep than 37.5%? Well, you'll have plenty of time to ponder that on your cycle up – if you can manage to stay upright.

The top end of Ffordd Pen Llech, i.e. the end you want to be at. Note the 40% sign – you don't see that too often.

12 June

Remember the doubling sequence for grains of rice on a chessboard: 1, 2, 4, 8, 16, …? This is called a *geometric* sequence, because there is a multiplying factor that takes you from term to term – in this case it's 2 ($1 \times 2 = 2$, $2 \times 2 = 4$, $4 \times 2 = 8$, etc.). Compare this to the classic Fibonacci sequence: 1, 1, 2, 3, 5, 8, … This is called an *additive* sequence

---

* Please don't write in, steep-road fans: Baldwin Street in Dunedin is officially the world's steepest street *on average*, but it doesn't have any parts as steep as Ffordd Pen Llech's steepest section.

because two successive terms add together to give the next. Could a sequence be both geometric and additive?

Let's say the sequence starts with a 1, and then you keep repeatedly multiplying by some common ratio, which for argument's sake we'll call r. Then the sequence would look as follows: $1, r, r^2, r^3, r^4, \ldots$

Because the sequence also needs to be additive, we can take any two terms and require that they add up to the next. This gives the following set of equations:

$$1 + r = r^2$$
$$r + r^2 = r^3$$
$$r^2 + r^3 = r^4$$

All of these equations are essentially duplicates of $1 + r = r^2$, and the only positive number that solves this equation is – can you guess?– the golden ratio, φ: 1.618…

13 June

Yesterday we established that $1 + \varphi = \varphi^2$, and we can use this to find higher powers of φ as simple multiples of φ, as follows:

$$\varphi^2 = \varphi + 1$$
$$\varphi^3 = \varphi\varphi^2 = \varphi(\varphi + 1) = \varphi^2 + \varphi = \varphi + 1 + \varphi = 2\varphi + 1$$
$$\varphi^4 = \varphi\varphi^3 = \varphi(2\varphi + 1) = 2\varphi^2 + \varphi = 2(\varphi + 1) + \varphi = 3\varphi + 2$$
$$\varphi^5 = \varphi\varphi^4 = \varphi(3\varphi + 2) = 3\varphi^2 + 2\varphi = 3(\varphi + 1) + 2\varphi = 5\varphi + 3$$

What do you know – we see the familiar Fibonacci sequence appearing in the terms on the right.

14 June

1, 1, 2, 3, 5, 8, 13, 21, 34, 55, 89, 144

NEAT FIBONACCI TRICK #1

Adding together any ten consecutive terms is the same as multiplying the seventh term by 11!

For example: 2 + 3 + 5 + 8 + 13 + 21 + 34 + 55 + 89 + 143 = 374

34 × 11 = 374*

---

15 June

1, 1, 2, 3, 5, 8, 13, 21, 34, 55, 89, 144

NEAT FIBONACCI TRICK #2

Start from the first term and add up to any other term. The sum you find will be 1 less than the term 2 on from where you stopped adding.

For example: 1 + 1 + 2 + 3 + 5 + 8 + 13 = 33. Look on two terms from the 13 and you'll find 34: 1 more than our sum of 33.

---

* Give yourself a gold star if you remembered that to multiply 34 by 11, you separate the 3 and the 4 and insert the sum of 3 and 4 between: 3(7)4

16 June

1, 1, 2, 3, 5, 8, 13, 21, 34, 55, 89, 144

NEAT FIBONACCI TRICK #3

Take any three consecutive terms in the sequence. Squaring the term in the middle will always be 1 more or 1 less (alternately) than multiplying the two terms around it.

For example: $5^2 = 25$, which is 1 more than $3 \times 8 = 24$.

$8^2 = 64$, which is 1 less than $5 \times 13 = 65$.

$13^2 = 169$, which is 1 more than $8 \times 21 = 168$.

And so on...

---

17 June

Terms in the Fibonacci sequence can be used to create a Pythagorean triple. Feel free to have a look back to early March to remind yourself of what Pythagorean triples are. Here's how you do it. Take four consecutive Fibonacci terms, say 1, 2, 3 and 5.

- Multiply the smallest and largest numbers: $1 \times 5 = 5$
- Multiply the two middle numbers, but then double it: $2 \times 3 \times 2 = 12$
- Square the two middle numbers and then add: $2^2 + 3^2 = 13$

This example produces one of the Pythagorean triples we saw back in March: (5,12,13).

18 June

Here are some multiples of the golden ratio, φ, and also of φ^2 (remember that $\varphi^2 = \varphi + 1$)

Multiple n	$\varphi \times n$	$\varphi^2 \times n$
1	1.618033989	2.618033989
2	3.236067977	5.236067977
3	4.854101966	7.854101966
4	6.472135955	10.47213595
5	8.090169944	13.09016994
6	9.708203932	15.70820393

If we pair up the numbers in each row and ignore anything after the decimal points, we get the following pairs: (1,2), (3,5), (4,7), (6,10), (8,13), (9,15), ... Do you notice anything interesting here? At least they aren't all Fibonacci numbers for once. It turns out that **these paired integers will account for every integer once and once only**, and the smaller number in each pair is the smallest number that has not yet appeared in the list. Also, the gaps between the paired numbers are increasing by 1 every time (this is inevitable because $\varphi^2 = \varphi + 1$).

So if we wanted to find the next pair of numbers, we simply have to look for the smallest number that hasn't appeared yet, which is 11. The gap between the previous pair of numbers is 6 (15 – 9), so the gap between our next pair should be 7, and the pair we're looking for is (11,18).

19 June

Here's a game you might like to try playing with a friend and a bag of counters. Put the counters into two piles, not necessarily of the same size. When it's your turn you may take any number of counters from either pile, or from both piles – but if you take from both piles you have to take the same number from each. The winner is the person who takes the last counter.

Here's a neat thing: the pairs of numbers from yesterday's table represent 'winning positions' for this game. Say you were playing a friend and facing piles of eight and ten counters. The optimal strategy for your first move is to reach one of the pairs in the list above: (1,2), (3,5), (4,7), (6,10), (8,13), (9,15), (11,18), …

With piles of eight and ten counters, the optimal move is to remove two counters from the pile of eight, leaving pile sizes (6,10). Your partner – who doesn't know the strategy – then decides to remove five counters from the large pile, leaving pile sizes (6,5). Now you need to get the piles back to a listed pair, and the way to do this is to take four from each pile, leaving the arrangement (1,2). From here, your partner is stuck: whatever they do next, you can make the final move and win.

20 June

One more visit to our list of 'good pairs' from yesterday's game of counters: (1,2), (3,5), (4,7), (6,10), (8,13), (9,15), (11,18). Also remember that we can extend the sequence by starting a pair with the smallest number that hasn't occurred yet, and adding one to the gap between the previous pair of numbers: (12,20), (14,23), (16,26), ...*

Now we're going to divide the larger number in each pair by the smaller:

a	b	b/a
1	2	2
3	5	1.666…
4	7	1.75
6	10	1.666…
8	13	1.625
9	15	1.666…
11	18	1.636…
12	20	1.666…
14	23	1.643…
16	26	1.625

It's a very slow convergence from above, but the ratio of these pairs of numbers will eventually converge to the golden ratio of 1.618…

21 June

A doughnut is the same as a coffee cup, if you ask a topologist. Topology is the study of spaces and shapes that are invariant under continuous deformation, such as stretching and twisting but not creating or opening holes. Since a doughnut and coffee cup each just

---

* There's another equivalent version of the counters game called *Wythoff's game* that leads to these same number pairs occurring; I highly recommend James Grime's video on the subject.

have one hole – the centre of the doughnut or the looped handle of the coffee cup – one can be deformed into the other.

22 June

A fun idea from topology is the *hairy ball theorem*, which states that **it is impossible to comb a hairy ball so that every hair lies flat** – there will always be some hair that sticks up or lies on top of some other hair. Imagine trying to comb a coconut: you will always reach some point where you're combing hair against other hair to form a cowlick. You *can*, however, comb a hairy torus (that's a hairy ring doughnut shape – mmm, delicious).

The hairy ball theorem was proved by Henri Poincaré in 1885 (year of the formation of the world's finest football club) and if you are an absolute child and can't say 'hairy ball' without sniggering, you are welcome to call it by its other name: the hedgehog theorem.

23 June

It has often been said that eating too many bananas could cause death by potassium overdose, even sometimes reported that the figure could be as low as half a dozen bananas. In reality it seems that **the required lethal dose of bananas would be more like 400**, and eating this many would probably kill you in a far more disgusting way than the potassium hit.

Bananas of course are the chosen snack for tennis players, and some players seem to put one away every single time they return to their seat. But even the longest tennis match of all time, between John Isner and Nicolas Mahut, which involved a staggering 118 games on the middle of three days' play (23 June 2010), would have required one of the players to eat three or four bananas between every single game in order to commit potassicide.

24 June

Earlier in the chapter we saw that the ratio of one Fibonacci term to the previous term (1, 1, 2, 3, 5, 8, ...) converges upon the 'golden ratio' of around 1.618, and this is very close to the ratio of kilometres to miles: most people use multiplication by $\frac{8}{5}$ or 1.6 to convert miles to kilometres, but the true conversion rate of 1.60934 is actually closer to the golden ratio than it is to 1.6. This means that **the Fibonacci sequence can be used to accurately convert kilometres to miles, or vice versa**. If you are driving in Europe and see a distance on a road sign that is a Fibonacci number of kilometres, you can convert it to miles by switching to the previous Fibonacci number of miles. For example, if you see 55 km on a road sign, just think through your Fibonacci numbers (1, 1, 2, 3, 5, 8, 13, 21, 34, 55), find the previous number and that converts it to miles: 34. Likewise, if you see a Fibonacci number of miles on a British or American road sign, convert it to kilometres by switching *up* to the next Fibonacci number.

25 June

Earlier in the book we also observed the happy coincidence that the length of a light-year in kilometres (95 followed by a whole load of zeros) converted very neatly to the length of a light-year in miles (59 followed by the same load of zeros) simply by switching round the 9 and the 5. We can now see why this works, when comparing it to yesterday's miles/kilometres conversions; it's because 95/59, despite neither number being in the Fibonacci sequence, is very close to the golden ratio: $95/59 = 1.610...$, $\phi = 1.618...$

26 June

This is called a *tree* for four *nodes* (a node is just another word for a point or vertex):

A

It joins all the nodes together without creating a loop anywhere. A tree for *n* nodes should always have *n* – 1 edges, so a tree for four nodes should have three edges. Here are some more trees for four nodes:

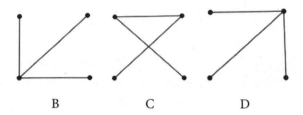

B   C   D

The first of these is a new tree, but the second and third are *not* new. That's because if you pulled the nodes around you could transform them into one of the other trees (the 'picnic bench' in C can be made into the shape of A by uncrossing the 'legs'; D is simply a rotation of B). C and D are *isomorphic* to A and B respectively. A and B represent all the unique trees on four nodes – so there are two different trees in total. I call A a 'snake' and B a 'spider', but please don't expect to find these terms in any other book.

Before you read on, try drawing all the possible trees for five nodes. They're under this sentence, so close the book quickly if you want to try for yourself first…

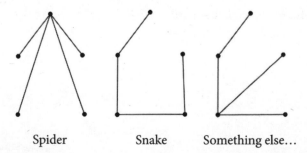

Spider   Snake   Something else…

There are three possible trees for five nodes – the spider, snake, and something that isn't either – if you found any others you have made an isomorphic tree. It should now be fairly obvious that there is just one possible tree for two nodes and for three nodes:

Two-node snake   Three-node snake (or spider)

Let's summarize these results.

Nodes	Trees
2	1
3	1
4	2
5	3
6	?

Care to hazard a guess how many trees there are for six nodes? No, not five: **there are six trees**. Remember when I told you not to jump to conclusions? This looks as though it's going to be a sequence of Fibonacci numbers, but it falls apart on six nodes. If you don't believe me, they're drawn in the Further Notes at the back of the book.

27 June

1/89 is an interesting fraction. Honest! It is equal to 0.01123595595618. It seems that the decimal expansion of 1/89 is made up of Fibonacci numbers, but starting with a zero. After the 5 we might expect to see an 8, but we see a 9, which at first looks like an error. However, consider lining up values from the Fibonacci sequence in the following way, splitting tens from units when appropriate:

```
1
  1
    2
      3
        5
          8
          1   3
              2   1
                  3   4
                      5   5
```

Add down the columns and we have 1123595…, which is indeed the decimal expansion we saw above. There's a bit more about why this happens in the Further Notes at the back of the book.

28 June

Today is the only *perfect* day of the year, that is, a date made of two perfect numbers: 6 and 28. Both of these numbers are mathematically perfect, because each is the sum of its factors:

$6 = 1 + 2 + 3$

$28 = 14 + 7 + 4 + 2 + 1$

This is almost certainly what Lou Reed was thinking of when he wrote the classic song 'Perfect Day' in 1972.

29 June

There are very few perfect numbers: the list starts 6, 28, 496, 8128, 33,550,336, and then gets enormous very quickly. All other numbers are either *abundant* or *deficient*, depending on whether the sum of their factors adds up to more or less than the number itself, respectively. Numbers with lots of factors are abundant:

Sum of factors of $24 = 1 + 2 + 3 + 4 + 6 + 8 + 12 = 36$

Numbers with very few factors are deficient:

Sum of factors of $22 = 1 + 2 + 11 = 14$

30 June

One more sequence to end the month. What comes next in this sequence? 1, 2, 3, 4, 5, 6, 7, 8, 9, 10, … Give yourself a pat on the back if you said 11, 13, 12, 17, 15. Remember, don't jump to conclusions! Here's why:

Start with a solitary 1, and then keep drawing numbers in a clockwise spiral…

$$1 \ 2$$
$$3$$

Here's the rule though: when you place a new number, it has to be the lowest number that doesn't share a factor (other than 1) with the numbers already placed to its north, south, east or west. A 4 needs to be placed next, and it doesn't share a factor with 1 or 3, so we're all good. Carrying on the spiral up to 11 causes no problems:

```
 7  8  9 10
 6  1  2 11
 5  4  3
```

But when 12 needs to be placed, it can't be because it shares a common factor with 3. So 13 goes in instead, and 12 can take the next place because we only need to check it against the 13 directly north of it. The next number to be placed, however, can't share a factor with 3 or 12. This rules out 14 (common factor of 2 with 12), 15 (common factor of 3 with both 3 and 12), and 16 (common factor of 2 with 12), so the next number to be placed is 17. Continuing this gives the following spiral:

```
25 22 21 20 27
18  7  8  9 10
23  6  1  2 11
16  5  4  3 13
19 14 15 17 12
```

It is conjectured, but not proved, that every number will eventually be able to be placed in the spiral. This is sequence number A257340 on the online encyclopaedia of integer sequences (oeis.org): definitely one of the best sites on the internet.

JULY

PRIME TIME

1 July

<u>Prime numbers</u> are those whole numbers that have exactly two factors: the number itself and 1. You might like to think of them as numbers that can't be broken down into equally sized groups, unless those groups are just a load of 1s. So 5 is prime because it cannot be broken down into any smaller groups (other than five 1s), but 6 is not prime because it can be broken into three 2s, or indeed two 3s. The number 1 is not a prime number because it has only one factor: 1. Some people think 1 is a prime number, but they're wrong.

Oh OK, here's why. The fundamental theorem of arithmetic says that every number can be broken down into its prime factors in one unique way. So $12 = 3 \times 2 \times 2$, and there's no other way to multiply primes to make 12. If 1 was a prime number, then 12 could be written as a product of primes in infinitely many ways: $3 \times 2 \times 2 \times 1$, $3 \times 2 \times 2 \times 1 \times 1$, and so on.

I have a very clever rhyme for remembering this: **Remember, remember, one's not a prime number.** Thank me later.

The first prime number, therefore, is 2. And 2 is the 'odd' prime number because it's the only even prime number.

2 July

Eratosthenes of Cyrene was a Greek mathematician born in 276 BC. He was also a poet, astronomer, music theorist, geographer and chief librarian at the Library of Alexandria (big bloody show-off). He developed a neat, systematic way of listing all the prime numbers. Start with a large 1–100 number grid, shade all the multiples of 2 except for 2 itself. Then do the same with multiples of 3. No need to do the same with 4 as every multiple of 4 is itself a multiple of 2, so these squares are already covered. Keep doing the same with multiples of all the prime numbers and you'll end up with something like this:

	2	3	4	5	6	7	8	9	10
11	12	13	14	15	16	17	18	19	20
21	22	23	24	25	26	27	28	29	30
31	32	33	34	35	36	37	38	39	40
41	42	43	44	45	46	47	48	49	50
51	52	53	54	55	56	57	58	59	60
61	62	63	64	65	66	67	68	69	70
71	72	73	74	75	76	77	78	79	80
81	82	83	84	85	86	87	88	89	90
91	92	93	94	95	96	97	98	99	100

The numbers left unshaded are the prime numbers. Generally speaking they get more sparse as you move through the number grid, but frustratingly it happens in quite a chaotic way. For example, there are only two primes in the 20s row but three in the 70s row. Twenty-five of the numbers from 1 to 100 – exactly a quarter – are prime and if we counted up to 1000 we would find 168 primes (please don't actually do it unless you have a very long car drive and no podcasts to listen to). Coincidentally **168 is also the number of hours in a week, and the number of dots on a set of double six dominoes.**

3 July

The sieve of Eratosthenes can seem like a long-winded process, but it's worth noting that to find all the prime numbers up to n, we need to check prime factors only up to √n. So, in the example above, working with a grid size of 100, we need to sieve for multiples of primes up to only 10, that is, 2, 3, 5 and 7.

Why is this? Say we didn't realize and started shading in multiples of 11, as 11 is the next prime after 7. We will find that the multiples of 11 – 2 × 11, 3 × 11 – etc., have already been crossed off as multiples of 2, multiples of 3, and so on. Every multiple of 11 up to 100 will involve multiplying 11 by a smaller number that has already been considered, so there's no need to consider multiples of 11 at all.

4 July

Perform a sieve of Eratosthenes with a number grid that's just six columns wide instead, and we come to a curious result. Crossing off the 2 times table takes out columns 2, 4 and 6, and the 3 times table removes the third and sixth columns (though the sixth has already been crossed out):

	2	3	4	5	6
7	8	9	10	11	12
13	14	15	16	17	18
19	20	21	22	23	24
25	26	27	28	29	30

Because columns 2, 3, 4 and 6 will all be crossed out, no matter how far down we draw the table, we can say for sure that every prime number appears in either column 1 or column 5. In other words, **every prime number larger than 3 is either 1 more or 1 less than a multiple of 6**. There are some non-primes in these columns, such as 25, which would be removed later in the process, but every prime larger than 3 is definitely in column 1 (1 more than a multiple of 6) or column 5 (1 less than a multiple of 6).

For example: 37 is prime, and it's 1 more than 36 (6 × 6); 71 is prime, and it's 1 less than 72 (12 × 6). You'll never find a prime number, other than 2 and 3, that isn't either 1 more or 1 less than a multiple of 6.

5 July

Eratosthenes is probably best known for finding an incredibly good approximation for the circumference of the earth, in an age when many people still thought the earth was flat (no, not 2019).

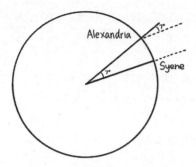

Eratosthenes observed a well at Syene (now Aswān) that caused no shadow when the sun shone above it at midday, so he realized that the sun must be directly above the well. At the same time of day but 900 km away,* at Alexandria, he planted a stick in the ground, which formed a shadow at an angle of 7.2° to the vertical. Eratosthenes used knowledge of corresponding angles (see the diagram) and proportion to work out the circumference of the earth. Since 7.2° is one fiftieth of a whole turn (360°), the distance between Syene and Alexandria must be about one fiftieth of the earth's circumference, i.e. the circumference of the earth must be about 50 × 900 = 45,000 km; remarkably close to the true figure of almost exactly 40,000 km.

6 July

Here is a different twist on the sieve of Eratosthenes that doesn't result in a list of prime numbers. Start with a list of all the <u>counting numbers</u> and remove all the even numbers:

---

* Actually he measured it as 5000 *stadia* – metres and kilometres weren't close to being in common use. A stadium was equivalent to about 185 m.

1, 3, 5, 7, 9, 11, 13, 15, 17, 19, 21, 23, 25, 27, 29, 31, 33, 35, 37, 39, 41, 43, 45, …

The first remaining number in the list that isn't 1 is 3, so next remove every third number from the remaining list:

1, 3, 7, 9, 13, 15, 19, 21, 25, 27, 31, 33, 37, 39, 43, 45, …

The first number remaining after 1 and 3 is 7, so now remove every seventh number:

1, 3, 7, 9, 13, 15, 21, 25, 27, 31, 33, 37, 43, 45, …

Next remove every ninth number, and so on:

1, 3, 7, 9, 13, 15, 21, 25, 31, 33, 37, 43, …

The list you're left with has been christened the *lucky* numbers. Is your lucky number in the list?

7 July

An *emirp* is the name that mathematicians give to prime numbers that remain prime when written backwards (because mathematicians are very witty). This is of course true for any prime that happens to be palindromic, such as 11, 101, 313, etc., but there are also many primes that give a completely different prime number when read backwards. The first couple of emirps that aren't palindromic are 13 and 17.

The mother of all emirps is

3,139,971,973,786,634,711,391,448,651,577,269,485,891,759,419,122,9
38,744,591,877,656,925,789,747,974,914,319,422,889,611,373,939,731

Remarkably, when this is written out as a 10 × 10 grid, it gives a 10-digit emirp in every row, column and diagonal:

3	1	3	9	9	7	1	9	7	3
7	8	6	6	3	4	7	1	1	3
9	1	4	4	8	6	5	1	5	7
7	2	6	9	4	8	5	8	9	1
7	5	9	4	1	9	1	2	2	9
3	8	7	4	4	5	9	1	8	7
7	6	5	6	9	2	5	7	8	9
7	4	7	9	7	4	9	1	4	3
1	9	4	2	2	8	8	9	6	1
1	3	7	3	9	3	9	7	3	1

8 July

How many balls do you think are used at the Wimbledon tennis tournament every year? Before you guess, I will give you one piece of information to get you started: the men's and women's draws each begin with 128 players. Decide on your guess, then I'll show you how I made mine...

A total of 128 players in each draw means 127 games each. You could calculate this by adding together the games in each round (64 + 32 + ... + 1), and you might cut down on your work if you remember that the sum of powers of 2 is always one short of the next power of 2 (1 + 2 + 4 + ... + 64 = 127). Or you might just logically deduce that since every game produces exactly one loser, and every player bar one has to lose the tournament in order for one person to win it, there must be 128 − 1 = 127 games.

Therefore 127 games for men and women is roughly 250 games. But there are also doubles matches, youth matches and veterans' friendly matches, though fewer of these. My guess is that all of these matches put together make no more than another 250 matches, so let's call it 500 matches in total.

From experience of watching tennis it feels like there are about twenty balls in use at any time – a couple with each ball boy or ball girl and maybe a few in the pockets of the players. But I'm also aware that every now and then the umpire says 'new balls please' and they rapidly change all the worn balls for brand new ones – it's terribly wasteful. This seems to happen three or four times per match, so I'll go for 100 balls per match. So 100 balls in each of 500 matches is 50,000 balls, and **the Wimbledon tournament's website says that the true figure for balls used each year is 55,000**. Well done me!*

This method is called a *Fermi estimate*, where with very little information but some nous and common sense, it is possible to make a good estimate for a problem that at first seems far from simple.

9 July

Cicadas are a species of forest-dwelling insect that live the majority of their lives underground, before emerging for a few weeks for furious mating activity and dying shortly after creating the next cicada

---

* Of course it's possible that the Wimbledon tennis tournament did not actually count how many balls were used per year, but simply ran their own Fermi estimate in more or less the same way that I have, coming up with more or less the same conclusion!

generation. Interestingly, **most species of cicada spend a prime number of years underground before coming up for their last hurrah: usually 7, 13 or 17 years.**

What do cicadas love so much about prime numbers? How do they even know what a prime number is? The answer of course is that they don't, but rather they have probably naturally evolved to spend a prime number of years underground to avoid predators. We know that a prime number has no factors other than itself and 1, so cicadas emerging at prime number intervals are unlikely to coincide with predators that return to the forest at standard intervals.

Imagine a species of cicada that emerged every 12 years. They would find themselves bumping into predators that returned every 2, 3, 4 or 6 years, since these numbers are all factors of 12. However, a 13-year cicada would find themselves faced only with, say, a 5-year predator every 65 years, since $13 \times 5 = 65$. Of course there are more complicated factors at play, but most scientists are agreed that this is the nub of the cicadas' prime-number obsession.

10 July

If you start from the number 7 and create a sequence of numbers by adding 30 each time (an *arithmetic sequence*), it's possible to construct a string of primes: 7, 37, 67, 97, 127, 157. Unfortunately the sequence breaks down at this point because the next number in the sequence, 187, is 11×17 and therefore not prime. If you found that short sequence of primes quite satisfying then you'll love this: **using only prime numbers, an arithmetic sequence of any length can be found**: that is, a sequence of primes with equal gaps between each, stretching on and on as far as you wish. This is the *Green–Tao theorem*, as found by Ben Green and Terence Tao in 2004.

Admittedly you do have to look at some *very* large numbers to find even a relatively short string of primes (the first string of ten equally spaced primes is 199, 409, 619, …, 2089), but it's still a fairly incredible finding.

11 July

Here's a neat formula that generates primes: $n^2 + n + 41$. Replace the 'n' in this formula with successive numbers from 1 upwards and you'll always generate a prime result:

n	$n^2 + n + 41$
1	43
2	47
3	53
4	61
5	71
6	83
…	…

Or will you? Unfortunately this is not actually true (no need to write to the publisher) because, although this formula gives an exceedingly long string of primes, the list will eventually run out when $n = 40$ and 41:

$$40^2 + 40 + 41 = 40^2 + 40 + 40 + 1 = (40 + 1)^2 = 41^2$$
$$41^2 + 41 + 41 = 41(41 + 1 + 1) = 41 \times 43$$

In each of these cases we arrive at a *composite number* (i.e. not a prime).

This so-called *prime-generating polynomial* was discovered by the genius eighteenth-century mathematician Leonhard Euler – we met him and his polyhedra formula a few months ago.

12 July

Leonhard Euler is possibly the greatest and most prolific mathematician who ever lived, but as is often the case with mathematicians, some of his most important work lies beyond the grasp of the layperson (or even the reasonably learned maths student). But if, in a moment of boredom, you've ever tried to draw this picture without taking your pen off the paper or going over a line twice, you share some mathematical common ground with the great Euler:

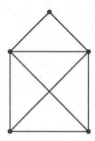

If you haven't tried this for a while, or indeed ever, I invite you to find a pencil and have a go before reading on. Can it be done? Does it matter where you start?

With a bit of playing around, you should find that it's possible to draw the shape without taking your pen off the page or repeating an edge, but only if you start at a bottom corner (node) and end up at the other one. If you try to start from one of the top three nodes you will definitely fail. Euler realized that this is because the bottom corners are *odd* nodes, because an odd number of edges meet there, whereas the top three corners are *even* nodes. Say you choose to start from the bottom left, where three edges meet. You will use one edge to leave, one to return and the third to leave again. The bottom right corner also has three edges that meet there, so one can be used to arrive on, one to leave again and the third to finally arrive on at completion. All the other nodes are even, so they can all be visited as many times as they are left, which is what we want to achieve.

Indeed a whole graph of even nodes is an ideal situation, because you can start and leave from anywhere. Try this one – you should be able to start from any node, go over every line once and return to your starting point:

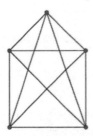

Most people can visualize a solution to this one quite quickly: start from any node, go around the outside of the pentagon and then around the five points of the internal star.

So if a graph has all even nodes you can start anywhere and end up back there, but if it has a pair of odd nodes then you must start at one and end at the other.* If there are two pairs of odd nodes or more, we cannot draw the graph without repeating a line; the graph is *non-*

---

* I will leave it as an open challenge as to why the odd nodes must come in pairs – this is explained in the Further Notes at the back of the book.

Eulerian. Because odd nodes are essentially 'unstable' and have more ways in than out (or vice versa) they can make up only the start or end of your route, never a middle part. No route can have more than one start and end, so more than a pair of odds is an insurmountable problem.

13 July

Yesterday's discovery about which graphs can and can't be drawn without repeating an edge came as a result of the *Bridges of Königsberg* problem, in which residents of the town of Königsberg (now Kaliningrad, in that strange bit of Russia sandwiched between Poland and Lithuania but not connected to the rest of Russia) tried to walk over all seven bridges in the town without going over a bridge twice. When this problem is reconfigured as a graph, in which each bridge is an edge and the four main land masses connected by the bridges are represented as nodes, it becomes clear that every 'island' of land is an odd node, so it cannot be done.

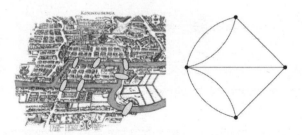

A map of the town and its equivalent as a graph. The left-hand node, with five edges coming out of it, represents the central island and its five connected bridges.

14 July

Leonhard Euler often corresponded with the German mathematician Christian Goldbach, who is best known for the *Goldbach conjecture* – a legendary problem in mathematics that is as easy to describe as it is difficult to prove.

Every even number except 2 can be written as the sum of two prime numbers.* That's it! For example:

$10 = 7 + 3$ $50 = 43 + 7$ $100 = 53 + 47$ and so on.

A car game I enjoy is finding pairs of primes that add to even numbers spotted on motorway mileage signs. You'll all be doing it now.

St Helens 7 + 5, Wigan 11 + 3, Preston 17 + 13

The Goldbach conjecture perfectly captures the frustrating and captivating nature of mathematical proof: even though the problem is basic to explain and play around with, it cannot be proved by trying

---

* Goldbach didn't have to worry about the 'except 2' part, because he considered 1 to be a prime number, and $2 = 1 + 1$. This is an outdated stance, but it's important to view it within the context of the era.

lots and lots of even numbers and eventually stopping. Nor can every even number be checked – since there are infinitely many – so a general proof must be found. Such a proof has eluded the combined might of all mathematicians to have ever lived.

Lev Schnirelmann appeared to have found a near-proof in 1939, but rather than proving that every even number is the sum of two primes, he proved that every even number can be written as a sum of *no more than 300,000 primes*. Some may belittle this achievement by suggesting that 300,000 is a lot larger than 2, but I would counter that 300,000 is a lot smaller than infinity. The longest journey starts with the smallest step, as they say.

15 July

3^2 can be written as the sum of 3 consecutive numbers.
3^4 can be written as the sum of 3^2 consecutive numbers.
3^6 can be written as the sum of 3^3 consecutive numbers.
And so on. Like this:

$9 = 2 + 3 + 4$ (3 numbers)
$81 = 5 + 6 + ... + 13$ (9 numbers)
$729 = 14 + 15 + ... + 40$ (27 numbers)

16 July

Happy 197th day of the year! 197 is a prime number; we can use Eratosthenes's method to verify this by checking if 197 is divisible by any prime number up to its own square root, which is just over 14.

Divisible by 2? No: it's clearly not even.

Divisible by 3? No: its digits add to 17, which is not divisible by 3.
    Every multiple of 3 has the sum of its digits also divisible by 3.

Divisible by 5? No: it doesn't end in 0 or 5.

Divisible by 7? No: 210 *is* divisible by 7, but 197 is 13 less than this, and 13 is *not* divisible by 7, so 197 can't also be divisible by 7.

Divisible by 11? No: alternately subtract and add the digits and you don't get zero; $1 - 9 + 7 = -1$.

Divisible by 13? No: count up from 130 *in thirteens* and you miss it: 130, 143, 156, 169, 182, 195, 208.

Divisible by 14? No, $14^2 = 196$.

197 is also the sum of the first twelve primes.

17 July

For any prime number p greater than or equal to 5, $p^2 - 1$ is a multiple of 24.

$5^2 - 1 = 24$
$7^2 - 1 = 48 = 2 \times 24$
$11^2 - 1 = 120 = 5 \times 24$
$13^2 - 1 = 168 = 7 \times 24$

...

This is a consequence of the fact we encountered on 4 July; there's a proof of how to get from one to the other in the Further Notes at the back of the book.

18 July

It seems that prime numbers get more sparse as we move along the number line – for example, after 523 they seem to die out altogether, the next prime not occurring until 541 – but the list will never stop altogether. The following beautiful proof shows that primes are a bit like LEGO® pieces on the living room carpet: **no matter how sure you are that you've found all the prime numbers, there is always one more.**

Say we thought the largest prime number was 11. Consider what would happen if we multiplied together all of the primes we have found up to this point, but then crucially we add 1:

$$2 \times 3 \times 5 \times 7 \times 11 + 1 = 2310 + 1 = 2311$$

Since 2310 is the product of all the primes from 2 to 11, it must be divisible by 2, 3, 5, 7 and 11. Therefore 2311 is *not* divisible by 2, because it's 1 more than a number that is divisible by 2. And it's *not* divisible by 3, because it's 1 more than a number that is divisible by 3. The same logic can be applied to deduce that 2311 is not divisible by 5, 7 or 11, and indeed it transpires that 2311 is prime. We assumed the primes ran out at 11, but by taking perfectly logical steps we have found another one.

Sometimes it goes a bit differently – consider what happens when we do the same with the list of primes up to 13:

$$2 \times 3 \times 5 \times 7 \times 11 \times 13 + 1 = 30,030 + 1 = 30,031$$

30,031 therefore isn't divisible by 2, 3, 5, 7, 11 or 13, but it turns out it *isn't* prime: it is the product of two larger prime numbers: 59 × 509. But this is fine; the original point we were trying to make is that if you assume a list of all primes, you will always be able to find at least one more. In both of the above cases we were able to use simple logical steps to find at least one larger prime than those in our original list.

19 July

Here's something that seems paradoxical: even though the primes never run out, **a list of consecutive non-primes (*composite numbers*) of any length can be found**. Want a list of 20 non-primes in a row? No sweat. Fifty composite numbers back to back? Piece of cake. Earlier we saw a list of seventeen composite numbers from 524 to 540, but how would you know where to look for such a list?

Here's a way to do it. Start with a <u>factorial</u>, say 6! = 6 × 5 × 4 × 3 × 2 × 1 = 720 (there's more about factorials back on 25 March if you need to remind yourself). So we can say for certain that 720 is a multiple of 2, 3, 4, 5 and 6. Adding 1 to this gives a number that may or may not be prime (it turns out that 721 isn't prime, but there was no guarantee of that). But 722 definitely is not prime, because it's 2 more than a multiple of 2. 723 can't be prime because it's 3 more than a multiple of 3, and the same can be said for 724 because it's 4 more than a multiple of 4. Carrying on this logical process gives us a list of five non-primes: 722, 723, 724, 725, 726; but starting with a larger factorial number could have given us any length of list of non-primes. Here's a list of nine non-primes in a row:

10! + 2, 10! + 3, 10! + 4, 10! + 5, 10! + 6, 10! + 7, 10! + 8, 10! + 9, 10! + 10

Can you see the potential flaw in this method? To find a list of composite numbers of length n, you must start by calculating $(n + 1)!$ So to find a list of seventeen non-primes you would need to start searching around 18!, which is about 6,000,000,000,000,000. But we already established that there's a list of 17 composite numbers as low as the 500s, so this method appears to be extremely inefficient. But if you are willing to imagine – or even enjoy – numbers so enormous that they could never have any practical use, there is a list of non-primes of any length waiting for you.

20 July

Here's a prime number that doesn't at first look particularly interesting: $10^{6400} - 10^{6352} - 1$. It was discovered by Harvey Dubner in 1991 and consists of over 6400 digits, all of which are 9s *except for one*. With the number written out, we can play the world's least exciting version of *Where's Wally?* Here's the first couple of hundred digits: luckily the non-9 occurs reasonably early – can you spot it?

99999999999999999999999999999999999999999998999999999
99999999999999999999999999999999999999999999999999999
99999999999999999999999999999999999999999999999999999
99999999999999999999999999999999999999999999999999999
99999999999999999999999999999999999999999999999999999
999999999999…

21 July

Fans of satanic ritual will be pleased to hear that the 'number of the beast' (666) can be achieved by squaring the first seven primes and adding them:

$$2^2 + 3^2 + 5^2 + 7^2 + 11^2 + 13^2 + 17^2 = 666$$

There are more devilish goings-on amongst the primes though – behold *Belphegor's prime*:

1000000000000066600000000000001

Yes, that's a palindromic prime with 666 sitting between 13 zeros either side. Very evil. Are we sure it's prime? Can we check using Eratosthenes's method of testing whether any smaller primes divide exactly into it? Remember from 3 July that we only need to check up to the square root of Belphegor's prime, so that should cut our work down a bit.

We can tell just by eye that Belphegor's prime isn't a multiple of 2 (the last digit isn't even), or a multiple of 3 (its digits don't add up to a multiple of 3) or a multiple of 5 (the last digit isn't a 5 or a 0). There are quite a few more primes to check though…

Belphegor's prime is very close to 10^{30}, so its square root will be just over 10^{15}. The approximate number of primes up to a certain number n is given by the formula $n/\ln(n)$, where ln is the natural logarithm – we'll learn more about this next month. $10^{15}/\ln(10^{15})$ comes in at about 30 trillion, so… still quite a lot of primes to check. In fact, even if you could check one prime per second, it would take about a million years to check all the primes up to 10^{15}.

Luckily there are much more efficient ways of checking if a number is prime than the sieve of Eratosthenes, but it is still an incredibly time-consuming pursuit – I wouldn't recommend it as a hobby.

22 July

The number 1808010808 doesn't look particularly exciting. It looks a little bit like that number you remember from school that says 'BOOBIES' when you turn it upside down on a calculator, but it isn't that one. Here's what it is: if you repeat this number 1560 times and then pop another 1 on the end, you'll have an enormous prime number that remains unchanged if you read it from right to left, *and* remains unchanged if you look at it upside down.

23 July

The excellent writer and maths communicator Alex Bellos once carried out a mass survey of people's favourite numbers, and unsurprisingly lucky 7 came in tops with nearly 10% of the total vote. Low numbers feature most strongly, with 5% of people choosing 13, the cheeky scamps. But charging in at 11th place – well ahead of its time – with 2.8% of the vote was the number 42.

You may recognize 42 as the answer to the 'ultimate question of life, the universe and everything' from Douglas Adams's *The Hitchhiker's Guide to the Galaxy*. As much as I enjoy the book, I'm personally more of a fan of 43: the chicken nugget number (and that's despite being a vegetarian).

43 is the largest number of chicken nuggets that you could not buy from the well-known red-and-yellow fast-food chain. Nuggets are sold only in lots of 6 (regular size), 9 (king size) and 20 (James Acaster size)* so clearly there are some low nugget-numbers that could never be achieved: 11 nuggets is impossible but 12 can be done (2 lots of 6).

We can show that 43 nuggets cannot be achieved by systematically working through all the possibilities. 43 can't be made with just 6s, 9s or 20s alone, so let's try combining them. Using two 20s clearly takes us too close to 43, and a single 20 leaves 23 nuggets, which can't be made with 6s and 9s. So the 20 box is out. Subtracting 9s from 43 gives the sequence 34, 25, 16, 7, and none of these are divisible by 6, so we have exhausted all possibilities: 43 nuggets can't be bought.

But how do we know that 43 is the *largest* number of nuggets that can't be made? Let's try making the numbers immediately larger than 43:

$44 = 20 + 6 + 6 + 6 + 6$
$45 = 9 + 9 + 9 + 9 + 9$
$46 = 20 + 20 + 6$
$47 = 20 + 9 + 9 + 9$
$48 = 6 + 6 + 6 + 6 + 6 + 6 + 6 + 6$
$49 = 20 + 20 + 9$

Clever bit coming! Because we've found solutions for six consecutive numbers, and the smallest nugget box is also of size 6, we can simply add 6 to each of the solutions above to continue the pattern indefinitely:

$50 = 20 + 6 + 6 + 6 + 6 + \mathbf{6}$
$51 = 9 + 9 + 9 + 9 + 9 + \mathbf{6}$
$52 = 20 + 20 + 6 + \mathbf{6}$

And so on.

---

* I have been told that a kids' meal has four nuggets, but since I'm far from a regular fast-food customer and have never seen it with my own eyes (and also because it spoils the maths), I am going to overlook this.

24 July

Another little (non-chicken) nugget that gives me great pleasure as a mathematician but no pleasure as a vegetarian is the *ham sandwich theorem*, which states that **for every ham sandwich there exists a cut that will split both slices of bread and the ham exactly in half,** no matter how unevenly the bread and ham are placed. Indeed it's true even if the ham sandwich has been constructed so poorly that the bread and ham are not even touching each other, or even in the same building.

Some better news for veggies is the two-dimensional version, which is called the *pancake theorem*. This is somewhat easier to imagine and understand: put two pancakes next to each other on a plate (remember there is no *on top of* in 2D, so they have to sit alongside each other) and there's one slice that would cut both pancakes in half. Good news also for fans of higher-dimensional sandwiches: n items in n-dimensional space can all be halved with a single slice – though you would need your knife to be $(n - 1)$-dimensional. It's no good trying to slice a four-dimensional sandwich with a bread knife, as the old saying goes.

25 July

The seventeenth-century French mathematician Pierre de Fermat discovered that every prime that is 1 more than a multiple of 4 (which could be described as primes that are *1 modulo 4*) can be written as the sum of two square numbers. For example:

$5 = 4 + 1$
$13 = 9 + 4$
$17 = 16 + 1$

If ever I'm arrested and held in solitary confinement (under false allegations, of course), this is one of the games I'll be playing in my head to stop myself from going mad.

26 July

Writing the counting numbers in a spiral leads to surprisingly long diagonal lines of primes:

This is known as an *Ulam spiral*, named after Stanislaw Ulam, who discovered this phenomenon in 1963 when doodling during a long and boring meeting. I'm sure his line manager was delighted.

27 July

All the lonely prime numbers, where do they all belong? Prime numbers often come in pairs, agonisingly separated by just one number between, such as 11 and 13 or 17 and 19. These are known as *twin primes*, and it seems that there are infinitely many pairs of twin primes in the same way that there are infinitely many prime numbers in general. However, this is another one of those frustratingly open problems in mathematics: **we don't know for certain if pairs of twin primes go on**

forever or eventually run out. This is called the *twin prime conjecture* – do feel free to have a go at cracking it on your coffee break.

28 July

28 is a rare and beautiful number: it is 'perfect', meaning that it is neither 'deficient' nor 'abundant': it is exactly the sum of its factors.

28 = 1 + 2 + 4 + 7 + 14

Numbers with this property really are few and far between – here are the first four: 6, 28, 496, 8128. If you think you've spotted a pattern – one with a single digit, one with two digits, one with three – you'd be in good company: the Greek mathematician Iamblichus thought as much. Unfortunately we can quickly put paid to that conjecture with the next few perfect numbers: 33,550,336 and 8,589,869,056.

Here's a recipe for making your own perfect number (do try this at home):

- Add up powers of 2 until you reach a prime number total. So, for example, 1 + 2 + 4 = 7 would be an acceptable place to stop, but 1 + 2 + 4 + 8 = 15 would not. (Prime numbers that take this form are called *Mersenne primes*.)
- Take your sum total and multiply it by the last number in your list of powers of 2. So if you started with 1 + 2 + 4 = 7, you would next do 4 × 7 = 28.

Since each Mersenne prime yields exactly one perfect number, it is therefore true that there are as many of one as the other. It is not known whether there are infinitely many Mersenne primes, so the same can therefore be said for perfect numbers too.

29 July

Did you notice that all of the perfect numbers mentioned yesterday were even? You might even think that they always will be, since they are formed by multiplying an odd by an even number, which always leads to an even product. So all perfect numbers will be even, right? Well, probably...

An odd perfect number could *theoretically* exist, but none has been found yet. This is one of the longest-standing unsolved problems in mathematics. It is known, however, that **if an odd perfect number exists, it is more than 300 digits long!** The chances look slim, but out of an infinity of numbers to choose from, you never know...

30 July

On the year of writing this book, 30 July is Earth Overshoot Day, the day on which humanity has used all the biological resources that Earth regenerates during the entire year. It is calculated by dividing Earth's ecological resources by humanity's ecological footprint, and dividing the year by that same proportion.

The first time Earth Overshoot Day occurred in July was 2018; 2005 was the first time it happened in August, the turn of the new millennium in 2000 marked the first Overshoot Day in September. When is it in the year you're reading this? Find out more at overshootday.org.

31 July

23,456,789 is the largest prime number with consecutive increasing digits.

AUGUST

'E'ASY AS PI

1 August

Find a small glass or mug that your index finger fits snugly across the top of, like this:

Now grasp the same vessel with the thumb and forefinger of one hand and a single forefinger from the other hand. You should find that your fingers just about meet, give or take the amount of faith I can reasonably expect from someone who has bought this book and read this far through it:

If we assume that your forefingers and thumbs are about the same length (yes, this is absolutely fine to assume – there's no need to check) then it appears that **the circumference of a circle – the distance around the outside – is about three times the diameter**: that is, the length from side to side, through the centre. In fact it is just slightly more than 3; it's 3.14159…

This value is of course *pi*, for which we use the symbol π. It's another *irrational* number (like $\sqrt{2}$ – see 18 March), meaning that the decimal expansion never repeats or terminates, leading to the popular (in certain circles, pardon the pun) hobby of memorizing digits of pi. More of this later.

A handy approximation to pi is 22/7, which works out at 3.142857…, a very near miss. π^2 happens to be very close to 10, another handy approximation.

2 August

There are various ways of memorizing the digits of pi, the most interesting of which is *piphilology*, the practice of writing a poem or even a story that contains the digits of pi. Here's a very short one:

How I wish I could calculate pi.

Count the letters in each word and you'll find the first seven digits of pi: 3, 1, 4, 1, 5, 9, 2. Piphilological poems and stories of various length have been written, including the 10,000-word novel *Not a Wake* by Michael Keith, which shows a borderline abnormal dedication to the art.

3 August

Turn your head 90° to the right. You didn't even need to think about it, did you? It's hard-wired that 90° is a quarter of a turn. (I didn't actually tell you to return your head to its initial position, but that's fine.)

Why is 360° a full turn though? What's the reason for it? Mathematicians will often argue over whether mathematics was discovered or invented, but in terms of using 360 degrees as a full turn there can be no doubt: the system was invented. It's a hangover from the Mesopotamian base 60 counting system, which the ancient Egyptians picked up and ran with. The Egyptians invented the degree symbol and the first 360-day calendar (close enough) but the reason the 360° circle has hung around since then is the same reason it was introduced in the first place: **360 is very divisible.**

360 can be divided evenly by 2, 3, 4, 5, 6, 8, 9, 10 – every number from 1 to 10 except for 7. This makes calculations easier, and who could argue with that? Plato had quite a love of highly divisible numbers,

suggesting that the ideal state should consist of 5040 people, so that they could be evenly split into groups of any number from 1 to 12 (except for 11).

4 August

Happy Birthday John Venn! Now omnipresent in both science and broader popular culture, **the Venn diagram was only popularized in the 1880s.** *Les Misérables* and Nottingham Forest Football Club are older than Venn diagrams.

Classic Venn diagrams have two or three overlapping circles (or one single circle if the categories are 'actors who played Dr Phil in *The Fresh Prince of Bel-Air*' and 'actors who voiced Shredder in *Teenage Mutant Ninja Turtles*') but it's impossible to draw a Venn diagram of four or more sets with circles. Drawing a four-set Venn diagram can be done, but you have to be very careful to create all of the necessary regions. For example, only one of these is a satisfactory Venn diagram:

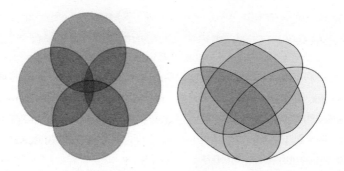

Take the example on the left. If the four circles represented, clockwise from top, 'two legs', 'TIME magazine cover stars', 'mammals' and 'dead things', then I would not be able to put myself into this Venn diagram. Nor would I be able to place any live two-legged person who hadn't been on the cover of TIME magazine, because there is no overlap of the top and bottom circles that doesn't involve crossing with another circle. The left version doesn't work as a four-part Venn diagram, but the one on the right does. Note that a correct diagram will have 2^n regions (including the outside), where n is the number of rings. So the left version can't be sufficient, as it only has 14 regions, whereas the version on the right has 16.

5 August

The fraction $\frac{355}{113}$, found by Chinese mathematician and astronomer Zu Chongzhi, gives an outrageously accurate approximation for π. Written as a decimal it is 3.1415929… accurate to six decimal places and within 0.000009% of the true value of π. It is the best rational approximation of π with a denominator of four digits or fewer, and is given the name 'milü' (密率) in China, meaning 'close ratio'.

6 August

22/7 gives a close approximation to pi that is easy to remember, and yesterday we saw that 355/113 gives a frighteningly good estimate. The mathematician Srinivasa Ramanujan (played brilliantly by Dev Patel in the film *The Man Who Knew Infinity*) popularized this particular approximation in the West during his correspondence with the mathematician G. H. Hardy. An even closer approximation is the fraction 104,348/33,215, but we do start to lose the ease of memorizing at this point.

Curiously though, **there are some infinite series that converge upon pi** – a <u>series</u> is simply the sum of a sequence of numbers. The best known of these is the *Leibniz* formula, named after Gottfried Leibniz (yes, the biscuits were also named after him – they both originate from Hanover):

$$\frac{\pi}{4} = 1 - \frac{1}{3} + \frac{1}{5} - \frac{1}{7} + \dots \text{ (where the denominators are all the odd numbers)}$$

I'm also a fan of the Euler formula (yes, Euler again, the Königsberg bridges guy):

$$\frac{\pi^2}{6} = 1 + \frac{1}{4} + \frac{1}{9} + \frac{1}{16} + \dots \text{ (where the denominators are all the square numbers)}.$$

7 August

The number 1729 holds a special place in the hearts of mathematicians; it is sometimes referred to as the *Ramanujan number*. When the mathematician G.H. Hardy visited Ramanujan in hospital towards the end of his young life, Ramanujan asked Hardy what the number of his taxi was. When Hardy replied that it was 1729 – surely not a very interesting number – Ramanujan quickly replied that, on the contrary, it was in fact the smallest number that can be written as the sum of two cubes in two different ways:

$$1729 = 1^3 + 12^3 = 9^3 + 10^3$$

Hardy once stated that if mathematicians could be scored out of 100 on their pure ability, that he himself would be a 25, the great German mathematician David Hilbert would be an 80 (more about him on 5 November) and that Ramanujan would be a 100. It is probably a bit weird to give your friends and colleagues ratings based on how clever they are, and I wouldn't recommend it if you're responsible for carrying out yearly staff appraisals, but there can be no doubt that Ramanujan was a mathematician of astonishing ability.

8 August

Move one matchstick to make this equation *approximately* correct... answer coming tomorrow.

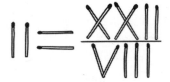

9 August

Yesterday's entry was a bit of fun – the solution is to move a matchstick from the 'eight' in the denominator on the right and use it to make the 'two' on the left into a 'pi', giving $\pi = 22/7$.

But here's a genuinely amazing way of finding pi with matchsticks (or indeed sticks, straws, or anything long and thin that you have very many identical copies of). Measure one matchstick and then draw a ladder-style grid of lines where the length between each 'rung' is the length of one matchstick, or whatever you used. Finally, throw your matchsticks randomly over the grid:

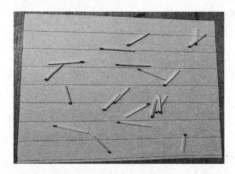

Now double the total number of matchsticks thrown and divide it by the number that touch a line. This should give you a decent approximation to pi. In the above diagram, with 20 matchsticks, that would be 40/14 = 2.9-ish: not too bad. Adding more matchsticks would make a better approximation.

This problem is called *Buffon's needle*, and it would hold even if the matchsticks were (somehow) wobbly. This sub-result is sometimes amusingly known as *Buffon's noodle*.

10 August

Imagine running a length of rope exactly around the circumference of the earth. Of course, in practice this is pretty much impossible given that huge oceans would get in the way, but imagine for a moment that it were possible. Now imagine placing volunteers so that they are standing all along the length of rope. Finally, imagine that they all lift the rope up by 1 metre at the same time.

Now, clearly there wouldn't be enough rope to go all the way around any more, but the question is this: how much more rope would you need? Or, to put it another way, how far would the two ends of the rope move away from each other?

We saw at the start of this chapter that the circumference of a circle is the diameter multiplied by just over 3, or π. Now, even if you can't remember Eratosthenes's calculations from the last chapter, we could just call the earth's diameter d. So the earth has a circumference of πd, and when we lift the rope by a metre we have a new, larger circle with diameter $\pi(d + 2)$, because the diameter has been extended by 1 metre at each side of the circle. The difference between $\pi(d + 2)$ and πd is:

$$\pi(d + 2) - \pi d = \pi d + 2\pi - \pi d = 2\pi$$

So the required amount of extra rope is 2π, or about 6.28 m. When I first saw this puzzle it did rather blow my mind that the required amount of rope was so small. What blew my mind a second time was that the same result would be true on any planet – be it Jupiter, Mars or a tiny tennis-ball-sized planet floating in your bedroom. **You always need just over 6 m of extra rope to be able to lift a circle of rope by 1 m all the way round any planet.**

11 August

It can sometimes appear that pi, like phi, pops up just about everywhere, but it's important to keep your wits about you for times when pi arrives unannounced and uninvited. For example, draw an alphabetic circle of capital letters, in English, and cross out those that have a vertical line of <u>symmetry</u>:

If you count the clumps of remaining letters, starting clockwise from the JKL bunch bottom right, you'll find clumps of 3, 1, 4, 1, 6, which is pi rounded to four decimal places. Although this is a bit of fun, it has nothing to do with circular measures whatsoever and is purely a contrived fluke.

12 August

314 and 31415 are examples of *early bird numbers*. If you were to write out all of the counting numbers in order with no gaps, you will find both 314 and 31415 well before they are 'due' to appear in natural order: 123456789101112131415161718192021222324…

The 314 arrives when the tail end of 13 meets 14; throw in the 15 as well and you have 31415.

13 August

Start reading through the digits of pi from the start, but stop at a different digit every time, and you'll find quite a few prime numbers early on:

3	Prime
31	Prime
314	Not prime
3141	Not prime
31,415	Not prime
314,159	Prime

But we saw earlier that prime numbers become generally more sparse as we move up the number line, and you'd better believe it: the next prime in pi after 314,159 is 31,415,926,535,897,932,384,626,433,832, 795,028,841.

14 August

Happy 14 August! I hope today holds some golden moments for you, because it does literally contain a golden moment: **if you divide the year into the golden ratio, so that the ratio of seconds elapsed to seconds still to come is φ (1.618-ish…) then the divide comes on 14 August**. In fact it happens at 1.58pm (and 39 seconds), which is quite possibly the time at which you're actually reading this. (If it's a leap year then the golden moment will come at a slightly different time tomorrow, but at least I've told you in advance…)

15 August

Here's a gorgeous series that generates half of π, first found by John Wallis in 1655: square every even number and divide it by the product of its adjacent odd numbers. Carry this on as far as you dare, multiply all the terms together and you have a great approximation for half of π:

$$\frac{\pi}{2} = \frac{2^2}{1 \times 3} \times \frac{4^2}{3 \times 5} \times \frac{6^2}{5 \times 7} \times \ \dots$$

16 August

Akira Haraguchi holds the unofficial record for memorizing digits of pi, reciting 100,000 digits in October 2006. (I have recited pi to 100 places, but I've never been invited back to any of those places (sorry).) Haraguchi recited 83,000 digits in one day – matching his own previous record – before returning the next day to top it off with another 17,000.

He took a five-minute break every two hours to eat, and his toilet breaks were filmed to make sure there was no cheating going on. Which feels like an invasion of pi-vacy (I'm really sorry).

17 August

In 2021, a new record for computer calculation of pi was set, with Swiss researchers calculating pi correctly to 62.8 trillion figures. To be clear, NASA require only a dozen or so digits of pi to keep satellites in orbit, so there is no benefit in knowing pi to 60 trillion figures. Records for computer calculation of pi are really about advancement in computer processing power, not the usefulness of the result.

Around the time that this record was set, Times Radio reached out to me to give an interview. I believe they regarded me as a reliable voice on the subject of mathematics, but since I had never heard of Times Radio I used the opportunity to cram in as many pi puns as I could in three minutes (the type you were subjected to in yesterday's entry). They have not approached me for an interview since.

18 August

I've been talking about pi for much of this month now, so you're probably used to the idea that it's simply a number slightly larger than 3. However, it's quite possible to show, with fairly logical steps, that pi is actually equal to 4. Strap in…

Here's a circle inscribed in a square. If the diameter of the circle is 1, then the circle has <u>perimeter</u> π, because the perimeter of a circle is π × diameter. The perimeter of the square would be 4, because it is 1 unit wide and 1 unit high (the sides of the square are the same length as the diameter of the circle). Now I'm going to 'cut in' towards the circle at some points on each side of the square. This results in a jaggedy shape that still has perimeter 4, because it still has all the same horizontal and vertical lengths, just rearranged.

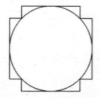

Can you see where I'm going with this? Next I'm going to repeat the process, giving a succession of jaggedy shapes that always have perimeter 4:

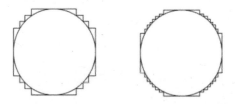

If I keep doing this, it feels like the long-term limit of the process is a circle. A circle with perimeter 4. But earlier on I found that the circle's perimeter is π. So... $\pi = 4$? What's the catch?

It's incredibly frustrating, but even though it looks like the jaggedy shape is converging upon a circle, it isn't really. The difference between the 'jaggedyness' of the outer shape and the smoothness of the curve is always the same as in the first diagram – it is not mathematically OK to say that the limit of the jaggedy process creates a circle (I don't think you will ever read the word 'jaggedy' as often as you have in today's entry).

19 August

Would you like to invest some money in my new bank? As an incentive, I'm going to offer you a free £1 to get you started. Not only that, but I'm going to offer you some options on how you'd like to invest the pound...

The simplest option is to take 100% interest at the end of the year. So when the year's up you get another £1 to add to your original pound. Another option is to take 50% interest but at two points in the year. So halfway through the year your £1 becomes £1.50, and at the end of the year the £1.50 becomes £2.25. You can actually choose any interest deal you like, as long as your interest rate is 100 divided by the number of splits:

Interest rate	Number of splits	End of year
100%	1	£2
50%	2	£2.25
10%	10	£2.59
1%	100	£2.70

As you can see, more splits seems to get you more money, but the increases seem to be slowing down. Even if you could split the year into a million parts, you'd still only take home £2.72, which is the most you can get out of my bank in a year, no matter how hard you try.

No matter how small the parts you split the year into are, you will never be able to get beyond £2.718281828459.* This number 2.71828…, where the digits go on forever, is a hugely important number that mathematicians call e, sometimes referred to as Euler's number (him again!), **The 'e' in Euler's number** **does not actually stand for Euler** but was simply chosen because a to d were already regularly used for other things in mathematics. Euler's number has countless uses and applications, from statistics to physics, but its original 'discovery' is

---

* Note that 2.7 is followed 1828 twice. Some remember this number as 'two point seven twice Tolstoy' in reference to the most famous person born in 1828, though Jules Verne, Henrik Ibsen and Josephine Butler might have something to say about that.

usually credited to Jacob Bernoulli in 1683, in the above context of compound interest.

20 August

Here's a fun game to play on a rainy afternoon: randomly generate numbers in the range 1–100, adding them up as you go. Stop when the total reaches 100 or more. Below are ten such trials from a <u>random number generator</u>:

Trial 1:	37	79		
Trial 2:	10	73	92	
Trial 3:	36	18	8	91
Trial 4:	24	47	92	
Trial 5:	94	72		
Trial 6:	22	50	30	
Trial 7:	56	44		
Trial 8:	23	43	98	
Trial 9:	26	78		
Trial 10:	46	23	38	

The computer took an average of 2.7 tries to reach 100 – you guessed it, the more trials you carry out, the closer the result will get to e. (Strictly speaking this should be done with real numbers between 0 and 1, and a target of 1, but the 100 target version is quicker and more inviting to carry out.)

Interestingly, when I asked 150 volunteers to 'randomly' generate the numbers, it took an average of 3.57 numbers to tip the total past 100 – a terrible estimate for e. We must put the disparity down to humans' preference for nice small numbers; a bias towards these small numbers meant that it generally took 'too many' trials for the humans to reach a total of 100.*

21 August

Euler's number – that is, e = 2.71828… – goes hand in hand with the *natural logarithm*, or 'ln' for short. The natural logarithm of a number is the power of e that is required to reach a given target number. Here are some powers of e:

$e^1 \approx 2.72$	$e^2 \approx 7.39$	$e^3 \approx 20.1$	$e^4 \approx 54.6$	$e^5 \approx 148$

So, working backwards, $\ln(20) \approx 3$ and $\ln(148) \approx 5$. How about $\ln(5)$? It must be somewhere between 1 and 2, because e^1 and e^2 fall either side of 5. It transpires that the accurate value of $\ln(5)$ is 1.609437, which is quite close to the golden ratio (1.618…) and quite close to 1.6, but (by chance) *extraordinarily* close to the conversion rate of miles to kilometres (1.60934). So the next time you're driving and need to convert miles to km, simply multiply by the natural logarithm of 5.

22 August

Take any whole integer, calculate $\sqrt{e^n}$, and round your answer up to the next whole number:

---

* Three people in the trial chose 100 as their first number, but this was cancelled out by *ten* people who hadn't even reached a total of 100 by their eighth number. The chances of choosing eight numbers from 1–100 that sum to less than 100, under true random choice, is absolutely minuscule.

$\sqrt{e^1} = 1.65 \rightarrow 2$

$\sqrt{e^2} = 2.72 \rightarrow 3$

$\sqrt{e^3} = 4.48 \rightarrow 5$

$\sqrt{e^4} = 7.39 \rightarrow 8$

$\sqrt{e^5} = 12.18 \rightarrow 13$

$\sqrt{e^6} = 20.09 \rightarrow 21$

$\sqrt{e^7} = 33.12 \rightarrow 34$

$\sqrt{e^8} = 54.60 \rightarrow 55$

Amazing – the Fibonacci sequence! Be careful not to jump to conclusions though – it breaks down at the next step and never works again:

$\sqrt{e^9} = 90.02 \rightarrow 91$ (should be 89)

23 August

Imagine you're on a game show where the final round involves choosing the best winning prize from a set of ten possible prizes. The prizes will come down a conveyor belt and all you have to do is choose the best one. There's a twist though, of course: you'll see the prizes one at a time, you've no idea what the best prize available is, when you choose your prize the conveyor belt stops, and if you pass up a prize you can't get it back.

So first comes a magnum of champagne. Pretty good, but there could be a speedboat or a luxury holiday coming later on, so you hold out. Next comes a voucher for a meal for two: maybe better, but not significantly so; you pass it up. Next comes a cuddly toy: clearly worse, you stick again, but now you're starting to worry that you should've taken one of the early prizes, especially when the fourth prize out is a bag of pick 'n' mix.

The fifth prize out is a pair of theatre tickets, and by this point you're nervous that you could wait all the way to the end and have to settle on a potentially awful tenth prize, so you take the tickets. It turns out prize ten was a new car, but you had no way of knowing that and to wait until the end is an incredibly risky strategy: there's only a one in ten chance that you'll win the best prize with this strategy. But is there a better strategy? What's the best strategy?

It turns out the best way to play is to watch a proportion of 1/e of the possible prizes, about 37%, and then take the first prize that beats what you've already seen. This will guarantee you taking away the best prize 37% of the time.

So in our example of ten items on a conveyor belt, your best bet is to view either three or four prizes from the list – that's 30% or 40% of the list, lying either side of 37% – and then choose the first prize that beats what you've seen so far.

24 August

Here's another unexpected place in which e raises its head: imagine a large theatre venue or cinema with unreserved seats, where customers can choose seats on a first come, first served basis. Oh, and the venue will be populated only by couples (this was absolutely not the case for any of the concerts my bands played).

As couples arrive they will start taking up empty seats, but they won't always use up every seat – people's inclination might be to leave the odd empty seat here and there to avoid the awkwardness of sitting right next to a stranger. And once some empty seats have been left alone, it's inevitable that others will crop up as a natural consequence of customers not being able to fill out rows. How much of the venue will be left as empty single seats if couples arrive and sit themselves fairly randomly?

The proportion is $1/e^2$, or about 13.5%.

25 August

Earlier I mentioned in passing that π^2 was very close to 10, but in fact π^2 is approximately 9.8696, which is even closer to g, the rate of acceleration due to gravity on Earth (measured in metres per second per second, or m/s² for short).

The equation for the time period of a hanging pendulum is:

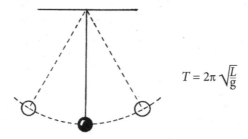

$$T = 2\pi \sqrt{\frac{L}{g}}$$

where T is the time for the pendulum to move back and forth once, and L is the length of the pendulum. Notice that the mass of the pendulum has no bearing on this formula.

Because π is almost indistinguishable from the square root of g, the above formula essentially boils down to $T = 2\sqrt{L}$. So if $L = 1$, $T = 2$; **a pendulum of length 1 metre has a time period of 2 seconds**, or 1 second to swing out and another second to swing back. Find a 1 metre string, tie something to the end of it (not the cat) and give it a try! 🐱

26 August

Usually a value of 9.8 or 9.81 m/s² is used for g, but gravity varies slightly depending on where on Earth you are, ranging from about 9.78 m/s² at the equator to around 9.83 at the poles. Since your weight is simply your mass multiplied by g, this means **you can literally make yourself lighter by taking a holiday near the equator**. And then you can eat and drink more – hurrah! This happens because the earth is not a perfect sphere, but instead ever so slightly egg-shaped.

27 August

A pendulum with a period of exactly two seconds – one second each way – is known as a *seconds pendulum*. In 1671 Jean Picard (not the one from *Star Trek*) proposed the length of a seconds pendulum as a measurement known as a 'universal toise'. This length is incredibly close to a metre, only differing from an exact metre because π^2 is not exactly the same as g. The universal toise would be 99.36 cm long, rather than 100, but of course it differs slightly depending on where on Earth you swing your pendulum – not ideal for a universal measurement.

In 1793 the length of a metre was first classified as one ten-millionth of the distance from the equator to the North Pole, but the modern classification is the distance that light travels in a vacuum in $\frac{1}{299,792,458}$ of a second. So if you're concerned that your metre ruler may have been cut overly long or short, simply check its legitimacy by holding it in a vacuum, shining a light along it and timing how long it takes the light to reach the other side. If it's about a 300 millionth of a second then you're all good.

28 August

Two months ago, on 28 June, many people (well, some people) were celebrating Tau Day, a day to honour the mathematical constant 'tau', with symbol the Greek letter tau, which looks like this: τ.

Tau is twice pi, in other words it's the ratio of the circumference of a circle to its <u>radius,</u> rather than its diameter (the radius is the direct distance from the edge of a circle to the centre, whereas diameter is the distance from one side of the circle to the other, through the centre). The diameter of a circle could fit around the circumference just over three times, whereas the radius could fit around the circumference just over six times – to be precise, 6.2831853… times.

Some people are very passionate that mathematicians should use tau instead of pi as the fundamental circular constant, reasoning that the radius and circumference are the fundamental features of a circle, and hence the circular constant should be derived from these measurements. There is even a 'tau manifesto' that can be found online, and tau purists use the inflammatory slogan 'pi is wrong' and support replacing all formulae involving pi with their tau-based equivalents. Personally I'm happy to leave all the textbooks alone, since they already contain more pi than a Chicago pizzeria, but it does amuse me to watch people argue about it.

29 August

e and π can be used to form a very accurate approximation for large factorial numbers, using the *Stirling formula:*

$$n! \approx \sqrt{2\pi n} \left(\frac{n}{e}\right)^n$$

To give you an idea, earlier we established that 13 factorial (13!) was a reasonable approximation for the world's population: 13! = 6,227,020,800

Using the Stirling formula to approximate 13! gives:

$$\sqrt{2\pi n} \left(\frac{n}{e}\right)^n = \sqrt{26\pi} \left(\frac{13}{e}\right)^{13} = 6,187,239,475$$

In this example, Stirling's approximation gives a result with an error of just 0.64%, and it only gets more accurate for larger values of n.

30 August

Here's another curious link between e, π and square numbers!

$$\frac{1}{\pi^2 + 1} + \frac{1}{4\pi^2 + 1} + \frac{1^2}{9\pi^2 + 1} + \ldots = \frac{1}{e^2 - 1}$$

31 August

This chapter has contained many references to both π and e, and eventually some links between them. Some other links between e and π can be found by pure chance, such as this:

$$\sqrt[9]{10e^8} = 3.141598\ldots$$

That's only approximately equal to π, although a very good fluke approximation indeed. The truly inspired link between π and e is *Euler's identity* (this is getting silly now), which states that:

$$e^{i\pi} = -1$$

Euler's identity has variously been described as the most beautiful in all of mathematics, and even a 'mathematical poem', which is a bit rich – it doesn't even rhyme. There is certainly a beauty to the way it perfectly links π and e – two fundamental mathematical constants – but to do so we must invoke i, an *imaginary* number. Now, imaginary numbers are lots of fun, but this so-called mathematical poem may be starting to lose the attention of the lay audience. In fact there are only a small proportion of people in the world (those with at least undergraduate level mathematics ability) who could truly understand and appreciate the implications of Euler's identity. I may be drummed out of the mathematicians' circle for saying this, but if we must have a 'most beautiful' mathematical identity, I'd rather it was something a little easier to understand.

Euler's identity is very much the $E = mc^2$ of mathematics: easy to remember but notoriously difficult to understand and explain.

SEPTEMBER

WHEN WILL I USE THIS IN THE REAL WORLD?

1 September

Put your hands together with your fingers crossed, as in this image. Do it quickly, don't overthink it:

Which thumb do you have on top? **60% of people cross their hands like this with left thumb on top**, and left- or right-handedness seems to have nothing to do with it.* So if ever you need to split a large group

---

* I've performed such trials several times and always hit roughly a 60:40 ratio. My most recent trial of 159 people came out at 64.2% in favour of left on top, with 65% of the right-handed people being left on top.

of people into three-fifths and two-fifths (perhaps you have two jobs that need doing but one is marginally more significant than the other?) this would be a good way of doing it.

2 September

Here is a method for publicly asking a large group of people an awkward or sensitive question, without them having to worry about other people knowing their innermost secrets. Let's say you were chairing a meeting of 80 local dog owners on the subject of dogs fouling on pavements. You want to know how many people at the meeting have ever let their dog do their business on the pavement without picking it up, but no one is going to come forward and confess to something like that. So you make the following request: 'Put your hand up if you have either let your dog foul on the pavement, or you have a birth date that ends in an even number.'

What you will then find is that slightly more than half of the room put their hand up: the half of the room that have even birth dates,* as well as some people born on odd dates but who let their dogs mess where they please. Let's say, for argument's sake, that you count 50 hands up out of 80.

Now you can disregard 40 of those people as essentially useless data – they may well be irresponsible dog owners but they are also born on even birth dates. However, the other 10 people with their hands up are useful to us: these people definitely let their dogs run wild. If we compare these 10 people against the 40 people in the

---

* Yes, in reality there are slightly more odd birth dates due to some months having 31 or 29 days, but it's close enough to a half to work well. First half vs second half of the year would be a cleaner split, but people would arguably be more likely to know each other's approximate birth date and hence spoil the confidentiality.

room who should statistically be born on odd birth dates, we find that very roughly one in four dog owners need to be reminded how to take their dog's mess home with them. Crucially though, you as the surveyor have no idea who those people are, and nor do the respondents know this about each other (unless they happen to know any other attendants' birth dates!).

3 September

Do you know anyone born in 1980? My sister was, and she and her fellow class of 1980 are the only humans alive who will ever be n years old in the year n^2 (in their case, turning 45 in the year 2025 – my sincere apologies if you're reading this after 2025 and missed it).

4 September

The mathematician John Conway developed an ingenious *doomsday method* for determining the day of the week of any day in the Gregorian calendar, past or future. It is based on the incredibly useful fact that **the dates 4/4, 6/6, 8/8, 10/10, 12/12, as well as 5/9, 9/5, 7/11 and 11/7, all fall on the same day of the week in any year**. In addition to this, the last day of February and Pi Day (3/14 in month/day format) also share the same so-called 'doomsday'. This gives a useful anchor date to work from for every month of the year.

Month	Date of 'doomsday' (month/day format)
January	1/3 in regular years, 1/4 in leap years
February	Last day of the month (either 28th or 29th in a leap year)
March	3/14 (Pi Day)
April	4/4

May	5/9 (think 'nine to five')
June	6/6
July	7/11 (think 'seven-eleven')
August	8/8
September	9/5 (think 'nine to five')
October	10/10
November	11/7 (think 'seven-eleven')
December	12/12

The trickiest month is January, but there is a mental method you can use: think 'the 3rd for 3 years, the 4th in the 4th year'. All we now need to know is the doomsday for any given year and we're away. There are mnemonics to remember these, but for the purposes of brevity, here are the doomsdays from the end of the Second World War up to 2030:

Doomsday	Years
Monday	1949, 1955, 1960, 1966, 1977, 1983, 1988, 1994, 2005, 2011, 2016, 2022
Tuesday	1950, 1961, 1967, 1972, 1978, 1989, 1995, 2000, 2006, 2017, 2023, 2028
Wednesday	1945, 1951, 1956, 1962, 1973, 1979, 1984, 1990, 2001, 2007, 2012, 2018, 2029
Thursday	1946, 1957, 1963, 1968, 1974, 1985, 1991, 1996, 2002, 2013, 2019, 2024, 2030
Friday	1947, 1952, 1958, 1969, 1975, 1980, 1986, 1997, 2003, 2008, 2014, 2025
Saturday	1953, 1959, 1964, 1970, 1981, 1987, 1992, 1998, 2009, 2015, 2020, 2026
Sunday	1948, 1954, 1965, 1971, 1976, 1982, 1993, 1999, 2004, 2010, 2021, 2027

To give an example of how it works: I was born on 2 June 1984, but what day of the week was that? The doomsday for 1984 is a Wednesday, which means that every anchor date in 1984 was a Wednesday. The 4–6–8–10–12 rule above tells me that 6/6 was a Wednesday, so I was born four days before a doomsday, on a Saturday. Try it yourself!

5 September

Here's a quirky method for multiplication that might appeal to big fans of square numbers. Take two numbers that you want to multiply, and then do the following:

- Square their sum.
- Square their difference.
- Subtract the second from the first.
- Divide by 4.

Say you wanted to work out 38×42. Their sum is 80 and their difference is 4. So:

$$\frac{80^2 - 4^2}{4} = \frac{6400 - 16}{4} = \frac{6384}{4} = 1596$$

Clearly this will hardly ever be easier than other multiplication methods, but if the two numbers you are multiplying are quite close to each other and add up to a multiple of ten, then it is just about possible to do in your head (and will impress friends at parties):

$$23 \times 17 = \frac{40^2 - 6^2}{4} = \frac{1600 - 36}{4} = \frac{1564}{4} = 391$$

6 September

Here's a trick for subtracting a number from a 100, 1000, 10,000 or any power of ten. For example, $1000 - 368$ will require a lot of awkward carrying. Instead we observe that $999 - 368$ will not involve any carrying at all, in fact it's quite easy to do in our head: 999 − 368 = 631. So 1000 − 368 must be 1 more than this: 632.

The method can be adapted to do any subtraction; say we wanted to calculate 542 − 389, this would ordinarily involve a lot of carrying from column to column. Instead we will do 999 − 389, add that to 542, and then subtract the 999. This might seem like going round the houses, but all of these steps could well be easier to do than subtracting and carrying in our heads:

999 − 389 = 610
610 + 542 = 1152
1152 − 999 = 153 (subtract 1000 and add 1)

7 September

A similar method to yesterday's can be used to subtract a decimal from a whole number. Say you wanted to subtract 0.74082 from 1. In each decimal place we'll calculate the 'complement to 9', but when we get to the last decimal place we'll calculate the 'complement to 10'.

1 − 0.74082 = 0.25918
(9 − 7 = 2, 9 − 4 = 5, 9 − 0 = 9, 9 − 8 = 1, 10 − 2 = 8)

8 September

The *rule of 72* gives a very good estimate of how long an investment will take to double, based on the interest rate. All you have to do is **divide 72 by the percentage interest rate and you'll have a great estimate**

for the number of years required for your investment to double (or alternatively for the size of a loan to double…).

At a 6% interest rate, it would take around 12 years for your investment to double, because 72/6 = 12. At a 10% interest rate it would take just over 7 years, because 72/10 = 7.2. Or you can work in the other direction: if you need to double your money in 5 years, you'll need to find an interest rate of about 14.4%, because 72/5 = 14.4.

9 September

Happy 9/9! To multiply the number 10,112,359,550,561,797,752,808, 988,764,044,943,820,224,719 by 9, simply move the last 9 to the front:

10,112,359,550,561,797,752,808,988,764,044,943,820,224,719 × 9 = 91, 011,235,955,056,179,775,280,898,876,404,494,382,022,471

10 September

Add together square numbers, starting from 1. You'll find it's quite hard to make another square number:

1 + 4 = 5	not a square
1 + 4 + 9 = 14	not a square
1 + 4 + 9 + 16 = 30	not a square

In fact you have to add all the way up to 576 to make a square number sum:

$$1 + 4 + 9 + \ldots + 576 = 4900 = 70^2$$

This is the first and only time that adding a string of square numbers, starting from 1, makes another square number.

11 September

Yesterday we saw the only solution to the *Diophantine equation* $1 + 4 + \ldots + x^2 = y^2$. A Diophantine equation is an equation that must have only integer (whole number) solutions; for example, solving the Diophantine equation $a^2 + b^2 = c^2$ is equivalent to finding Pythagorean triples.

The name comes from the third-century mathematician Diophantus of Alexandria. **Little is known of Diophantus beyond a rather neat biographical riddle** that was written about him and released in a Greek anthology of number puzzles a few hundred years after his death. As far as legacies go, it could be worse than having your life's story preserved for all time in a number puzzle (well, I think so anyway). Can you crack it? Answer in the Further Notes at the back of the book.

> Here lies Diophantus, the wonder behold
> Through art algebraic, the stone tells how old:
> 'God gave him his boyhood one-sixth of his life
> One twelfth more as youth while whiskers grew rife;
> And then yet one-seventh 'til marriage begun;
> In five years more there came a bouncing new son
> Alas, the dear child of master and sage
> Died at just half of his father's death age
> Four years after this, due to heartbreak and strife
> Came the end of the great Diophantus' life.'*

---

* Every translation of the riddle I have ever seen ceases to rhyme in its second half, which has always bugged me. So please consider this an original modern translation.

12 September

Place two identical coins side by side. In a moment you're going to roll one coin around the other one, keeping their edges intact, so that the coin on the right is now on the left. The question is, what will the coin on the right look like when it has been spun into its new position?

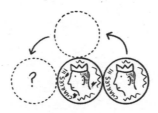

If you have two coins handy, I highly recommend doing this before you look at the answer. The coin on the right will be 'upside down' when in its new position, right? Because it's completed half a turn? Well…

The coin will be the 'same way up' when it has moved from the right side to the left side of the other coin. What's going on here then? The centre of the coin that's moving travels on a circular path, and the radius of this circle is the sum of the radii of the two coins – in this case, twice the radius of the stationary coin. And if the radius is twice as large, then the circumference is also twice as large. Since the moving coin is essentially moving around a path that's twice as large as its own circumference, it must have to travel through two full rotations to reach its original starting point.

You may prefer to think of the path that the leftmost point on the moving coin takes:

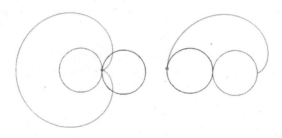

The shape of this path is called a *cardioid*, due to its similarity to the classic heart shape – this is shown in the left-hand image above. Look carefully at the right-hand image, showing the 'half turn' that you did a moment ago, and you'll see that the leftmost point on the moving coin (I've marked it with a dot) is also the leftmost point when the moving coin has moved from right to left. If the leftmost point is back to being the leftmost point, then the coin must have done a full rotation by that point.

A coin of radius r rolling around one of radius R would make R/r + 1 rotations. So if your inner coin had twice the radius of the outer, the outer coin would complete three full rotations while moving once around the larger inner coin.

13 September

Speaking of coins, in the UK why did the Queen's head used to face to the right on coins, but to the left on stamps? **Since the time of Charles II, the direction in which the British monarch's head faces on coins has changed with every succeeding monarch.** The same does not apply to stamps – the monarch always faces left. So Charles III faces left on both coins and stamps, but our next monarch will switch to facing right on coins only.

14 September

It's possible to make a biased coin into a fair one, or indeed to make anything two-faced (TV remote, piece of buttered toast, Nick Clegg) into a fair coin in the following manner.

Throw the coin/remote/toast twice and assign heads or tails to the following outcomes (I've used the buttered toast in my example):

Buttered up then buttered down = Heads
Buttered down then buttered up = Tails
Buttered up twice = Discard
Buttered down twice = Discard

Here's what happened when I repeatedly threw some buttered toast at home:

Up, Up, Down, Up

So much for the so-called phenomenon of toast always landing buttered side down. Because the first two throws landed butter up, we discard this pair of outcomes. But the next two throws landed butter side down then up, which according to my system corresponds to a tail.

This will work no matter how much more likely one outcome is than the other. It may be that buttered side down is more likely than buttered side up – who knows? – but up then down is equally likely as down then up, because toast has no memory.

15 September

Here is a neat trick for multiplying together two numbers in the 90s.* For example, say you need to multiply 92 by 97. The key step is to swap each number for how far it is from 100 – call these your magic numbers.

$92 \rightarrow 8$
$97 \rightarrow 3$

Multiply your magic numbers to give the last two digits of your final answer: In this case $8 \times 3 = 24$. Then subtract both magic numbers from 100 to find the first two digits of your answer: $100 - 8 - 3 = 89$. So 92 $\times 97 = 8924$.

Here's why it works:

$$(100 - a)(100 - b) = 10,000 - 100(a + b) + ab$$

---

* By which I mean two numbers between 90 and 100, not two numbers from thirty years ago.

16 September

If you're ever stuck in a maze, here's a more or less sure-fire way to find your way out: put either your left or right hand on the wall and keep walking forward. Eventually you'll find yourself escaping the maze. This works as long as the maze is simply connected (all the internal walls are joined to the outside) and the exit is on the perimeter of the maze, which is pretty much always true. Here's a blank maze map, and another showing an escape with the 'right-hand rule'; you're welcome to try out the left-hand rule too.

Since every internal wall is attached to the outer perimeter, walking through a maze in this way is essentially equivalent to walking around the perimeter either clockwise or anticlockwise, and covering every inch of wall that you encounter along the way. If the exit is on the perimeter somewhere, you will find it.

17 September

The number 17 is sometimes described as the 'least random number'. If you give a large enough sample of people the opportunity to pick a number from 1 to 20, 17 is meant to come out on top. It's hard to track any solid data for this phenomenon, but I did manage to replicate the result in a survey of 159 people, with 17 coming in as most popular, being picked 18 times (the next most popular were the ubiquitous lucky/unlucky numbers 7 and 13, with 14 and 15 votes respectively).

Humans are notoriously terrible at approximating randomness – for example, what's the longest run of heads or tails you'd expect from ten coin flips? Would you expect to get four in a row of either heads or tails? Few people will write four heads or tails in a row if they attempt to 'be the coin' and generate their best attempt at randomness,* but in fact it will happen about as often as not (it's actually a 46.5% likelihood – more on the calculations in the Further Notes at the back of the book). Below are 20 randomly generated strings of ten coin flips, with nine of them resulting in a four-in-a-row string (and one instance of a seven-in-a-row).

---

* In my survey of 158 people (one of the previous 159 decided not to answer this question) only 23% had a run of four or more of a type in a row, including three people who somewhat inevitably opted for ten in a row. This would happen only one time in 512 – not impossible, but very unlikely, as the brilliant illusionist Derren Brown showed when he filmed himself performing ten fairly flipped heads in a row. It took over nine hours.

T	H	T	T	H	T	H	T	H	T	No
H	H	T	T	T	H	T	H	H	H	No
T	T	T	T	H	H	T	T	T	T	Yes
T	T	H	T	T	H	H	T	H	H	No
T	H	H	T	H	T	H	T	T	T	No
T	T	T	T	H	T	H	T	T	T	Yes
T	H	T	H	T	H	H	T	H	H	No
T	T	T	T	T	T	T	H	H	T	Yes
H	H	T	H	T	H	H	T	T	T	No
T	T	H	H	H	T	H	T	H	T	No
H	H	T	T	T	T	H	T	H	T	Yes
T	H	T	T	T	T	T	T	H	T	Yes
T	T	T	H	T	H	T	H	H	T	No
H	T	H	T	T	T	T	T	H	H	Yes
H	T	H	T	H	H	T	H	T	T	No
T	T	H	T	T	T	H	T	H	H	No
T	H	H	H	H	T	H	T	H	T	Yes
T	H	T	T	H	T	H	H	H	T	No
T	H	T	H	T	T	H	H	H	H	Yes
H	H	T	H	H	T	T	T	T	T	Yes

18 September

It has been reported that around 10,000 people play the numbers 1, 2, 3, 4, 5, 6 in the weekly UK lottery. That means that if you were to play those numbers and win, you would have to knock four zeros off the jackpot before taking your personal winnings home. At time of writing the largest ever jackpot was £195 million: even that would be down to less than £20,000 a head by the time it had been shared 10,000 ways. The average jackpot of £4 million would be down to a measly 400 quid each.

Spare a thought for British jackpot winners from 14 January 1995, only nine weeks into the newly launched (to much fanfare) National Lottery, which still runs to this day. On this week there were a massive 133 winners, each taking home just £122,510. Not a bad day's work, no doubt, but not the life-changing sum that winners in the previous eight weeks took home. What made this week so bizarre and special? Here are the winning numbers from that week: 7, 17, 23, 32, 38, 42.

These winning numbers might not be consecutive, but notice how they are beautifully spaced out with gaps of around 6–10 each time, and spread right across the possible range of 1–49, which were the numbers that could be chosen at the time.* This set of numbers looks exactly like what humans do when attempting to approximate randomness – spread the numbers out fairly – which is why it proved to be hugely popular. This is similar to humans' inability to approximate the 'clumpiness' of heads and tails in a random string of ten flips.

19 September

Humans' misunderstanding of the 'clumpiness' of random numbers means that our suspicion is often raised when something perfectly possible but just very unlikely does happen. Take for example the following example: **In the South African lottery of 1 December 2020, the numbers 5, 6, 7, 8, 9, 10 were drawn.** This led to so many people complaining and alleging fraud that an official investigation was launched into the process, even though the jackpot was shared by 20 different players!

This is a classic example of how staggeringly unlikely events happen all the time in a world where millions of interactions are taking place

---

* In fact, all of these numbers lay in the central columns of the playslip, with none of the numbers falling in the outer columns.

every second. It may be monumentally unlikely for a consecutive string of six numbers to come up, but in all the lotteries in all the world in all the time since lotteries began, it's not unreasonable for it to happen. In the Bulgarian lottery in 2009, the same winning numbers were drawn two weeks in a row. Again, astonishingly unlikely in isolation, but in the wider context of thousands of lottery draws taking place all over the world every week, not unreasonable.

20 September

As I write this in 2022, the iPod has recently been discontinued by Apple after 21 years. It was the last mass-produced portable music-playing device before smartphones became ubiquitous, and over 400 million iPods were sold. Perhaps the most unique selling point of the iPod was the ability to randomize your entire music collection with the 'shuffle' mode, meaning that Slayer could flow seamlessly on from Elvis and absolutely terrorize your visiting grandparents.

There was a problem though: the random shuffle feature would regularly play two or even three songs from the same artist in a row. Sometimes it would even play three songs from the start of an album in the intended sequence – surely a mistake? **Hundreds of Apple customers complained about the shuffle feature, leading to Apple altering their random algorithm to be... less random**. Apple introduced Smart Shuffle, which allowed users to adjust the likelihood of the same artist being played twice in a row. It seems that what people wanted was not true randomness, but for the songs to be 'spread out nicely' so that the same artist doesn't get played back to back as often as they should under real randomness. It really sums up everything you need to know about humans and their understanding of true randomness: the algorithm was made less random, so that it would feel more random.

21 September

Here's a useful way of mentally finding a <u>mean average</u>. Say you wanted to find the average of these five teacher salaries (in thousands of pounds):

95   112   98   105   110

Adding them up and dividing by 5 will be a little tedious. We might instead notice that some numbers are under 100 and some are over 100, so maybe 100 is the mean? Instead of adding the original values, we'll replace each value with how far above or below our guess of 100 it is, and average those values:

−5 +12 − 2 + 5 + 10 =   +20

We have an error of +20, spread across 5 values. So the 'average error' is +4 (20 divided by 5). Adding the +4 to the 100 that I assumed the average to be gives 104, which is the correct mean average.

22 September

How many people do you reckon share your PIN – that special four-digit number that means so much to you and allows you to verify your card purchases on the odd occasion that contactless payments don't work? Some combinations are more popular than others, and some are outlawed altogether (most banks won't allow you to have four of the same number like 2222 or four consecutive numbers forwards or backwards, such as 1234 or 6543) but that still allows plenty of scope for all of our own idiosyncrasies and quirks, right? (Personally, I heard a rumour that hardly anyone starts their PIN with a zero, so all of my bank cards have the PIN 0666, which allows me to honour Satan appropriately but still have a number that nobody could guess.)

But a simple bit of analysis makes it clear that our precious PINs are nowhere near as special or personal as we may think they are. There are fewer than 10,000 possible numbers from 0000 to 9999 once the previously described handful have been removed, and about 50 million adults in the UK. But each of those adults probably has at least two different bank cards with PINs, so let's use two per head as a lower bound. That means 100 million PINs spread across 10,000 possible combinations: in other words, **if you live in the UK, there are at least 10,000 other people that have each of your PINs**. If you live in the United States, make that 50,000 people. Probably the only countries in the world where every adult could have their own unique PIN for every bank card are Tuvalu and Vatican City. You're not as special as you thought you were.*

---

* It was incredibly difficult, throughout this entry, not to write 'PIN number' – this of course would be a tautology, since the 'N' in 'PIN' already stands for the word 'number'. But we all fall into the trap of accidentally using tautologies, especially when popping to the ATM machine to use our PIN number to draw out cash to pay for some naan bread and chai tea.

23 September

1001 is a very cool number indeed. First of all, multiplying a three-digit number by 1001 is as simple as writing it out twice:

$682 \times 1001 = 682,682$

Multiplying a number by 1001 is equivalent to multiplying by 1000 and then adding on the number once; multiplying by 1000 'shifts' the number three places to the left, and these places will be filled by the original number itself when you add it on once.

1001 is also $7 \times 11 \times 13$, which leads to a few neat tricks, including the following: take a large number – say, 13,576,717 – and chunk it into groups of three starting from the right side. So here that would be 717, 576 and 13. We can ascertain in one fell swoop whether 13,576,717 is a multiple of 7, 11, 13 (some or all of the these) or none of them. Subtract and add the alternating 'chunks' of numbers, starting from either the right or the left, whichever you prefer:

$717 - 576 + 13 = 730 - 576 = 154$

If this remaining number is divisible by 7, 11 or 13, then the original number is also. 154 is $140 + 14$, i.e. twenty 7s plus two 7s, so it is divisible by 7. It's also $110 + 44$, so ten 11s plus four 11s; it is divisible by 11. But counting on from 130 gives 143, 156, …, so 154 is *not* a multiple of 13. Therefore, 13,576,717 is divisible by both 7 and 11, but not by 13.

24 September

As we move into a cashless society we may mourn the loss of small-value coins, but the producers of said coins certainly won't, as **low-value coins often cost more to make than their actual monetary value**. Up until 1990, penny coins in the UK were made of pure copper, but the price of copper meant that they began to be worth more melted down than if you kept them and spent them. At this point the Royal Mint began to make pennies from copper-plated steel, which for a while meant that new pennies were magnetic but old ones weren't. Even this didn't entirely keep a lid on the problem though: in 2006 a rise in the price of copper meant that for a while 2p coins were worth 3p.

It has been variously reported in the US that 1 cent coins cost around 1.5 cents to make, and nickels (5 cent coins) cost around 6 cents, costing the US Mint tens of millions of dollars a year.

25 September

You've read a good amount of this book by now (unless you flicked straight to this page because it's your birthday; hello Michael Douglas and Catherine Zeta Jones!) but is it any good? Is it decent? Amazing? Fantastic? Dreadful? *Abysmal?* And what do these words even mean? Which ones are five-star reviews; which are two-star reviews? How good is good?

Fortunately the UK polling website YouGov took on the task of classifying such words in 2018, leading to the following gorgeous data visualization:

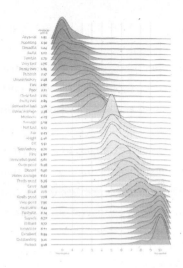

Respondents were asked to rate the adjectives given from 0 to 10, with 0 being 'very negative' and 10 being 'very positive'. There are some fascinating insights: for example **'perfect' scores just 9.16 out of 10**. How exactly should one improve on perfect? If perfect is worth a 9, then what is worth 10? Americans were even harsher, rating 'perfect' as just 8.75.

I'm also drawn to the word 'unsatisfactory', the only adjective to draw a bi-modal (two-humped) response. It seems that some people think it means really bad, and some think it means just worse than average.

26 September

Anscombe's quartet is an ingenious group of four data sets that are clearly all completely different, but have the same descriptive statistics (the same average x-position, average y-position, amount of variance in both x and y, the same line of best fit (or regression line) and the same level of correlation to this line).

The graphs were created by the statistician Francis Anscombe in 1973 to show the importance of visualizing data, not just making judgements based on the summary statistics. Clearly these graphs all tell very different stories, but if viewed only through the lens of summary statistics, they are all identical.

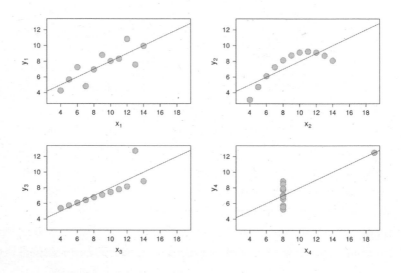

27 September

An even more stunning example of the point made by Anscombe's quartet was created in 2017 by Justin Matejka and George Fitzmaurice; this example is known as the *Datasaurus dozen*. These twelve data sets, as well as the dinosaur-looking data set originally created by Alberto Cairo, all have exactly the same summary statistics.

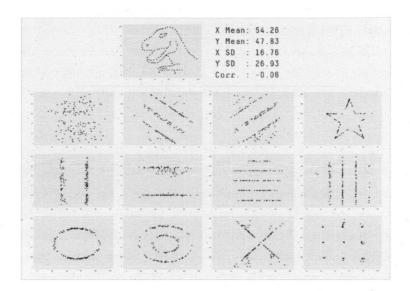

X Mean: 54.26
Y Mean: 47.83
X SD : 16.76
Y SD : 26.93
Corr. : -0.06

28 September

You will probably remember from school that the internal angles of a triangle always add up to 180°, so it's impossible to have a triangle with two right angles (90°). But what if I told you **it's perfectly possible to construct a triangle with *three* right angles** – all you need is a sphere. In fact, since we live on a giant sphere, let's start here on Earth.

Imagine you were standing at the North Pole and walked directly south until you hit the equator, around 10,000 km later (thanks Eratosthenes!). Then turn left and walk along the equator for 10,000 km. Finally, turn left again and you'll find yourself facing directly north; walk another 10,000 km and you'll be back where you started. What do you know, you've just charted an equilateral triangle with three internal right angles.

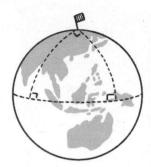

Working with shapes on a sphere is known as *elliptic geometry*, in which the surface 'bulges outwards' so we say it has positive curvature. The opposite is *hyperbolic geometry*, in which the surface 'bulges inwards', which we call negative curvature. Next time you're eating Pringles (other snacks with negative curvature are available) consider what a triangle drawn on its surface would look like; it would have 'inwards bulging' edges, resulting in a total internal angle of *less* than 180°.

29 September

Adding together every other odd number results in a triangle number, regardless of where you stop adding:

$1 + 5 = 6$
$1 + 5 + 9 = 15$
$1 + 5 + 9 + 13 = 28$

Here's a cute visual proof:

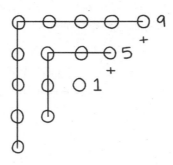

30 **September**

It's impossible to lose on a roulette table. Sort of. Here's how you do it.

All you're going to do is bet everything on black until it comes in. So, to begin with, bet £1 on black. If it comes in, the casino will pay out £2, since half of the numbers on a roulette wheel are coloured black, and the rules of roulette stipulate that every outcome pays out the equivalent odds corresponding to its likelihood of the occurrence.*

If you lose though, you simply double your stake. So in your second play you bet £2, and you stand to win £4 if successful; enough to cover your loss from the first game as well as your stake in the second game. If you lose again, just keep doubling your stake:

Win on 1st game: £2 win – £1 stake = £1 winnings
Win on 2nd game: £4 win – £2 stake – £1 loss from 1st game = £1 winnings

---

* Traditionally there are 36 squares on a roulette wheel – half black, half red – plus a 37th green square. The 37th square is the only reason that the house makes any money out of roulette; without it, every game would be as likely to fall in favour of the players as the house.

Win on 3rd game: £8 win – £4 stake – £2 loss from 2nd game – £1 loss from 1st game = £1 winnings

You can guarantee to always win £1 this way. Not bad! This is usually known as the St Petersburg paradox, and it isn't too hard to see the problem: you can only ever win £1 with this strategy, and the potential losses given an (albeit very unlikely) long string of reds could be ruinous. Casinos instigate a maximum stake, so it would not be possible to keep doubling your stake indefinitely. Is it worth the risk of financial devastation to probably win £1? Probably not.

A legendary long streak occurred in Monte Carlo casino in 1913, when a run of 26 consecutive blacks came in, costing gamblers millions of francs in assuming that a red would *surely* come up soon. This is known as the *gambler's fallacy* – the false assumption that, because something has not happened for a long time, it is more likely to happen soon. Of course, the odds of red or black never change, regardless of what has gone before.

OCTOBER

THAT'S ENTERTAINMENT!

1 October

One of the most popular and addictive computer games of all time is Tetris, so called because every piece is made up of four blocks. Similarly a tetrapod is a four-legged creature, a tetrahedron has four faces, and a Tetrapak carton has four, erm, flappy closey bits.

The seven Tetris pieces, each made up of four squares,
that players move around to attempt to fill a grid.

I was never very good at Tetris, so I take some pleasure from knowing that **every game of Tetris is statistically doomed to end**, no matter how skilled or fast the player. This was proved in 1992 by John Brzustowski.

2 October

Though it's hard to know for certain, it is likely that **the Shia LaBeouf film *Man Down* is the least successful film in the history of British cinemas, selling one ticket in one cinema on its opening weekend in 2017.** The film did pull off the unlikely feat of increasing its weekly box office sales by 200% later that week when two more tickets were sold, but fans of rice on chessboards will be disappointed to hear that it couldn't pull off the doubling twice: no more tickets were sold; total gross $26.19.

The least successful film in US history in terms of box office sales is the Katherine Heigl thriller *Zyzzyx Road*, which sold three tickets at one cinema in 2006, grossing $30. Clearly filmgoers are more keen on vowels than the producers had anticipated, or perhaps new releases were listed alphabetically and nobody got that far down the list.

3 October

Through most of the 1940s and 1950s, over a billion cinema tickets were sold per year in the UK. This peaked in 1946, when over 1.6 billion cinema tickets were sold; with a population at the time of around 50 million, that means 32 cinema visits per man, woman and child. Occasionally a film is touted as 'saving cinema' by tempting people away from streaming services – often it's a new James Bond film or a similar popular franchise – but it's hard to overstate just how different the culture is now: in 2019 there were 178 million tickets sold in the UK; around three tickets per person.

4 October

The 1939 movie *Gone with the Wind*, despite its outdated and racially insensitive themes, will almost certainly remain a record-breaker for as long as feature films continue to be made. **At 3 hours and 58 minutes** (including the overture, intermission, entr'acte,* and exit music), *Gone with the Wind* **is the longest movie ever to win the Academy Award for Best Picture**. With the general public's waning attention span (they need even their books to be broken down into bitesize daily chunks...) it's hard to see that length ever being surpassed. In terms of box office receipts, it is also the most successful film in history when accounting for inflation.

5 October

The twenty-first century is truly the age of the sequel – **since the year 2000 there have been only three occasions that the year's highest grossing film worldwide was an original story**: *Avatar* in 2009, *The Avengers* in 2012† and *Frozen* in 2013. The highest grossing movie of 2020 was the Japanese animation *Demon Slayer: Mugen Train*, which is a movie sequel to a television series. However, even if you were to include this as an original film, its gross box office sales are minuscule compared to years before and since, because cinemas were closed for most of 2020 due to the Covid-19 pandemic, so 2020 should probably be excluded from the data set altogether. Actually the entire year 2020

---

* No, I did not have a clue what an entr'acte was either; apparently it's a piece of music played between two acts in a play. I don't remember this happening, but I admit I may have fallen asleep somewhere around the middle two hours.

† *The Avengers* is not strictly a sequel, but it is the sixth movie in the Marvel cinematic universe that had been established in 2008, so you may choose not to include it.

should be excluded from official records altogether – who do we need to speak to about that?

6 October

Telephone numbers beginning with 555 have long been used in American TV and film for the phone numbers of fictitious characters and institutions. This system stops people from being bothered with curious callers when their real-life phone number is assigned to, say, the character of God in the film *Bruce Almighty* (this actually happened).

Universal Studios also owns a genuine phone number, (212) 664-7665, which it uses to give a sheen of authenticity now that people are used to the ubiquity of 555 numbers. This number has appeared in films such as *The Adjustment Bureau, Definitely Maybe, Munich* and *Scott Pilgrim vs. the World*, but if you dial it in real life it just rings endlessly.

Musicians seem less cagey about giving out their real-life numbers, and artists from the sublime to the ridiculous (Tom Waits, Alicia Keys, Razorlight's Johnny Borrell) have all given out their phone numbers, or supposed numbers, in song lyrics.

7 October

3435 is a *Munchausen number*, for the following reason:

$$3^3 + 4^4 + 3^3 + 5^5 = 3435$$

The only other numbers to fit this pattern are 1, 438,579,088 and possibly 0, though we would need to have a debate about zero raised to the power of zero. The name 'Munchausen number' comes from the literary character Baron Munchausen, who was based upon the very much real-life eighteenth-century baron of the same name. The fictional baron's outrageous claims and exaggerations include saving himself from drowning by pulling himself up by his own ponytail; in a similar way, we could say these numbers are 'pulling themselves up by their own base'. The term *Munchausen's syndrome* is, of course, also used to describe patients who overstate or lie about their state of physical health.

8 October

Happy World Octopus Day! It's quite clear that octopuses are an intelligent species: one need only think of the wise, compassionate star of Netflix's Oscar-winning *My Octopus Teacher*, or the legendary octopus Paul who predicted football scores.*

If an octopus could count, it would make sense that they do so in base 8, given that they have eight tentacles. This is sometimes known as *octal* counting. Counting in base 8 would involve having eight digits from 0 to 7 and using a new column whenever necessary. So, to an octopus, the number of years in a human century would look like this: 144. What? 144 years? No, this number still describes the same hundred that we expect it to, but in base 8 the rightmost digit counts 1s, the next column counts 8s, the next column counts 64s, and so on. So to convert 144 from base 8 to base 10:

$$144 \rightarrow (1 \times 64) + (4 \times 8) + (4 \times 1) = 64 + 32 + 4 = 100$$

---

* Of course I don't think Paul the octopus could actually predict scores; I'm a rational man. But I'll be honest, I was struggling to think of a second intelligent octopus.

There are some cultures that count in base 8, such as Native Americans using the Yuki language in California or the Parmean language in Mexico. When counting, they count the gaps between their fingers rather than the fingers themselves.

9 October

Halving the length of a plucked string results in hearing the same note but an octave higher, because halving the length of the string doubles the frequency at which it vibrates. Many musical styles have formed in different cultures around the world, but all of them are built on this fundamental fact – Pythagoras (yes, the triangle guy with the golden thigh) experimented with strings around 500 BC and found this pleasing occurrence. It also explains why the bodies of many pianos have a roughly 'exponential' curved shape, with the longer strings on the left and the length of string halving every twelve keys.

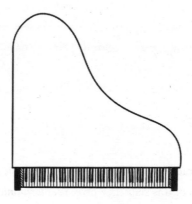

10 October

There's a cheeky Fibonacci (1, 1, 2, 3, 5, 8, 13, …) element to the piano too: there are *eight* notes in an octave – C, D, E, F, G, A, B, C – across *thirteen* piano keys including sharps and flats (that's *five* black keys and *eight* white), and the black keys are always arranged in *threes* and *twos*.

11 October

Musical notes of interest can also be found by dividing a string into three, four, five or any integer division.

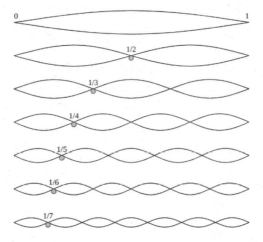

This sequence of fractions is often called the *harmonic sequence*; adding together the terms of this sequence gives the *harmonic series*:

$$1 + \tfrac{1}{2} + \tfrac{1}{3} + \tfrac{1}{4} + \tfrac{1}{5} + \dots$$

What do you think will happen with this series in the long term? Clearly each term is smaller than the previous term, but does that mean the series will eventually get closer and closer to some grand total (a convergent series)? In fact the opposite is true: the harmonic series can grow as large as you want it to, as long as you have a lot of patience.

We're going to prove this by grouping the fractional terms into sections, each of which contains twice as many terms as the previous group:

$$1 + \tfrac{1}{2} + \left(\tfrac{1}{3} + \tfrac{1}{4}\right) + \left(\tfrac{1}{5} + \tfrac{1}{6} + \tfrac{1}{7} + \tfrac{1}{8}\right) + \left(\tfrac{1}{9} + \tfrac{1}{10} + \tfrac{1}{11} + \tfrac{1}{12} + \tfrac{1}{13} + \tfrac{1}{14} + \tfrac{1}{15} + \tfrac{1}{16}\right) + \left(\tfrac{1}{17} + \cdots\right)$$

Look at the second group: a third plus a quarter. A third is more than a quarter, so this group adds up to more than two quarters, i.e. more than a half. In the next group of four, the smallest fraction is one eighth, so the four fractions together sum to more than four eighths, in other words more than a half again. The next group is more than eight sixteenths, so again more than a half. This same process could be continued indefinitely so that the harmonic series can contain as many halves as you wish, in other words it grows indefinitely (albeit very very slowly); this is called a divergent series.

12 October

Plot twist! What would happen to the harmonic series if you remove every term with a zero in it? This would be the same sum as yesterday, but with no 1/10, no 1/20, no 1/100, etc.:

$$1 + \tfrac{1}{2} + \tfrac{1}{3} + \tfrac{1}{4} + \tfrac{1}{5} + \tfrac{1}{6} + \tfrac{1}{7} + \tfrac{1}{8} + \tfrac{1}{9} + \tfrac{1}{11} + \tfrac{1}{12} + \cdots$$

My expectation was that this series would also be divergent, since it contains almost all of the original series. In fact, *it is convergent!* The sum of this infinite sequence will never get beyond about 23.1 – there's more of this at the back of the book.

13 October

Happy Ada Lovelace Day (approximately, depending on which year you're reading this)! Ada Lovelace Day is an international celebration of the achievements of women in science, technology, engineering and maths. The only legitimate daughter of the poet Lord Byron and Lady Byron, **Augusta Ada King, Countess of Lovelace, is chiefly remembered as the first computer programmer**.

Lovelace worked with Charles Babbage on the Analytical Engine, an early precursor to the computer, and published the first algorithm intended to be used by such a machine. She died in 1852 at the tragically young age of 36, from uterine cancer. To find out more about Ada Lovelace Day, and the precise day it's on this year, visit findingada.com.

Augusta Ada King, Countess of Lovelace, English mathematician

14 October

The excellent UK indie pop band ME REX released an album entitled *Megabear* in 2021, which consists of 52 short songs that fit together seamlessly without gaps to create a half-hour movement. Here's the clever bit though: the album is intended to be played on random, so that there are 52! (52 factorial) ways to hear the album.* This number is so large that it means no two people who have ever listened to *Megabear* have heard the same sequence of songs.

You may be thinking: two people *could* hear the same sequence of songs, it's just very unlikely. Well, yes, but only in the same way that all the air particles in a room *could* all move over to one side and leave you to suffocate in the other. **The probability of hearing the same**

---

* Chapter skippers – pop back to March for an explanation of factorial numbers.

Megabear **twice in a row would be less likely than winning the UK lottery nine times in a row.**

To put it another way, if every person currently living had existed at the birth of the universe, and they had all listened to *Megabear* continuously since the dawn of time (honestly, what better thing would there be to do while waiting for the primordial soup to cough up something interesting?), *and* each person had a trillion computers to play it on simultaneously *and* they played the album at 1 trillion times the intended speed (kids these days have no patience), then they would by now have got through one billionth of one billionth of 1% of all the possible versions of the album.

15 October

Next time you're at a thrash metal or hardcore punk show and wish it could all just be a little bit more mathematical, fear not: research has shown that **human behaviour in mosh pits, especially the popular and intimidating 'circle pit' type, follows a similar pattern to molecules in an ideal gas.**

The fantastic title of the research paper in question is 'Collective Motion of Humans in Mosh and Circle Pits at Heavy Metal Concerts', by J. L. Silverberg, M. Bierbaum, J. P. Sethna and I. Cohen, published in the journal *Physical Review Letters* (2013).

16 October

The White Stripes played the shortest concert in history on 16 July 2007, when they played one single note at St John's in Newfoundland, Canada. You can watch the set – in its entirety – as part of the 2009 documentary *Under Great White Northern Lights*. However, Guinness World Records have stopped recognizing this as a record, as they have been inundated with bands suggesting they had done a set with a shorter note, or even no music at all. If a band plays no notes at a venue, and there is nobody there to hear it, is it even a gig? Actually don't ask, it brings back too many memories of my own musical career...

The longest gig ever is much harder to quantify: both Bruce Springsteen and The Cure have surpassed the four-hour mark in recent years, and the notoriously well-lubricated cult indie rockers Guided By Voices played a 100-song set on New Year's Eve 2019 (and drank nearly as many beers). DJ Obi played a ten-day DJ set in 2016, but since DJing is just pressing buttons and waving your hands around (kidding!) let's give the accolade to Chilly Gonzales, who in 2009 played a 27-hour solo piano concert without repeating any material ('I will break the record without sounding like a broken record'). He did, however, change into pyjamas, eat cereal and shave mid-song with his non-playing hand. Not bad.

17 October

A musician friend of mine was once unfortunate enough to be mugged while on tour; they asked their friends and family to support them by leaving their songs on repeated play on Spotify overnight. This seems like a supportive thing to do until you realize that **Spotify pay around $0.003–$0.005 per stream**, which then has to be split between the artist, record label and any other contractual stakeholders. Assuming my friend's songs are all four minutes long, and that I sleep for eight hours a night, that's 120 plays totalling $0.48. It's quite hard to calculate, but depending on your model of computer or laptop it may well cost you more than that to power the machine that is idly playing the songs.

18 October

Google 'golden ratio' and you will find some fairly wild suggestions and conjectures flying around, not least the 'golden point' in a song or classical piece, which supposedly occurs 62% of the way through and divides the song into the golden ratio.

I tested this theory on the song 'Buddy Holly' by Weezer, which has been one of my favourite songs since I was ten years old and contains the single greatest moment in the history of recorded music: a two-second isolated guitar solo when the song crashes from the middle section into the final chorus. If you know the song, you just sung that bit in your head. There are many approximations and subjective opinions in this book, but it is an empirical objective fact that this is the greatest moment in the history of rock, if not all of music, if not the greatest achievement in human history altogether.

Disappointingly though, said solo takes place 129 seconds into the 159-second song – 81% of the way through. You're very welcome to test the theory on your own favourite song, but don't hold out too much hope.

19 October

The Beatles may well be the most legendary and influential band of all time, but their understanding of semaphore leaves something to be desired. Their 1965 *Help!* album sleeve (and accompanying film poster) features an iconic image of the band holding flags to display the semaphore symbols for the album's name.*

---

* Fortunately, where copyright is concerned, this album cover is so ubiquitous and well known that there's no need to display it here.

Just one problem though: cover photographer Roger Freeman didn't think the symbols for 'HELP' looked pleasing to the eye, so he just told the lads to hold the flags wherever they wanted to and that no one would bother checking the accuracy of the semaphore. (The Beatles, of course, were infamous for their indifferent and dispassionate fans.) So it turns out the UK version of the album is really called 'NUJV', while the US version, where the boys were rearranged into a different order on the cover, is entitled 'NVUJ'.

20 October

The Beatles were not alone with their album code faux pas; Coldplay – who it's unsettling to realize have existed as a band for about three times as long as the Beatles did – have had their own problems. The cover image of their 2005 *X&Y* album is meant to display the album's title using the *Baudot code*, a sort of precursor to Morse code originating in the 1870s. Unfortunately they seem to have written 'X9Y'.

My personal favourite of this particular genre is the sleeve of British pop phenomenon Girls Aloud's greatest hits album *The Sound of Girls Aloud*, which intends to display a Union Flag and an Irish tricolour flag to honour the nationalities of the band members. Unfortunately the Irish flag was printed backwards, so the sleeve of this number one million-selling album actually displays the flag of the West African nation of Côte d'Ivoire.

I should give a successful example of an album sleeve code: New Order's classic single 'Blue Monday' was designed by Peter Saville to resemble a 5¼-inch floppy disk with the words 'FAC 73 BLUE MONDAY AND THE BEACH NEW ORDER' written in a code that could only be deciphered by using the key contained as part of the band's *Power,*

Corruption and Lies album. Legend has it, however, that the floppy disk sleeve cost so much to produce that the band lost money with every copy sold: not ideal for an all-time classic that shifted over 700,000 copies.

21 October

In my twenties I was a struggling musician, and at a particular low point I had lost all faith in my lyric-writing ability and decided to steal lyrics from the pop music greats instead. After all, as a great man once said, 'talent borrows, genius steals'. And that great man is me, Kyle D. Evans.*

But, being a man of science, I wanted to plagiarize with statistical correctness, so I gathered the lyrics to the 100 most successful songs in British history and piled them into a spreadsheet. I quickly realized that the most common words were fairly bland connecting words such as 'I', 'and', 'to', etc., so I decided to rank the words proportionally against their general everyday usage. I compared my list against the Corpus of Contemporary American English (COCA), which contains more than one billion words of text, 25 million words from each year 1990–2019, from eight genres: spoken, fiction, popular magazines, newspapers, academic texts, TV and movie subtitles, blogs and other web pages.

The following words were those that occurred with the highest frequency when compared to COCA; in other words, they are the words that occur much more frequently in pop music than anywhere

---

* Of course it's actually usually attributed to Oscar Wilde, or sometimes Mark Twain, but it's fairly certain that neither originated it. It may have come from T.S. Eliot's 'Immature poets imitate; mature poets steal', but given the subject matter of the quote I don't think it matters too much.

else (relative frequency in brackets). Writers of pop music, please feel free to use these words readily and watch the cash flow in!

ha (69×)	ah (59×)	uh (55×)	lonely (38×)
love (38×)	found (37×)	happiness (37×)	hey (36×)
oh (34×)	Christmas (34×)	lost (33×)	killing (32×)
baby (26×)	burning (26×)		

In case you were wondering, no, this did not lead to me becoming a world-conquering superstar pop songwriter. But at least I tried.

22 October

When I did create my huge spreadsheet of commonly used pop words, something strange stood out: around half of the words in my list were used only once. Just one single occurrence across all of the top 100 songs in British chart history. At first that seemed far too low, but it's nothing more than *hapax legomenon* in action.

Hapax legomenon (let's be honest – it's just fun to say) is the name for a word that occurs just once in a large piece of text or body of work. In a lengthy piece of work, around half of all words will be hapax legomena (the plural is fun too). For example, around 44% of the words in the classic novel *Moby-Dick* are hapax legomena, such as 'soberly', 'marling-spikes' and 'whale'.* The book you're currently reading has around 7500 words, and about 3500 of them are single-use hapax legomena.

Essentially, around half of the words in any book, film, article or conversation will be repeated uses of a small bank of common words, and the other half will be unique single instances of other words. So I

---

* That's a joke of course. 'Whale' is used twice.

shouldn't have been too surprised by all the single-use words in my pop spreadsheet (Beelzebub, Lineker, backbeat, etc.).

23 October

Zipf's law states that, in any lengthy piece of writing, **the frequency of any word is inversely proportional to its rank in the frequency table**. The easiest way of describing this is that the most common term will occur about twice as often as the next most common, around three times as often as the next most common word, and so on. Take a different corpus of American English text, the Brown Corpus. The two most common words are 'the' and 'of', with about 70,000 and 36,000 occurrences respectively; almost entirely in line with Zipf's law. 'And' comes in third, with about 29,000 occurrences, not far off one third of 70,000.

Here's a graph of the words used in *Moby-Dick*, with the frequency of word use on the vertical axis and word ranking on the horizontal axis. If the raw data were plotted then the graph would be a curve, but with logarithmic axes (which means the values on the axes jump in powers of ten: from 1 to 10 to 100 and so on) we see a linear graph. Zipf's law says that the gradient of this graph should be -1.

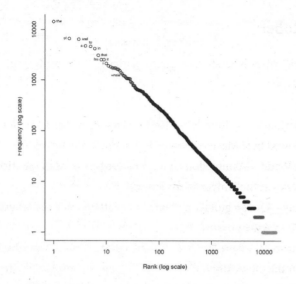

The big flat wedge in the bottom right represents the hapax legomena.*
The reason the wedge is quite small is because of the logarithmic scale –
on a regular scale that wedge would take up half of the horizontal axis.

24 October

Something like Zipf's law holds reasonably well for the sizes of the
largest cities in a given country, with the largest being about twice as
big as the next largest, about three times as big as the next largest, and
so on. New York is about twice as highly populated as Los Angeles, and
has three times the population of Chicago, and so on (full disclosure –
it breaks down a little beyond that point but still holds reasonably well).

---

* I have intentionally used the words 'hapax' and 'legomena' more than once in this
  book, so that neither are hapax legomena. How's that for a paradox? In fact, I've now
  used them more than twice, so they aren't even *dis legomena* (words used twice only.)
  But one of those words I just wrote in italics *is* a hapax legomenon! Phew…

25 October

Some celebrities who studied mathematics before (or during) finding fame:

Reed Hastings – Co-founder of Netflix. Degree in Mathematics, followed by a Masters Degree in Computer Science.

Virginia Wade – Wimbledon champion. Degree in Mathematics and Physics at the University of Sussex.

Brian May – Queen guitarist. Degree in Mathematics and Physics, PhD in Astrophysics.

Glen Johnson – Ex professional footballer. Studied for a maths degree with the Open University while playing. Anything to distract from the fact that you play for Portsmouth, I suppose.

Sergey Brin – Co-founder of Google. Degree in Mathematics and Computer Science, PhD in Computer Science. This one is not too surprising.

Jonny Buckland – Lead guitarist, Coldplay. Degree in Astronomy and Mathematics.

Lee Hsien Loong – Prime minister of Singapore at time of writing. Degree in Mathematics. Note that in some parts of the world not every leading politician needs to have done PPE at Oxford.

26 October

The phrase 'six degrees of separation' originates from an experiment carried out by the psychologist Stanley Milgram in the 1960s. (It is probably Milgram's second-best-known social experiment, after the one where people were convinced to administer supposedly fatal or near-fatal electric shocks to a stranger in another room, just because an authoritative scientist in a white coat told them to.) In the 'small-world' experiment, random American citizens in backwater towns such as Omaha and Wichita* were given a letter with the name of a person in a super-metropolitan location such as New York City. Either they knew the person on a first-name basis (very unlikely) or they knew someone – probably geographically closer to the target – who might be more likely to, and they forwarded the letter on to them instead.

Most letters failed to reach their intended destination due to a person in the chain not cooperating or a wrong address being used, but of the letters that reached their intended destination, the average number of links in the chain was about 5.5 to 6. Most people in the United States were separated by no more than six personal links; in the modern era of social media it would almost certainly be much shorter than this, though the conditions for 'knowing' someone you are linked to on social media are undoubtedly somewhat looser than being on letter-sending terms in the sixties.

---

* Not my choices of backwater town – don't write in! My favourite band comes from one of those towns, and the best song of all time is named after the other…

27 October

Stephen Hawking is one of the most well-connected people in the history of the universe, which is apt considering he helped us to learn so much about it.

You have probably heard of the 'Kevin Bacon number': the number of steps it takes to connect an actor to Kevin Bacon, who is apparently the centre of the Hollywood universe. For example, Scarlett Johansson has a Bacon number of 2, because she appeared in *Just Cause* with Ed Harris, who was in *Apollo 13* with Kevin Bacon. Most well-known actors have a Bacon number of 2, but if you scrape hard enough you can even find Stephen Hawking a Bacon number as low as 2: he appeared in *Masters of Science Fiction* with Sean Astin, who was in *White Water Summer* with Kevin Bacon.

A less well-known but similar game (and a little harder to play on long car journeys) is based on how removed mathematicians or scientists are from the mathematician Paul Erdős – legendary for his prolific output of collaborative papers.* Everyone who ever co-authored a paper with Erdős has an 'Erdős number' of 1, anyone who collaborated with those authors has an Erdős number of 2, and so on. Hawking has an Erdős number of 4:

Name	Collaborated on	With
Stephen Hawking	Origin of time asymmetry	Raymond Laflamme

---

* He was equally legendary for his eccentric mannerisms, such as drinking copious amounts of coffee, living out of a suitcase for most of his adult life and rarely changing his suit. Please note that adopting similar quirks will not necessarily make you an instant mathematical genius.

Raymond Laflamme	Compiling gate networks on an Ising quantum computer	Emanuel Knill
Emanuel Knill	Minimal residual method stronger than polynomial preconditioning	Vance Faber
Vance Faber	Sets of natural numbers of positive density and cylindric set algebras of dimension 2	Paul Erdős

Hawking also has a 'Sabbath number' of 2: this measures how removed a musician is from the legendary Birmingham heavy metal originators Black Sabbath. Why Black Sabbath were chosen as the supposed centre of the musical universe is unclear; they are less legendary than, say, The Beatles, and have far fewer collaborations to their name than serial collaborators such as Snoop Dogg or Elton John. But, in a similar way to Kevin Bacon probably not actually being the most well-connected actor, the game has stuck and it's too late to argue now.

Hawking's voice was sampled on the Pink Floyd track 'Keep on Talking', and Pink Floyd guitarist Dave Gilmour played alongside Sabbath's Tony Iommi on a recording of 'Smoke on the Water' for the collaborative record *The Earthquake Album* by Rock Aid Armenia.

Combining these scores gives Hawking an *Erdős–Bacon–Sabbath* number of 8, one of the lowest on record.

28 October

Having an *Erdős–Bacon–Sabbath* number at all puts you in quite an elite club: Richard Feynman, Natalie Portman and Brian May are some other polymaths to be on the select list. But, if you are *very* loose with the rules, anyone can muster themselves a soft E–B–S number. Here's mine:

Erdős number 5: I wrote a chapter of *If I Could Tell You One Thing*, published by the Mathematical Association in 2022. Another chapter was written by Colin Foster, who has an Erdős number 4 (his very genuine contribution trail goes: Johnny Griffiths → Graham Everest → Kálmán Győryco → Paul Erdős).

Bacon number 2: We've both been on BBC Breakfast, albeit fifteen years apart.

Sabbath number 4: I sang on a Frank Turner album; Frank has toured many times with the Gaslight Anthem; they've regularly collaborated with Bruce Springsteen; Springsteen's original band Steel Mill once supported Black Sabbath.

Total (very loose) E–B–S number 11.

29 October

A Semihemidemisemiquaver is a unit of brief musical time: it's $\frac{1}{128}$ of a note. How one can tell if they are playing a $\frac{1}{128}$ note and not a $\frac{1}{64}$ note is beyond me, but then I have never been much of a musician. This is the shortest that a note can go though... just kidding! You can have a note half this long, it's called a demisemihemidemisemiquaver and it is of course a $\frac{1}{256}$ note.

There seems to be literally no end to this madness: Anthony Philip Heinrich's *Toccata Grande Cromatica*, written around 1825, contains a spate of 256th and 512th notes (that's a hemidemisemihemidemisemiquaver of course), and even some 2048th notes, though it's possible that they were intended to be 1024th notes and were mis-transcribed. How on earth you're meant to tell if the piece is being played correctly or not is anyone's guess.

30 October

A joke: why do computer scientists celebrate Hallowe'en on Christmas Day? To find out we will have to do a bit more octopus counting in base 8. What's base 8 again? Well, to quote the great Tom Lehrer: base 8 is just like base 10 really – if you're missing two fingers.

In base 10 we use the ten digits 0–9, before rolling over into the next column to count lots of 10, then the next column to count 100s, and so on. In base 8 there is no 8 or 9, just eight digits from 0 to 7, so we use the second column to count lots of 8, and the next column to count 64s, and so on. You might remember from earlier this month that this is called *octal* counting, rather than decimal. To give an example, if we use the abbreviations 'oct' and 'dec' to show which base we're working in:

132 oct → $(1 \times 64) + (3 \times 8) + (2 \times 1) = 64 + 24 + 2 = 90$ dec

Or…

31 oct → $(3 \times 8) + (1 \times 1) = 24 + 1 = 25$ dec

So why do computer scientists celebrate Hallowe'en on Christmas Day? Because 31 oct = 25 dec. Yes, I know it's not as funny when you have to explain it.

31 October

Happy Hallowe'en! If you go to your local pumpkin-picking patch and measure a few hundred pumpkins, you will find that there is an average size that most of them conform to. There will be some enormous pumpkins and some teeny pumpkins, but overall the majority will fall closest to the mean average, and the further you get from the mean, the fewer pumpkins you will find. Put this data into a graph and you will get something like this:

This is called a **normal distribution**, as opposed to the following, which is called a paranormal distribution:

NOVEMBER

THE CHAPTER THAT GOES ON AND ON...

1 November

Welcome to the infinity chapter. Some of this is really going to hurt your head, but that's absolutely fine. In fact, I'm deeply sceptical of anyone who is completely happy and comfortable with infinity. I do this for my day job and I still get freaked out every time I need to talk about infinity.

We begin with the best-known analogy for the concept of infinity, the so-called *infinite monkey theorem*. You've probably heard of the idea: **a monkey, given an infinite amount of time and a typewriter, will eventually write out the entire works of Shakespeare**. Or just *Hamlet*, if you prefer. Or indeed any classic work that you care to name – even this one.

I've never been a huge fan of the monkey–typewriter problem, mostly because the 'eventually' is doing an enormous amount of work. Just writing the opening line of *Hamlet* – 'Who's there?' – would require the monkey randomly making 11 correct keystrokes in a row. There are 44 keys on a classic typewriter, so that's a 1 in 44 chance, eleven times in a row. That would be a one-in-a-quintillion chance, or one in a billion billion. And that's just the first line. It's reasonable to suggest that a monkey typing since the dawn of time would never have got past the first line of *Hamlet*, never mind the rest.

2 November

There are as many even numbers as there are numbers. What? This can't be right... if you went along your road counting all the even-numbered houses, it wouldn't be all the houses, would it? It would be half of the houses. But that's because we're used to counting from a *finite* set. When we're talking about infinity, things are a little different.

The mathematician Georg Cantor established that if a one-to-one mapping can be found between any set of numbers and the counting numbers (1, 2, 3, ...) then that set of numbers is of equal size, or cardinality, as the counting numbers. The even numbers can be paired together infinitely with the counting numbers, so the sets of numbers are the same size:

$1 \rightarrow 2$

$2 \rightarrow 4$

$3 \rightarrow 6$

...

$n \rightarrow 2n$

So, if we're counting all the way up to infinity, there are as many even numbers as there are counting numbers. In fact, all of these sets are the same size: integers, even integers, odd integers.

3 November

Yesterday we saw that there are as many even numbers as there are counting numbers, if we're counting all the way up to infinity. We can use the same logic to determine that there are as many square numbers as counting numbers, and also as many cube numbers:

$1 \rightarrow 1$ $1 \rightarrow 1$
$2 \rightarrow 4$ $2 \rightarrow 8$
$3 \rightarrow 9$ $3 \rightarrow 27$
$\ldots$ $\ldots$
$n \rightarrow n^2$ $n \rightarrow n^3$

All of these sets – even numbers, square numbers, cube numbers, rational numbers (that's anything that can be written as a fraction) – are said to be *countably infinite*; even though it would take you forever to count them, there is at least a strategy for counting them.

4 November

You're probably starting to wonder if, in fact, *all* infinite sets of numbers are the same size. But, no: **some infinities are more infinite than others**, as George Orwell wrote. Consider all the numbers between 0 and 1, written as decimals. I can't really start counting from 0, since the next largest number is impossible to jump to. Is the next smallest number 0.1? Well, of course not, because 0.01 exists. But what about 0.001? And 0.000000001? Where to even start?

Instead of trying to count from the smallest number, let's just list out a whole load of numbers between 0 and 1 in any old order:

0.0000010000000
0.142857142857...
0.14159265359...
0.300000000000
0.11111111111111...
0.1234567891011...

Some of these will be rational numbers that terminate, like 0.3 and 0.000001. Some will be rational numbers that never terminate, like 0.142857... and 0.111..., which are 1/7 and 1/9 respectively. Some are irrational numbers that never terminate and *can't* be written as a fraction such as 0.14145... (which is π – 3), and 0.123456... (which is all the integers written out in order after a decimal point). Try to write all the numbers between 0 and 1 in this way and you'll have a gargantuan list, but it will never be complete. To see why, we invoke **Cantor's diagonal argument.**

Take the same list as the one above but increase by 1 the first digit in the first number, the second digit in the second number, the third digit in the third number, and so on. Then use all these new digits to create a brand new number and write it beneath:

0.**1**000010000000
0.1**5**2857142857...
0.14**2**59265359...
0.300**1**00000000
0.1111**2**111111111
0.12345**7**7891011
0.**152127**...

This new number cannot be the same as any number in the original list, however long that list may be, because it differs from every number in the original list in at least one place. So, however we try to count the numbers between 0 and 1, there will always be a number that has evaded our counting system. The real numbers between 0 and 1 are *not* countably infinite; it is a larger infinity!

5 November

It's possible to fit an extra guest into a full hotel – but only if the hotel has infinitely many rooms... Imagine you were the manager of this full hotel with infinitely many rooms, and a very important guest arrived. You don't want to turn them away, but there isn't an empty room number you can send them to. What to do? Simply give the instruction to every guest to pack their bags, add 1 to their current room number and move to that room. So the guest in room 1 moves to room 2, room 2 to room 3, and so on. This leaves room number 1 free and available for your important new guest, and all other guests have clear instructions on how to re-room themselves.

This lovely thought experiment – which shows that infinity plus one is still infinity – is known as *Hilbert's Hotel*, after the German mathematician David Hilbert, owner of the most splendid hat in the history of mathematics.

David Hilbert, German mathematician (1862–1943)

If you're worried about the logistics of building a hotel with infinitely many rooms, there is no need: room 1 is really quite spacious, but room 2 is half its size, room 3 is half that size again, …

6 November

Our full hotel of infinite rooms can even find space for an infinite number of new guests. Here's how you do it…

A bus arrives on your hotel forecourt containing an infinite number of prospective guests; a great money-spinning opportunity, but sadly your infinite hotel is still full. What to do? It's a case of your current guests packing their bags once again, but this time they're going to *double* their current room number and move to it, so room 1 moves to room 2, room 2 to room 4, and so on. Since there are as many even numbers as there are odd numbers as there are counting numbers, we can move all the current guests to the even-number rooms and give the infinity of odd-number rooms to the coach passengers. In other words, two lots of infinity is still infinity. Problem solved.

7 November

One last visit to the infinite hotel, this time to squeeze in an infinite number of buses, each holding an infinite number of hopeful guests. And our infinite hotel is still full.

There are several ways of doing this, but here is my favourite. Once again it begins with packing up our current occupants and sending them onwards to a higher-numbered room, but this time they'll have a longer walk; we're sending each occupant to room 2^n, where n is their current room number. This means the current occupants in rooms 1, 2, 3, 4, end up in rooms 2, 4, 8, 16, etc.

We then assign every bus on the forecourt with a different prime number (we saw on 18 July that there are infinitely many primes) and every person on the bus takes a different power of that prime. So the eventual room numbers look a bit like this:

Current occupants: 2, 4, 8, 16, 32, …
First bus: 3, 9, 27, 81, …
Next bus: 5, 25, 125, 625, …
Next bus: 7, 49, 343, 2401, …
…

Powers of primes can never coincide at the same room, so there will be enough rooms to go round. The startling thing about this method is that it also creates infinitely many unused empty rooms, such as 6, which is neither a prime number nor a power of primes. So a hotel with infinitely many full rooms is able to fit in an infinite number of infinitely full buses, and still have infinitely many rooms left over. That's enough of that, I think!

8 November

Happy Birthday Edmond Halley! Halley of course gives his name to Halley's Comet, visible from Earth every 75–79 years and the only comet that can be seen with the naked eye twice in a human lifetime.

Mark Twain was born in November 1835 when the comet was visible in the sky, and in his 1909 autobiography, he wrote: 'I came in with Halley's Comet… It is coming again next year. The Almighty has said, no doubt, "Now there are these two unaccountable freaks; they came in together, they must go out together."' Sure enough, he died in April 1910.

9 November

We've encountered various interesting decimal expansions: recurring decimals like 0.08333..., which is 1/12; non-recurring irrational numbers like 3.141592..., which is π; and strange numbers like 0.123456789101112... (all the integers lined up after a decimal point) which we can describe but which have no real mathematical use.

But there are numbers that do not fall into any of these categories – the *non-computable* numbers. They exist, but unlike any of the numbers described above, a computer program could never write out their full decimal expansion because they essentially have no logical structure. I can't write one of these numbers as an example for you, because, to paraphrase the mathematician Greg Chaitin, once I've shown it to you, it's not non-computable! (He called these numbers *Omega*, which certainly is a little shorter and pithier.)

Rather upsettingly, **there are vastly more of these non-computable numbers than there are computable numbers**; it's a larger infinity. So all the numbers that you or your computer could ever see or describe make up a single grain of sand in a desert of non-computables.

10 November

The number 142857 has the curious property that, when multiplied by the numbers from 1 to 6, the result always uses the same six digits but in a different order. It all falls apart for 7 though (albeit in a pleasing way):

$142857 \times 1 = 142857$
$142857 \times 2 = 285714$
$142857 \times 3 = 428571$
$142857 \times 4 = 571428$
$142857 \times 5 = 714285$
$142857 \times 6 = 857142$
$142857 \times 7 = 999999$

Impress your friend(s) by asking them to multiply 142857 by any number from 1 to 6, then ask them to read out their answer but to leave out one digit. If you remember the digits '142857' you can tell them the digit they left out. It's no coincidence that 142857 is also the recurring decimal part of the fraction $\frac{1}{7}$:

$$\frac{1}{7} = 0.142857142857\ldots$$

11 November

Happy 11/11! As a teacher for many years I enjoy spotting interesting quirks in the six-digit date, but when teaching on this day in 2011* I was saddened to realize that 11/11/11 was the last *binary date* I would ever see in my lifetime. These are dates that can be made up of just 1s and 0s, and they had been liberally spread across the previous few years to the extent that I would often remark upon it with classes and we would convert the date from binary to base 10 for a quick mental workout (go back to 19 January for a reminder of how to do this). But on 11/11/11, both I and my class of 17-year-olds had to accept that this would be the last one we would ever see (certainly for me but probably also for them, as the next one will be 01/01/00; the first day of the next century).

The last ternary date of the century has also passed: these are dates that can be made with just 0s, 1s and 2s, the last of which was 22/12/22. Sequential dates are also good fun, but the last one of these this century has also passed: 11/12/13.

---

* Please feel free to use Conway's doomsday method from 4 September to check that this really was a teaching day.

12 **November**

Imagine an equilateral triangle, and then imagine removing the middle third of each edge and replacing it with two new sides of a smaller equilateral triangle of the same length as the removed line, forming a new vertex as shown in the diagram:

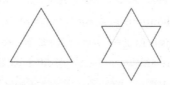

We now have a 'snowflake' with twelve edges of equal length. We will next continually remove the central third of each edge and replace it with two sides of a smaller triangle, as before:

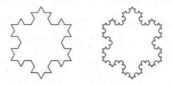

This shape is known as a *Koch snowflake*,* and its perimeter is a <u>fractal</u> curve. A fractal is essentially any shape with *self-similarity* (the whole has the same shape as its parts). You can make the snowflake infinitely detailed by carrying out more and more iterations of the same procedure. But the long-term behaviour leads to an infuriating paradox.

---

* I believe 'Koch' is pronounced with a hard 'ch', but if you are teaching 16-year-olds it's definitely better to pronounce it with a soft 'ch'.

Consider the perimeter of the infinite snowflake. Moving from one iteration of the snowflake to the next increases the length of its perimeter by a factor of 4/3, because the central section of each edge is replaced by two similar sections, so that each edge is split into three parts and replaced with four parts. Multiplying by 4/3 repeatedly will lead to a perimeter that is infinitely long.

Confusingly, however, although the area of the Koch snowflake also increases with each iteration, it is limited to 8/5 of the area of the original triangle (proof of this is in the Further Notes at the back of the book). As we carry out more and more iterations, **the Koch snowflake's area could be easily shaded with the ink in your pen, but its perimeter becomes so long that all the ink in the world could not draw it.**

13 November

Another beautiful and befuddling fractal is the Sierpinski triangle, which is formed by starting with a black equilateral triangle, bisecting each edge and removing the resultant triangle formed, then endlessly repeating the process on each remaining black triangle:

This time the head-scratcher is that **the black area tends to zero in the long term, but the perimeter of the black area – including all internal lines – becomes infinitely long.** So you'd be using up infinite amounts of ink to draw the border of a shape with no area.

14 November

The mother of all paint/ink paradoxes is *Torricelli's trumpet*, sometimes less excitingly known as Gabriel's horn. This shape is formed by starting with the relatively straightforward graph of $y = 1/x$ for some positive x and revolving it around the x-axis to form a trumpet shape:

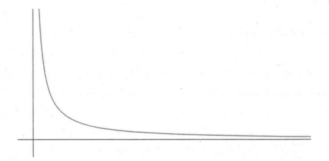

The graph of $y = \dfrac{1}{x}$.

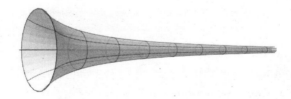

The shape formed by rotating the graph of $y = 1/x$ around the x-axis.

The resultant horn has finite volume but infinite surface area: that's right, **you could fill Torricelli's trumpet with paint but you couldn't paint its outside with all the paint in the universe.**

15 November

6174 is one of the most strange and mysterious numbers in mathematics. To uncover why this is, simply pick your favourite four-digit number. Mine is 1885 because that's the year the world's greatest football club was founded. Next you rearrange the digits into both ascending and descending order and subtract the smaller from the larger:

1885:   8851 − 1588 = 7263

With your new answer, do exactly the same thing. In fact, keep repeating the process until something interesting happens:

7263:   7632 − 2367 = 5265
5265:   6552 − 2556 = 3996
3996:   9963 − 3699 = 6264
6264:   6642 − 2466 = 4176
4176:   7641 − 1467 = 6174
6174:   7641 − 1467 = 6174

And we appear to have converged upon a would-be endless string of 6174s. It turns out that this result occurs no matter which 4-digit number you start with (unless all four digits are the same). Very satisfying, isn't it? This is known as the Kaprekar operation, and 6174 is the Kaprekar number, as devised in 1949 by the mathematician D. R. Kaprekar from Devlali, India. Every number will converge to 6174 within seven iterations or fewer, so if you've calculated more than seven steps you did something wrong. But even if you do make an error, since 6174 is the only four-digit number that rearranges with this property, you will still end up at 6174. I'd encourage you to have a play around with working out *why* it works; there's some more about this in the Further Notes at the back of the book.

16 November

6174 is also a *Harshad number*, which is the name given to any number that is divisible by the sum of its digits. $6 + 1 + 7 + 4 = 18$, and the very fact that the digits add up to a multiple of 9 tells us that 6174 is divisible by 9 (because **any number with a digits sum divisible by 9 is also itself divisible by 9**).

So 6174 is definitely divisible by 9, and because it's even it must be divisible by an even number of 9s. If a number is divisible by an even number of 9s, by definition it is divisible by 18.

17 November

Happy Birthday August Ferdinand Möbius! This mathematician and astronomer was born on 17 November 1790 and made many great contributions to both fields, but is probably best known for the *Möbius strip*, a curious mathematical object that has only one face but is very much not a sphere. To make a Möbius strip, simply cut a long strip of paper, twist it in the middle and glue the two ends together.

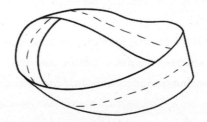

Start colouring the Möbius strip and you will quickly find that you only need one colour – both sides are in fact the same side. An ant walking along the centre of the strip, marked with a dotted line, would walk around both sides of the strip before returning to where it started from. These are great fun to make with small kids – if they're really enjoying it, ask them to guess what will happen if you cut the strip in half along the dotted line.

18 November

The correct name for the recognizable infinity symbol (∞) is the *lemniscate.* Sometimes more charmingly called a 'lazy eight', the symbol was first used to describe infinity by the English mathematician John Wallis in the mid-seventeenth century.

19 November

Every power of 6 ends in a 6. Indeed, raise any number ending in 6 to any power and you will have a resultant answer that ends in a 6. For example, I know without calculating that $53,180,086^3$ will definitely end in a 6, even though there will be a huge number of digits before the 6. Here it is, if you were wondering:

$$53,180,086^3 = 150,399,747,086,179,158,476,056$$

This leads us to the following number, sometimes called the *ultrahex* (though I call it a 'super sleepy six'), which is perfectly possible to write in power notation, but could probably not be written down in full in the entire remaining life of humans on Earth. If they ever got there though, they would find that it ends in a 6.

20 November

Happy Birthday Benoit B. Mandelbrot! The *Mandelbrot set* is a set of points that satisfy a certain geometric property relating to complex numbers. Complex numbers are a little more advanced than I intend to go into in this book, but if you're familiar with them I recommend further exploring the Mandelbrot set. Notice that round shapes seem to reappear around the edges, and that the outside of the shape looks a little fuzzy. If you zoom in on the perimeter of the shape you will see endless repetitions of these repeated circles, of tinier and tinier size but always exactly similar to the larger Mandelbrot set. Yep, it's another one of those fractal images that have self-similarity.

21 November

What's the sum of this infinite sequence?

$$1 - 1 + 1 - 1 + 1 - 1 + \ldots$$

Your first instinct might be that the answer is 0, since we subtract as much as we add:

$$(1 - 1) + (1 - 1) + (1 - 1) + \ldots = 0$$

But a similar argument could be applied to suggest that the answer is 1:

$$1 + (-1 + 1) + (-1 + 1) + (-1 + 1) + \ldots = 1$$

The second version might feel like a trick, but mathematically it's no less sound than the first. So the sum can be either 0 or 1 depending on how you add it up? That can't be right can it? How about this then:

$$\text{Let} \quad A = 1 - 1 + 1 - 1 + 1 - 1 + \ldots$$
$$\text{Then} \quad 1 - A = 1 - (1 - 1 + 1 - 1 + \ldots)$$
$$1 - A = 1 - 1 + 1 - 1 + 1 + \ldots$$
$$1 - A = A$$
$$1 = 2A$$
$$\frac{1}{2} = A$$

So, without breaking any logical rules, we've found this infinite sum to be 0, 1 and ½. I apologize if you're reading this first thing in the morning as I may have spoiled your day. It's possible to use a similar argument to show that adding the infinite list of integers from 1 upwards gives a sum of –1/12, but this result – apparently genuinely useful in string theory – is so upsetting that I've put it in the Further Notes at the back of the book.

22 November

Zeno's paradoxes are a set of philosophical thought experiments dating back to about 500 BC. Perhaps the most famous of these suggests that Achilles could never overtake a tortoise in a race, as long as the tortoise has a head-start.

It goes like this: the tortoise starts the race somewhere ahead of Achilles, and we pause the race when Achilles has reached the point the tortoise set off from. By this point, however, the tortoise will have moved forward somewhat. So we continue the race and pause once again when Achilles has reached this new point that the tortoise has reached. A snag though: once again, the tortoise has moved forward and is ahead of Achilles:

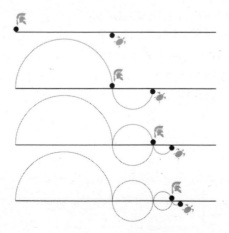

The paradox doesn't stand up to too much scrutiny: clearly the time periods between the pauses in the race very quickly converge to zero, and the tortoise can be overtaken. But Zeno's real point was that to actually overtake the tortoise you would have to pause the race infinitely many times, which can never be done.

23 November

Another of Zeno's paradoxes suggests that a man can never walk across a room: before crossing the room you must walk halfway, but before this can be done one must walk a quarter of the way, and similarly this cannot be done until one has walked an eighth of the way, and so on.

Apparently this claim was challenged by an audience member who got out of their seat and walked across the floor and out of the room, which is actually quite witty on two levels. This happened about 400–500 years before Christ but it is the last recorded account of a genuinely intelligent heckle.

24 November

1/243 is a curious fraction: the physicist Richard Feynman seems to have been the first person to notice that it's made up of increasing pairs of digits, separated by another sequence of single digits: 0.004115226337448559…

25 November

If you calculate 1/998,001, the decimal expansion will list every three-digit number from 000 to 999, except for 998:

1/998001 = 0.000001002003004005006007008009010011012013014 0
150160170180190200210220230240250260270280290300310320330 3
403503603703803904004104204304404504604704804905005105205 3
054055056057058059060061062063064065066067068069070071072 0
730740750760770780790800810820830840850860870880890900910 9
209309409509609709809910010110210310410510610710810911011 1
112113114115116117118119120121122123124125126127128129130
131132133134135136137138139140141142143144145146147148149 1
501511521531541551561571581591601611621631641651661671681 6
91701711721731741751761771781791801811821831841851861871 88
189190191192193194195196197198199200201202203204205206207 2
082092102112122132142152162172182192202212222232242252262 2
722822922302312322332342352362372382392402412422432442452 46
247248249250251252253254255256257258259260261262263264265 2
662672682692702712722732742752762772782792802812822832842 8
528628728828929029129229329429529629729829930030130230330 4
305306307308309310311312313314315316317318319320321322323 3
243253263273283293303313323333343353363373383393403413423 4
334434534634734834935035135235335435535635735835936036136 2
363364365366367368369370371372373374375376377378379380381 3
823833843853863873883893903913923933943953963973983994004 0
140240340440540640740840941041141241341441541641741841942 0
421422423424425426427428429430431432433434435436437438439 4
404414424434444454464474484494504514524534544554564574584 5

946046146246346446546646746846947047147247347447547647747 8
479480481482483484485486487488489490491492493494495496497 4
984995005015025035045055065075085095105115125135145155165 1
751851952052152252352452552652752852953053153253353453553 6
537538539540541542543544545546547548549550551552553554555 5
565575585595605615625635645655665675685695705715725735745 7
557565775785795805815825835845855865875885895905915925935 94
595596597598599600601602603604605606607608609610611612613 6
146156166176186196206216226236246256266276286296306316326 3
336346356366376386396406416426436446456466476486496506516 5
265365465565665765865966066166266366466566666676686696706 71
672673674675676677678679680681682683684685686687688689690 6
916926936946956966976986997007017027037047057067077087099 71
071171271371471571671771871972072172272372472572672772872 8
973073173273373473573673773873974074174274374474574674774 8
749750751752753754755756757758759760761762763764765766767 7
687697707717727737747757767777787797807817827837847857867 7
877887897907917927937947957967977987998008018028038048058 0
680780880981081181281381481581681781881982082182282382482 5
826827828829830831832833834835836837838839840841842843844 8
458468478488498508518528538548558568578588598608618628638 6
486586686786886987087187287387487587687787887988088188288 3
884885886887888889890891892893894895896897898899900901902 9
039049059069079089099101191291391491591691791891992092192 9
292392492592692792892993093193293393493593693793893994094 1
942943944945946947948949950951952953954955956957958959960 9
619629639649659669679689699709719729739749759769779789799 8
098198298398498598698798889989990991992993994995996997999 ...

26 November

If you enjoyed yesterday's fact about the strange fraction 1/998,001, you might also like to know that 1/998,999 gives all three-digit Fibonacci numbers except for 987 (I won't give the whole thing this time):
0.000001001002003005008013021034055089144233377610…
And 1,000,000/997,002,999 lists all the three-digit triangle numbers, only going wrong when it lists 991 instead of 990 (again, just a handful of digits for your enjoyment):

0.001003006010015021028036045055066078091105120136…

27 November

A number 1 followed by one hundred zeros is known by what name?

A: Googol　　　B: Megatron
C: Gigabit　　　D: Nanomole

This question reached infamy when, in September 2001, it was the final hurdle facing Major Charles Ingram on the popular TV quiz *Who Wants to Be a Millionaire?* Ingram answered correctly and took away the £1 million cheque, before it was later revealed that he had utilized an assistant in the audience who had coughed at strategic times to give the answers away. Would you have required a coughing co-conspirator? Perhaps this question is easier in the modern era, as Google – the name of which is derived from the correct answer – has risen to prominence as one of the biggest and most recognizable companies in the world.

That's right, the answer is A: **Google takes its name from a misspelling (possibly intentional, possibly not) of googol, which is an enormous number made of a 1 followed by a hundred zeros.**

1000000000000000000000000000000000000000000000000000000000000000000000000000000000000000000000000000

Give yourself a gold star if you counted them all.

28 November

The term 'googol', from yesterday's entry, was coined by Milton Sirotta, nephew of the American mathematician Edward Kasner. Sirotta also suggested the name 'googolplex' to describe 1 followed by zeros 'until your hand gets tired', but this isn't quite exact enough for fusty old mathematicians so the accepted googolplex is 10^{googol}, that is ten multiplied by itself a googol times. **The googolplex number is so enormous that, if printed on paper, the book would weigh more than all of the stars in the observable universe combined** (that's even more than *The Goldfinch*).

29 November

The most zeros ever printed on a banknote was on the Zimbabwean hundred trillion dollar note. It happened in 2016, during a period of extreme hyperinflation, resulting in the quite bizarre spectacle of a banknote with fourteen zeros. Imagine counting the change for that.

This is not the largest denomination ever issued; immediately after the Second World War, Hungary had a 100 quintillion pengő note (1 followed by twenty zeros) and even a 1 sextillion pengő note (ten times bigger at a whopping twenty-one zeros). The latter of these was printed but never issued, and both notes had the amount printed in words rather than numbers, so the Zimbabwean hundred trillion still takes the record for literal zeros on a note. These notes sell for £200–£300 on eBay, which is either a great deal or a terrible deal, depending on which way you look at it.

30 November

About a billion people are currently looking at their phone. According to Statista, there are more than 6.6 billion smartphone users in the world: more than 80% of the global population. Various surveys have found the average daily smartphone use to be around 3–5 hours, so if we take 4 hours as an average, that means the average person spends one sixth of their time looking at their phone. If we assume phone-use habits to be broadly similar around the world, and accept the fact that at some times there will be more people awake than at others, then we can similarly assume that one sixth of smartphone users worldwide are looking at their phone at any given time. One sixth of 80% of 7.75 billion (at time of writing) comes in at pretty much bang on a billion people. Put your phone down! (Unless you're reading this book on it...)

DECEMBER

THE 31 DAYS OF CHRISTMATHS

1 December

Here's a method to work out how many people in the world are doing what you're currently doing. This only works if it's something that everyone in the world does every day. Here it is: multiply the time it takes to complete, in minutes, by 5.5. That gives you the number of million people who are currently doing it.

How many people are currently brushing their teeth? If we assume that everyone in the world brushes for four minutes per day, $4 \times 5.5 = 22$, so 22 million people are currently brushing their teeth. Getting out of bed takes three seconds, which is one twentieth of a minute. One twentieth of 5.5 is roughly 0.25, so a quarter of a million people are currently getting out of bed. I'll let you calculate how many people are currently going to the toilet.

2 December

In 2015, Sheffield University Maths Society (SUMS, of course) came up with the following formulae that will help you to obtain a mathematically perfect Christmas tree, where the height of the tree is in centimetres:

$$\text{Length of tinsel} = \frac{13\,\pi}{8} \times \text{height of tree}$$

$$\text{Length of lights} = \pi \times \text{height of tree}$$

$$\text{Number of baubles} = \frac{\sqrt{17}}{20} \times \text{height of tree}$$

They call this tree-gonometry (that's not my pun, so no apologies). The Trafalgar Square Christmas tree is usually about 25 metres tall, meaning it would need 515 baubles, over 100 metres of tinsel and 78 metres of lights to be perfect.

3 December

Don't tell your family this secret, but **the best properties to buy in the game of Monopoly are the orange ones**. I know everyone has their favourites – being a fan of the underdog I'm quite partial to the brown properties – but statistically it's best to buy orange when you can.

The most visited property in a game of Monopoly is Jail, as there are many ways of ending up there: 'just visiting' by landing on the square in regular play; being sent to jail by a Community Chest or Chance card, or rolling three doubles in a row (the 'pride comes before a fall' clause). After leaving Jail you can of course roll any number from 2 to 12, but not all of these outcomes are equally likely:

Outcome	Possible dice combinations
2	(1,1)
3	(1,2) (2,1)
4	(1,3) (2,2) (3,1)
5	(1,4) (2,3) (3,2) (4,1)

6	(1,5) (2,4) (3,3) (4,2) (5,1)
7	(1,6) (2,5) (3,4) (4,3) (5,2) (6,1)
8	(2,6) (3,5) (4,4) (5,3) (6,2)
9	(3,6) (4,5) (5,4) (6,3)
10	(4,6) (5,5) (6,4)
11	(5,6) (6,5)
12	(6,6)

Therefore, on leaving Jail you are most likely to travel seven spaces to Community Chest, but the orange properties lie 6, 8 and 9 spaces from Jail – all likely outcomes that combined give you a better than one-in-three chance of catching a reformed jailbird upon release.

4 December

I have some exciting news for you: we're going out for Christmas lunch, and there are four items on the menu: Soup, Roast Dinner, Trifle, Cheese (henceforth S, R, T, C). You can choose any three items. Yes, I know, I'm very generous.

How many different meals could you make? It really depends on what the rules are on forming a meal. If items can be ordered more than once (triple trifle!!) then it's quite easy to calculate: there are four possibilities for each of the three courses, so $4 \times 4 \times 4 = 64$ possible meals.

Let's change the rules slightly: this time, no repeat orders. You can have one order of each course at most. Now there are four possibilities for the first course, but only three for the second course and two options for the third course: $4 \times 3 \times 2 = 24$ possible meals. Let's have a look at them:

SRT	RST	TSR	CSR
SRC	RSC	TSC	CST
STR	RTS	TRS	CRS
STC	RTC	TRC	CRT
SCR	RCS	TCS	CTS
SCT	RCT	TCR	CTR

This is not ideal either though, because SRT and TRS are both in the list. Is Soup – Roast – Trifle a different meal from Trifle – Roast – Soup? If you think not then we need to remove the repetitions of SRT (underlined below):

SRT	<u>RST</u>	<u>TSR</u>	CSR
SRC	RSC	TSC	CST
<u>STR</u>	<u>RTS</u>	<u>TRS</u>	CRS
STC	RTC	TRC	CRT
SCR	RCS	TCS	CTS
SCT	RCT	TCR	CTR

Essentially we want to count SRT once, not six times, so we counted six times too many SRT meals. But we also counted six times too many SRC, STC and RTC meals. This means the overall count of 24 was six times too high: we should have counted four possible meals in total. In fact, these four meals may have been obvious from the start: simply leave out Soup, leave out Roast, leave out Trifle or leave out Cheese.

This last rule, where repetition is not allowed and the order matters, is called finding the number of <u>combinations</u>. The notation $^{n}C_{r}$ is often used for choosing r items from a possible n. So in our dinner example we found that $^{4}C_{3} = 4$ (there are four ways to choose three meals from four), but also that $^{4}C_{1} = 4$ (four ways to choose one meal from four; leaving out one item from four is identical to choosing three items from four).

5 December

Times are hard. We're all tightening our belts: the Christmas dinner I promised you is now down to two courses: the options are still Soup, Roast, Trifle and Cheese, but now you can choose only two courses out of the possible four, and still no repetition. What might you choose?

It turns out there are slightly more options here: if you start with Soup you could follow it by Roast, Trifle or Cheese; if you start with Roast you could follow it with Trifle or Cheese, which just leaves the final possibility of Trifle and Cheese (the option for true rebels).

SR   ST   SC   RT   RC   TC

We've now established that $^{4}C_{3} = 4$, $^{4}C_{2} = 6$ and $^{4}C_{1} = 4$. Once we have established $^{4}C_{4}$ and $^{4}C_{0}$ we have the full set, and clearly they are both 1: there is only one way of choosing everything, but similarly there is only one way to choose nothing.

6 December

Once more to the Christmas dinner table: I am taking away the cheese option; we will investigate all the possible meals that can be made from three possible courses (Soup, Roast, Trifle). It's all quite easy to calculate: there's still one way of having no meal, but three ways of having a stingy one-course meal (Soup, Roast or Trifle), three ways of having a two-course meal (*leave out* Soup, Roast or Trifle) and just one possible three-course meal. I'm going to collate this all into a table for ease (along with some more basic options that you may wish to think about yourself):

Available courses	0-course meals	1-course meals	2-course meals	3-course meals	4-course meals
1	1	1			
2	1	2	1		
3	1	3	3	1	
4	1	4	6	4	1

If we just take the numbers from the table and offset them in a convenient way, we get something that looks more like this:

```
                    1
                1       1
            1       2       1
        1       3       3       1
    1       4       6       4       1
  1     5      10      10      5       1
1     6     15      20     15       6      1
1   7     21      35     35      21      7      1
```

I've added a 1 at the very top (because there's one way of having a no-course meal from an empty menu...) and also some rows below. The easiest way to find numbers in any row is to add the two numbers to the left and right in the row above. For example, the 21s in the bottom row can both be found by adding the 15 and 6 in the row above. These values represent the 21 ways there are to have either a two-course lunch or a five-course banquet from seven course options.

This arrangement of numbers is known as *Pascal's triangle*, after the seventeenth-century French mathematician and philosopher Blaise Pascal. As is so often the case in mathematics though, evidence of discussion of these numbers and their properties can be found in various world cultures dating back at least a thousand years – long before Pascal.

7 December

Adding across the rows in Pascal's triangle gives an interesting outcome: the first row adds to 1, the second row 2, followed by 4, 8, 16, 32 and so on.

If we think in terms of our meal analogy, it's possible to see why this is so. Imagine there are three courses available to you: starter, main and dessert. When we add across the third row we are counting all the possible no-course, one-course, two-course and three-course meals. But another way of looking at the same problem is that each of the three courses can either be chosen or not chosen, like a light switch that is either on or off. So there must be $2^3 = 8$ ways to select a meal from three possible courses.

Starter	Main	Dessert	Total courses
No	No	No	0
Yes	No	No	1
No	Yes	No	1

Starter	Main	Dessert	Total courses
Yes	Yes	No	2
No	No	Yes	1
Yes	No	Yes	2
No	Yes	Yes	2
Yes	Yes	Yes	3

8 December

Blaise Pascal's name is associated with many things – Pascal's triangle, the standard unit for pressure, the lizard in Disney's *Tangled* – but his best-known contribution to philosophy is *Pascal's wager*, in which he uses his mathematical background to argue in favour of belief in God. If God doesn't exist but you spend your life believing in God, then you have made only a finite loss (wasting time going to church, buying Bibles, watching *Songs of Praise*, etc.) but if God exists and you don't believe in God then you could be missing out on the potentially infinite gain of eternity in Heaven.

Many would argue that if God really exists and is a truly superior being, they would reward good-hearted people regardless of whether they happened to believe in them. But this isn't a theology or philosophy book, so you'll have to make your own mind up.

9 December

Happy Hanukkah (somewhere around this date)! Hanukkah is always on the 25th day of Kislev in the Hebrew calendar, but **the Hebrew calendar is *lunisolar*, meaning that it is based on both the sun and**

the moon. A lunar month is about 29.5 days, and adding 12 of these together will land you well short of 365 days – more like 354.

Rather than add on another 11 or 12 days every year, the Hebrew calendar is adjusted by adding a 'leap month' every two or three years: in fact it happens on the 3rd, 6th, 8th, 11th, 14th, 17th and 19th years of every 19-year cycle. And you thought it was complicated keeping track of when leap years happen! The 'leap month' adjustment is made by adding an additional month after the month of Adar (around March time), called 'Adar II'. Great news if your birthday is in Adar – two birthdays for you!

Oh, and each year on the Hebrew calendar is deemed either 'deficient', 'regular' or 'complete': the lengths of Hebrew months are slightly tweaked depending on what kind of year it is, in order to have Hebrew months beginning with a new moon. The upshot of all of this is that Hanukkah can occur any time from 28 November to 27 December.

10 December

On the tenth day of Christmas my true love gave to me… oh, I've forgotten what the tenth day is. Is it lords a-leaping? That's a strange gift. Where would you put them all? And, lest we forget, you'll receive more than ten of them. You actually get ten of them every time that line comes round, which is on the tenth, eleventh and twelfth day. Good lord!

It begs the question: which gift would you receive the most of over the course of the 12 days of Christmas? You'll get a partridge in a pear tree every day, but you only ever get one, so that's not many. Similarly you get a whopping 12 drummers drumming on the 12th day of Christmas, but those are the only drummers you ever receive. Somewhere between must be the sweet spot that maximizes gifts. Time for a table!

Gift	Number received each time the lyric is sung	Times the lyric is sung	Total received
Partridge in a pear tree	1	12	$1 \times 12 = 12$
Turtle doves	2	11	$2 \times 11 = 22$
French hens	3	10	$3 \times 10 = 30$
Calling birds	4	9	$4 \times 9 = 36$
Gold rings	5	8	$5 \times 8 = 40$
Geese a-laying	6	7	$6 \times 7 = 42$
Swans a-swimming	7	6	$7 \times 6 = 42$
Maids a-milking	8	5	$8 \times 5 = 40$
Ladies dancing	9	4	$9 \times 4 = 36$
Lords a-leaping	10	3	$10 \times 3 = 30$
Pipers piping	11	2	$11 \times 2 = 22$
Drummers drumming	12	1	$12 \times 1 = 12$

It turns out that **in 'The Twelve Days of Christmas' song, swans a-swimming and geese a-laying are the most commonly received gifts**, with 42 of each received.

11 December

Add up all the gifts in the right-hand column of yesterday's table and you'll find the grand total of all gifts received over the 12 days of Christmas according to the song. Using the symmetry from top to bottom to save us a little bit of work, that's two lots of 12 + 22 + 30 + 36 + 40 + 42, which is 364: that's right – **in 'The Twelve Days of Christmas' song, there is one gift for every day of the year except Christmas**.

12 December

'The Twelve Days of Christmas' lyrics make an appearance in Pascal's triangle too, as long as you know where to look:

```
                1
              1   1
            1   2   1
          1   3   3   1
        1   4   6   4   1
      1   5  10  10   5   1
    1   6  15  20  15   6   1
  1   7  21  35  35  21   7   1
```

If you look at the first diagonal that isn't just a load of 1s, you'll see 1, 2, 3, ..., in other words the days of Christmas, the counting numbers. In the next column you have the triangle numbers – 1, 3, 6, 10, 15 – those are the total numbers of gifts received on each day of the song:

Day 1: 1 partridge
Day 2: 2 turtle doves + 1 partridge = 3
Day 3: 3 French hens + 2 turtle doves + 1 partridge = 6

Piles of gifts like this would literally look like triangles, as we saw back in March:

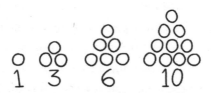

The next diagonal shows the <u>cumulative</u> running total of gifts received:

Day 1: 1 gift
Day 2: 3 new gifts + 1 from yesterday = 4
Day 3: 6 new gifts + 4 from yesterday = 10

The cumulative pile of gifts would look like a 3D stack of triangles on top of each other – these are called *tetrahedral numbers*:

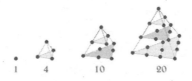

Sure enough, the 12th tetrahedral number is 364: this would represent a giant tetrahedral stack of all the gifts given in the song.

13 December

Since the second diagonal in Pascal's triangle represents a two-dimensional stack of counting numbers, and the third diagonal represents a 3D stack of 2D triangle numbers, it follows that the next diagonal must be... a four-dimensional stack of 3D tetrahedral numbers?! What on earth would that look like?

This sequence, 1, 5, 15, 35, ..., is known as the *pentatope* numbers, and admittedly it's pretty hard to find an everyday application for a 4D stack of 3D objects; what does a 'stack' even mean when we move into four dimensions? The pentatope numbers do have a use in biochemistry though: they represent the possible arrangements of polypeptide subunits in a tetrameric, or tetrahedral, protein. So there!

14 December

The *hockey stick identity* says that any diagonal line on Pascal's triangle, starting from a 1, always adds up to the next square below but in the opposite direction. See below: 1 + 6 + 21 + 56 = 84.

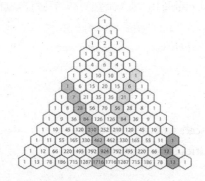

15 December

Colour the odd or even numbers in Pascal's triangle and we have another fascinating property:

Yup, it's the fractal Sierpinski triangle that we first saw in November!

16 December

In fact Pascal's triangle can be linked to a theme in almost any chapter in this book. What about the prime numbers from July, you say? Well on every prime row in Pascal's triangle – but only the prime rows – you will find that every entry in the row (except for 1) is divisible by the row number. So everything on row 5 (5, 10, 10, 5) is divisible by 5, every value in row 7 is divisible by 7 (7, 21, 35, 35, 21, 7). Row 7 also contains three numbers with equal gaps (7, 21, 35), which happens infinitely often but also *incredibly* rarely – the next one is (1001, 2002, 3003).

17 December

Read off from Pascal's triangle at a slightly different diagonal angle and something else curious happens:

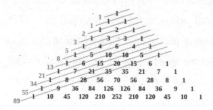

That's right, it's our old mates the Fibonacci numbers from June. I told you they got everywhere!

18 December

Christmas is a time for giving, and what better gift for the special person in your life than a Galton board, otherwise known as a bean machine or quincunx.*

This is a device that consists of a vertical board and interleaved pegs, so that when a ball drops in at the top it has a 50/50 chance of falling left or right every time it hits a peg. Balls are collected in pots at the

---

* As ridiculous as 'bean machine' and 'quincunx' sound, I still prefer these to using the name of Francis Galton, pioneer of eugenics.

bottom, and by repeatedly dropping balls in we can learn by experience the most likely final position for a ball to fall into. Of course there are far fewer ways that a ball might fall to the outer edges than to stay near the centre, so we would expect to see more balls collecting in the central area. In the long term, the heights of the resultant pots of balls approximate the *normal distribution*, the 'bell curve' shape of graph that is often found when collecting measured data such as height, weight, IQ scores or pumpkin sizes, as we did back on Hallowe'en:

19 December

Consider dropping a bead into a quincunx and tracing all of its possible routes through to the bottom. When the ball hits the first peg it can either go left or right, so there are two possible positions the ball can end up in. But when the ball hits the next peg, there are more ways that the ball can end up in the central position, as it could go left then right or right then left:

Position 1: 1 way Position 2: 2 ways Position 3: 1 way
Left Left   Left Right or   Right Right
                   Right Left

If we trace the path one more step further we can see that there's still just one way of ending up on the far right or left, but three ways of landing in one of the central positions:

Position 1:	Position 2:	Position 3:	Position 4:
1 way	3 ways	3 way	1 way
Left Left Left	Left Left Right or	Left Right Right or	Right Right Right
	Left Right Left or	Right Left Right or	
	Right Left Left	Right Right Left	

Have you seen where this is going yet? If you imagine a quincunx superimposed over Pascal's triangle, the triangle tells us how many routes there are for each ball to find its way to that position:

```
                1
              1   1
            1   2   1
          1   3   3   1
        1   4   6   4   1
      1   5  10  10   5   1
    1   6  15  20  15   6   1
  1   7  21  35  35  21   7   1
```

20 December

The *68–95–99.7 rule* states that, on a normal distribution, 68% of data will fall within one <u>standard deviation</u> of either side of the mean, 95% within two standard deviations and 99.7% within three standard deviations. The 95% bit is the most important and useful fact: essentially, **in a group of twenty people you should expect to find one person who is tall or short enough to be two standard deviations from the mean.**

It's always worth remembering that when a statistical test passes at the 95% significance level, it could be that there's no genuine significant statistical connection at all, but rather that you have encountered the one time in twenty that a connection was found by pure randomness.

21 December

Chebyshev's inequality states that for many probability distributions, not just the normal distribution, no more than a certain fraction of values can be more than a certain distance from the mean. Chebyshev also found a similar rule for the distribution of prime numbers, finding that, for any n, there will always be a prime number between n and $2n$. Say $n = 5$, Chebyshev said there's at least one prime between 5 and 10, and indeed there is: 7. There's even a rhyme for remembering this:

Chebyshev said, and I'll say it again,
There's always a prime between n and 2n

22 December

It's pretty well hidden, but our old mate 'e' can be found in Pascal's triangle too (a reminder for chapter-skippers that e is an omnipresent mathematical constant that's approximately 2.7). Take any row and multiply together all of its terms, then square your answer. Then do the same for the rows above and below, and multiply your two answers together.

```
                    1
                 1     1
              1     2     1
           1     3     3     1
        1     4     6     4     1
     1     5    10    10     5     1
  1     6    15    20    15     6     1
1     7    21    35    35    21     7     1
```

4th row: $1 \times 4 \times 6 \times 4 \times 1 = 96$
5th row: $1 \times 5 \times 10 \times 10 \times 5 \times 1 = 2500$
6th row: $1 \times 6 \times 15 \times 20 \times 15 \times 6 \times 1 = 162{,}000$

Now $2500^2 = 6{,}250{,}000$, and $96 \times 162{,}000 = 15{,}552{,}000$. Divide the latter by the former and you'll get a rough approximation to e, in this case 2.49. But the lower down the table you go, the closer to e you'll get: one row lower down the calculation would be:

$$\frac{26{,}471{,}025 \times 2500}{162{,}000 \times 162{,}000} = 2.52$$

It's a pretty slow convergence compared to some of the other methods we've seen earlier, but it gets there.

23 December

As if Pascal's triangle wasn't Christmassy enough, here's the *Star of David theorem*: draw two triangles around any value in the following way, and the products of the three values on each triangle will be the same:

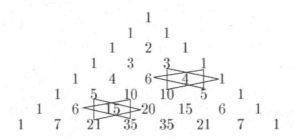

$3 \times 1 \times 10 = 1 \times 6 \times 5 = 30$
$5 \times 20 \times 21 = 10 \times 6 \times 35 = 2100$

24 December

One of the great challenges of Christmas is how long to roast the turkey for. Making this horribly dry and tasteless meat somewhere near edible is apparently a crucial component of a successful Christmas Day, and everyone seems to have their own advice on the best formula for success. The BBC's Good Food website suggests: 'roast for 40 mins per 1 kg for the first 4 kg, then 45 mins for every 1 kg over that weight, or until the internal temperature reaches 65–70 °C.'

Of course scientists have attempted to answer the question too, and the late Stanford University physicist Wolfgang Panofsky used the laws of heat conduction to come up with the following formula:

$$t = 1.13W^{\frac{2}{3}}$$

where t is the cooking time in hours and W is the weight of the turkey in kilograms. In terms of physics, this formula does of course assume that the turkey is perfectly spherical.*

If you asked me, I would say: have a nut roast, save on stress and save the turkey.

25 December

Merry Christmas! Some mathematical Christmas cracker jokes for your enjoyment:

Q: *What did zero say to eight?*
A: *Nice belt!*
Q: *How does a farmer count cows?*
A: *With a cow-culator!*
Q: *Who is the king of fractions?*
A: *Henry the $\frac{1}{8}$th!*

---

* If you were wondering, a 4.63 kg turkey is the weight at which Professor Panofsky and BBC Good Food are in agreement.

26 December

If you're feeling a little worse for wear after a heavy day of food and drink yesterday, spare a thought for Santa. Although households are divided on exactly what treat Santa should be left – for some it's milk and cookies, for others it's mince pies and a glass of brandy – with around 2 billion people worldwide celebrating Christmas that's a fair amount to put away.

Of course not every one of those 2 billion people puts out their own plate: most people live together as families. So let's assume each plate of snacks covers a family of four, meaning 500 million trays to get through. If half the people leave milk and the other half brandy, that means about 250 million shots of brandy and the same number of glasses of milk.

Let's say a glass of milk is 250 ml – about half a pint – that would mean Santa is drinking about 60 million litres of milk across the night. Defra states that an average dairy cow produces about 6,500 litres of milk per year, which means Santa is consuming the combined yearly yield of 10,000 dairy cows in one evening.

As for the brandy, if people leave Santa just a single shot – 25 ml – that would mean Santa is additionally downing 6 million litres of brandy on top of all that milk. That's 6 billion ml, and a millilitre of liquid takes up 1 cm^3, so 6 billion cm^3 of brandy, or 6000 m^3. For context, an Olympic swimming pool is 50 m $\times$ 25 m $\times$ 2 m, giving a capacity of 2500 m^3. You really should be grateful that those presents got to you in one piece.

27 December

The *Christmas Price Index* is worked out yearly by the American financial services company PNC. It is calculated based on the rising cost of obtaining all the gifts in the 'Twelve Days of Christmas' song. (Actually it's the cost of all the gifts that would be received on day 12, i.e. one partridge in a pear tree through to twelve drummers drumming, not the entire 364 gifts.)

Here's what the rising cost looks like over the last forty years or so:

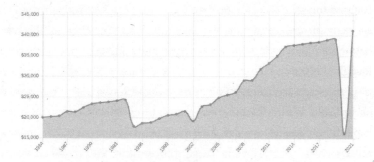

What happened in 2020? Well, there was a worldwide pandemic and anyone in the entertainment industry (leaping lords, drumming drummers, dancing ladies) could not perform and therefore could not be booked as a gift.

28 December

The United Kingdom has long been obsessed with the idea of 'Christmas Number One', that is, the last song before Christmas Day to top the weekly Top 40 singles chart. This is a festive tradition as well embedded as arguing with your family, burning the Christmas dinner and someone dying on *EastEnders*. There's only one problem: **there hasn't been a Christmas Number One that is actually about Christmas, and not a cover version, since 1990.**

Perennial Christmas chart-botherer and UK pop institution Cliff Richard took the accolade that year, with 'Saviour's Day', but since then the only instance of a Christmas-themed chart-topper was 'Do They Know It's Christmas?' by the collaborative act Band Aid 20, a song that had already topped the chart in previous guises in 1984 and 1989. Some near-misses in the intervening years include Mariah Carey's bona fide classic 'All I Want for Christmas is You' and The Darkness's pun-tastic 'Christmas Time (Don't Let the Bells End)', both of which fell short at number two.

29 December

As long as the music charts have existed there have been devious and nefarious methods of inflating a song's performance. From the 'payola' days of record labels bribing radio stations to play their latest releases, to record company workers driving round record shops buying up bootfuls of their own latest releases, right through to the popular 1990s practice of releasing a new single on multiple formats,* there has always

---

* This is apparently how Blur defeated Oasis in the legendary 'Battle of Britpop' in 1995, though you must also consider the fact that Blur were good and Oasis were rubbish.

been a way to game the system in your favour if you have the money and know-how to do it.

Since the charts have been rejigged to account for the inclusion of streaming, this has only become more weird. **The last British number one single of the 2010s was Ellie Goulding's cover of 'River' by Joni Mitchell, which topped the charts despite having almost zero promotion and being available on only two platforms: YouTube and Amazon Music**, both of which lag behind Spotify in terms of number of UK users. So how did a song that most people didn't even know existed manage to get to the top spot?

The song was an 'Amazon exclusive', so it was inserted into most of Amazon's most popular Christmas playlists (the song has a very loose festive connection). In the week when thousands of people around the country were asking their Alexa to 'play Christmas music', they would have been subjected to the song – quite possibly without even realizing it. More interestingly though, the song would have been the newest song on the playlist, meaning it benefited from a quirk in the algorithm behind the singles chart. Something called 'accelerated decline' is used to dampen the inevitable popularity of older songs and promote newer songs to higher positions, presumably for the purpose of keeping the chart fresh and stopping the same old songs from repeatedly topping the chart.* In the week of Goulding's success she achieved fewer plays than a host of other festive favourites by acts such as Mariah Carey, The Pogues and Wham!, but defeated them simply by being newer.

---

* The accelerated decline algorithm has been tweaked since, as a result of Kate Bush failing to dislodge Harry Styles from number one after the *Stranger Things* effect upon the renewed popularity of 'Running up that Hill'. Eventually the UK Chart company relented and Kate ran all the way up the hill to the top spot.

30 December

Born in 1940, Oliver R. Smoot spent his working lifetime as a lawyer, chairman of the American National Standards Institute (ANSI) and, later, president of the International Organization for Standardization. But his real claim to fame is having one of the most ridiculous units of measurement named after him.

In October 1958, as part of a university prank, Smoot lay down repeatedly on the Harvard Bridge between Boston and Cambridge, Massachusetts, so that it could be discovered how many of his length would be required to measure the whole bridge. He eventually became so tired of this process that his fraternity brothers had to pick him up and carry him from position to position.

The absurd story eventually broke into folklore, with the bridge now adorned with lovingly made markers at the 100, 200 and 300 smoot marks, and a commemorative plaque. **It turns out that the Harvard Bridge's length is 364.4 smoots**; a wonderful fact for the 364th day of the year. (A single smoot is exactly 5 ft 7 in, by the way.)

31 December

If the history of Earth, from its formation to the present day, were scaled down to one year, humans evolved somewhere around midday on 31 December. Recognizable *homo sapiens* wouldn't have been here until about half an hour before midnight. We have literally been here for half an hour and look what we've done to the place. The most primitive life forms took until around March to get going, but sexual reproduction was off the menu until around October. Dinosaurs, like George Michael, became extinct on Christmas Day.

In the Oscar-winning film *Birdman*, Emma Stone's character carries around a single sheet of toilet paper to remind her that, if the whole roll represented the history of Earth, the entirety of human existence would be contained within the final sheet. And yet when my daughter carries toilet roll around the house, we are told by the health visitor that it's unsanitary and inappropriate. It seems it's one rule for Emma Stone and another for the rest of us. Happy New Year!

AFTERWORD

What a year that was, huh? I can't believe humans finally made it to Mars, or that Elon Musk accidentally got left there. I can assure you that I was as surprised as you were that Prince Harry won *Strictly Come Dancing* though.

I'd like to congratulate the readers who made it to the end, regardless of which of these categories you fall into:

- Keen beans: maintain a strict reading rate of one entry per day, never reading ahead or getting behind, even if it means taking the book on holidays or business trips.
- Perpetual resolution breakers: start the year by intending to read an entry a day, but lose motivation somewhere in mid-January so that they become experts in the first half-chapter that they repeatedly read every year.
- Better-late-than-nevers: start the year off well, but then get distracted around March and have to smash through the last nine months of entries in December to hit the end of year deadline.

- Oddballs: just read it like a normal book with no regard to the dated entries, so that they're reading a whole lot of Christmas-themed entries somewhere in the spring.

I hope this veritable smörgåsbord of numerical nuggets has given you intellectual stimulation to last a lifetime, but I can assure you that the contents of this book merely scratch the surface of mind-melting maths out there. If you have managed to eke this book out over the whole year, I imagine you may well have forgotten everything from January and be ready to go round again. I highly encourage it – you don't even need to pay me again – just promise me one thing: go out and spread these little factoids into the world. Passing on knowledge is one of the kindest things you can do in this life, whether you're five or 105.

FURTHER NOTES

27 January

HEAD – HEAL – TEAL – TELL – TALL – TAIL. There may be other ways.

26 June

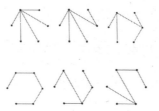

27 June

I'm going to work 'backwards', starting from the decimal expansion and hoping to end up at $\frac{1}{89}$. Let S be the sum of all Fibonacci numbers over successive powers of ten:

$$S = \frac{0}{10} + \frac{1}{100} + \frac{1}{1000} + \frac{2}{10,000} + \frac{3}{100,000} + \frac{5}{1,000,000} + \ldots \quad (1)$$

Now remove the $\frac{0}{10}$ term (0) and multiply everything by 100:

$$100S = 1 + \frac{1}{10} + \frac{2}{100} + \frac{3}{1000} + \frac{5}{10,000} + \ldots \quad\quad\quad (2)$$

Subtract (1) from (2):

$$100S - S = 1 + \frac{1}{10} + \frac{1}{100} + \frac{2}{1000} + \frac{3}{10,000} + \ldots$$

Subtract 1 from each side, tidy up and note the familiar Fibonacci numbers on top of the fractions. Pulling out a factor of 10 on the right-hand side gives:

$$99S - 1 = 10 \left(\frac{1}{100} + \frac{1}{1000} + \frac{2}{10,000} + \frac{3}{100,000} + \ldots \right)$$

The part in the brackets is our S from earlier, so:

$$99S - 1 = 10S$$
$$89S - 1 = 0$$
$$89S = 1$$
$$S = \tfrac{1}{89}$$

12 July

Every edge in a network must run from a node to another node, so it contributes 1 to the order of each node (the order of a node is simply how many edges meet there). For this reason, the combined order of all nodes put together must be a multiple of 2 – in other words, an even number. If the combined order is always even, then it's impossible to have just one odd node; every odd node must be accompanied by another odd node that 'levels it off' and keeps the total even. So odd nodes always come in pairs.

17 July

On 4 July we established that every prime number larger than 3 is 1 more or 1 less than a multiple of 6, so we can write every prime more than 3 in the form $6n + 1$ or $6n - 1$. Square these forms and you get two fairly similar results:

$$(6n + 1)^2 = 36n^2 + 12n + 1$$
$$(6n - 1)^2 = 36n^2 - 12n + 1$$

We're trying to show that subtracting 1 from either of these always gives a multiple of 24. Subtracting the 1 on the right-hand side of each of these gives $36n^2 + 12n$ or $36n^2 - 12n$, which can be written as (factorized as) $12n(3n + 1)$ or $12n(3n - 1)$. It's fairly clear that both of these will be multiples of 12, but we can do a bit better than that: $n(3n + 1)$ and $n(3n - 1)$ are both always even, because regardless of whether you input an odd or an even n, you always get an even output.

So both $12n(3n + 1)$ and $12n(3n - 1)$ are always even multiples of 12: in other words, multiples of 24.

11 September

Diophantus's youth lasts $\frac{1}{6}$ of his life; he grows a beard after another $\frac{1}{12}$ of his life; he marries after another $\frac{1}{7}$; five years later he has a son; the son lives for half of the eventual life of the father; Diophantus dies four years after his son. All of this can be put together into an equation:

$$D = \tfrac{1}{6} D + \tfrac{1}{12} D + \tfrac{1}{7} D + 5 + \tfrac{1}{2} D + 4$$

At this stage let's multiply everything by 84 to clear out all the fractions:

$$84\,D = 14\,D + 7\,D + 12\,D + 420 + 42\,D + 336$$

Tidying up, we have:

$$9\,D = 756$$
$$D = 84$$

Diophantus lived to 84. A more canny way of solving the problem might be to note that Diophantus's age of death must be divisible by 6, 12 and 7, so 84 is the only reasonable candidate.

17 September

This is much harder than you'd think to calculate. It's easy enough to first consider all of the possible runs of four coin flips, for which there are two which meet our requirement of four heads or tails in a row (underlined below):

<u>HHHH</u>	HTHH	**THHH**	TTHH
HHHT	HTHT	THHT	TTHT
HHTH	HTTH	THTH	TTTH
HHTT	**HTTT**	THTT	<u>TTTT</u>

When we move up to five flips, the two underlined runs each have a half chance of maintaining the 'at least four in a row' property, but the two bold runs above now also have a half chance of getting there in the next flip. As we add more flips it gets harder and harder to tally the successful runs, so a space-efficient way forward is for me to show you a *matrix*. Will you take the red pill?

$$\begin{bmatrix} \frac{1}{2} & \frac{1}{2} & \frac{1}{2} & 0 \\ \frac{1}{2} & 0 & 0 & 0 \\ 0 & \frac{1}{2} & 0 & 0 \\ 0 & 0 & \frac{1}{2} & 0 \end{bmatrix}^{9} \cdot \begin{bmatrix} 1 \\ 0 \\ 0 \\ 0 \end{bmatrix}$$

This is a transition matrix, and it gives the result [0.291016, 0.158203, 0.0859375, 0.464844]. If you've had n coins in a row and you flip the next one, half the time you'll now have $n + 1$ in a row, half the time you'll go back to 1 in a row. That's what the first three columns say. When you get to 4, you stay there (you've won), which is what the fourth column says. You start from 1 after the first flip (that's the (1, 0, 0, 0)), then go through this matrix nine times, and out pops your probability of being at score 1, 2, 3 or 4. So the probability of reaching four in a row at any stage is about 46%. I'd like to thank the brilliant Colin Beveridge for teaching me this.

12 October

We're trying to show that the infinite series $1 + \frac{1}{2} + \frac{1}{3} + \dots$ is convergent, not divergent, if you skip over all terms with a zero in the denominator. First note that there are nine terms with just a single digit in the denominator, from 1 to $\frac{1}{9}$. All of these terms are less than or equal to 1, so their sum is less than 9.

Next consider all the terms with a two-digit denominator. There are 81 of these (denominators from 10 to 99 but removing the 10, 20, 30, etc.), and each one is less than $\frac{1}{10}$. So their sum is less than $\frac{81}{10}$, or $\frac{9^2}{10}$. Continue this process that we've started and we'll find that the infinite sum we're looking for is less than:

$$9 + \frac{9^2}{10} + \frac{9^3}{100} + \dots$$

This is a *geometric* series with first term 9 and a *common ratio* of $\frac{9}{10}$ (each term is multiplied by this to find the next term), which converges to 90. So the sum of the series that we are considering is something less than 90; actually it converges to a much smaller sum of 23.1-ish, but that's a story for another day. Either way, it's convergent.

12 November

When the first set of new triangles are added, we add three triangles that are each one ninth of the area of the original triangle; they are a ninth of the original area because they are mathematically similar to the original triangle but have a base that's one third of the original, and making a shape one third as wide and one third as tall gives it one ninth of the area.

The next set of triangles we add are 12 in number and are one ninth of the previous triangle area, which means they're $\frac{1}{81}$ of the area of the original triangle. The third iteration of triangles are again one ninth of the previous triangle area, but this time there are 48 of them. Essentially we have a geometric series that looks like this:

$$3\left(\frac{1}{9}\right) + 12\left(\frac{1}{9^2}\right) + 48\left(\frac{1}{9^3}\right) + \ldots$$

This geometric series has first term $\frac{1}{3}$ and a common ratio of $\frac{4}{9}$, meaning its sum converges to $\frac{3}{5}$. In other words, all of the additional added triangles will add up to no more than three fifths of the original triangle.

17 November

To best understand why a Kaprekar sequence converges as it does, I recommend doing some calculations by hand. If you do, you will notice that you always have to 'carry' in the units and tens columns, and possibly in the hundreds columns, but definitely not in the thousands column. We can say this for certain because the numbers are arranged into ascending and descending order, so in the units column you'll always be subtracting larger from smaller, in the tens column you'll always be subtracting larger from smaller (the numbers in the tens column could have started the same but the top number will always have had one 'borrowed' from it) and in the hundreds column you'll usually be subtracting smaller from larger (the number in the top of the hundreds column will almost always be larger than the other number in the hundreds column, unless they started the same and the top number was a similar casualty of borrowing). Phew! Let's consider a totally general number made up of the digits a, b, c, d, where $a \geq b \geq c \geq d$, and a, b, c, d are all between 0 and 9 inclusive. Then we'll subtract $dcba$ from $abcd$, as follows:

$$\begin{array}{r} abcd \\ - \ dcba \\ \hline wxyz \end{array}$$

I've called the result $wxyz$. Now it must be true that $z = d - a + 10$ (we can't subtract a from d because a is greater than d, so we have to 'borrow' ten from the previous columns). Following similar (if trickier!) logical deduction we can reach the following set of equations:

$z = d - a + 10$ (see above)

$y = (c - 1) - b + 10 = c - b + 9$ (because some borrowing has definitely happened)

$x = b - 1 - c$ or 9   ($b - 1 - c$ in most cases, 9 only if b and c were initially the same)

$$w = a - d \text{ or } a - d - 1 \qquad (a - d \text{ in most cases, } a - d - 1 \text{ only if } b$$
$$\text{and } c \text{ were the same})$$

The number *wxyz* needs to consist of the same original four digits of *abcd*, perhaps in a different order. If we consider all the possible orderings of *a*, *b*, *c*, *d*, of which there are 24, and run them through simultaneous equations above, we find only one set of integers that satisfies all four equations: 7641 which deforms to 6174. Since this is the only four-digit number that is 'stable', and every other four-digit number remains a four-digit number under Kaprekar's operation (subtraction could never make the result longer), if we ever reach convergence it must be at 6174.

21 November

We showed that $1 - 1 + 1 - 1 + \dots = \frac{1}{2}$, so let's stick with that definition for the sum *A*. Next we're going to calculate the sum $1 - 2 + 3 - 4 + \dots$, which we call *B*. Constructing $A - B$ gives the following:

$$(1 - 1 + 1 - 1 + \dots) - (1 - 2 + 3 - 4 + \dots)$$

Collecting pairs of terms from each of the brackets gives:

$$(1 - 1) + (-1 + 2) + (1 - 3) + (-1 + 4) + \dots$$

which simplifies to:

$$0 + 1 + 2 + 3 - \dots$$

which we just defined as B.

So $A - B = B$

$\frac{1}{2} - B = B$

$\frac{1}{2} = 2B$

$\frac{1}{4} = B$

We're now ready to tackle $1 + 2 + 3 + 4 + \ldots$, which I will call C. This time we'll start with $B - C$, which gives us the following:

$(1 - 2 + 3 - 4 + \ldots) - (1 + 2 + 3 + 4 + \ldots)$

Again, pair across the brackets:

$(1 - 1) + (-2 - 2) + (3 - 3) + (-4 - 4) + \ldots$

Simplifying gives:

$0 + (-4) + 0 + (-8) + \ldots$

One last bit of simplification:

$-4(1 + 2 + \ldots)$

in other words, 4 lots of C.

So $B - C = -4C$

$\frac{1}{4} - C = -4C$

$\frac{1}{4} = -3C$

$-\frac{1}{12} = C$

It appears that the sum of all the natural numbers is not infinity, but rather a negative fractional amount, namely $-\frac{1}{12}$. It seems there is definitely some jiggery-pokery going on here, but apparently this result – known as the *Ramanujan* summation after the same legendary Indian mathematician we met back in August – actually is useful in something called Bosonic string theory.

GLOSSARY

Area – the part of a two-dimensional shape that is enclosed within a border.

Billion – a thousand million: 1,000,000,000.

Binary – related to counting in base 2, using only the **digits** 0 and 1.

Cardinality – the size of a **set**, in other words the number of elements in the set.

Circumference – the boundary length, or **perimeter**, of a circle.

Combination – a selection of objects from a **set**, without regard to order. For example, if choosing three letters from the alphabet, GOD and DOG would not be different combinations.

Complete graph – a **graph** where exactly one **edge** joins every **vertex** to every other vertex.

Completist – a person who reads a book from cover to cover, including the acknowledgements and the full glossary from start to end.

Composite number – a number that is not **prime**, that is, it has a **factor** other than itself and 1. For example, 15 is composite, because it is **divisible** by 3 and 5, as well as by 1 and 15.

Conjecture – a statement which is believed to be true, though no proof or disproof has yet been found.

Convergent – the property of a **sequence** in which the terms tend towards a limit, or the property of a **series** in which the **sum** of terms tends to a limit. For example, the halving sequence 20, 10, 5, … has terms which tend to zero in the long term, but a sum that tends to 40 in the long term.

Counting numbers – literally the numbers we use for counting; the positive **integers**: 1, 2, 3, 4, …

Cube – to multiply a number by itself, and then by itself again. 'Two cubed' = $2^3 = 2 \times 2 \times 2 = 8$.

Cube number – a number that is the **cube** of a positive **integer**: 1, 8, 27, 64, …

Cumulative – increasing by successive addition.

Cylinder – a three-dimensional solid with straight parallel sides and two circular **faces**, for example a soup can.

Data – the information, usually numerical, gained from an experiment, survey, etc. Data is the plural of *datum* but is often used in the singular.

Decimal – anything related to using **powers** of 10 or base 10.

Diameter – a straight line from one side of a circle to the other, through the centre. The diameter is twice the **radius**.

Digit – any of the ten Arabic numerals used in the decimal system: 0–9.

Divergent – a **sequence** or **series** that is not **convergent**. For example, the doubling sequence 1, 2, 4, … does not have terms that tend to some limit in the long term, nor a sum that tends to a limit in the long term.

Divisible – capable of being divided exactly by another stated number.

e (Euler's number) – a constant that is approximately 2.71, with a wide range of mathematical applications. It is the limit of the function $(1 + \frac{1}{n})^n$ as n tends to infinity.

Edge – a line along which two **faces** of a three-dimensional solid meet; part of a 3D solid that you could run your finger along. A dice has 12 edges.

Equation – a formula, usually solvable, that asserts that two expressions are equal in value.

Equilateral triangle – a triangle with three sides of equal length. This means the three angles will also be of equal size: 60°.

Exponential growth – an increase in the value of a quantity over time, where the rate of growth is proportional to the value of the quantity, rather than being proportional to the time elapsed.

Face (of solid) – a flat surface of a three-dimensional solid, bounded by **edges**. A dice has 6 faces.

Factor – a number (or algebraic expression) that equally divides another number (or algebraic expression). For example, 3 is a factor of 12.

Factorial – an operation that involves multiplying a positive **integer** by every smaller positive integer. For example, $5! = 5 \times 4 \times 3 \times 2 \times 1 = 120$.

Fibonacci sequence – a **sequence** that begins with two 1s (or sometimes a 0 and 1) and where each subsequent term is formed by adding the two previous terms: 1, 1, 2, 3, 5, …

Fractal – a shape or geometrical figure with self-similarity.

Golden ratio – see **phi**.

Gradient – the slope or steepness of a line; it is the **ratio** of the vertical change in height to the horizontal change in length.

Graph – usually a diagram that shows the relationship between two variables such as x and y (for example, the *graph* of $y = 3x$), but also a diagram that shows **vertices** and their connecting **edges** (in *graph theory*).

Highest common factor (abbreviated to hcf) – sometimes known as the *greatest common divisor* (abbreviated to gcd), it is the largest **integer** that is a **factor** of two other chosen integers. For example, 6 is the highest common factor of 12 and 18.

Index – a number, written as superscript, that indicates the **power** that a number is being raised to. For example, in the expression 2^3, '3' is the index. Also known as *exponent*.

Integer – a whole number, either positive or negative and including zero.

Light-year – the distance that light travels in one year: about 9.46 trillion kilometres.

Logarithm – the **power** to which a base (or number) must be raised to reach a required number. For example, if working in base 10, the logarithm of 100 is 2 (because $100 = 10^2$).

Mean average – this is what we usually mean by the word 'average' alone: the result of adding some **data** values and dividing by the number of values. For example, the mean average of 2, 3 and 10 is $(2 + 3 + 10)/3 = 5$. Also known as the *arithmetic mean*.

Median – the middle piece of **data** (or average of the two middle pieces of data) in an ordered list of data. For example, in the data 0, 1, 2, 2, 4, 5, 7, 9, 10, the median is 4.

Million – a thousand thousand: 1,000,000.

Millisecond – one thousandth of a second: 0.001 seconds.

Mode – the most common **data** value in a set of data. For example, in the data 0, 1, 2, 2, 4, 5, 7, 9, 10, the mode is 2.

Multiple – a number that would appear in the times table of another number (not necessarily an integer). For example, 12 is a multiple of 3, and 5 is a multiple of 2.5.

Negative number – any number less than zero.

Node – in graph theory, another word for a **vertex**. A point at which edges meet.

Normal distribution – a 'bell-shaped' statistical distribution, which has a symmetrical shape with the **mean**, **median** and **mode** all occurring at the same point.

Numeral – a symbol representing a number, a single **digit**.

Paradox – an apparently absurd or self-contradictory statement.

Perimeter – a line or curve enclosing a region or surface, or the length of such a line.

Permutation – an ordered arrangement of values from a **set**. For example, if choosing three letters from the alphabet, GOD and DOG are different permutations.

Phi (φ) – a constant that is approximately 1.62 and is referred to as the golden ratio; it appears in many natural contexts and has a wide range of mathematical applications. In exact form, it is $\frac{1+\sqrt{5}}{2}$.

Pi (π) – a constant that is approximately 3.14, with a wide range of mathematical applications. It is the **circumference** of a circle divided by the **diameter**.

Power – the number of times a number is multiplied by itself in a given operation. For example, 'three to the power of four' = 3^4 = 3 × 3 × 3 × 3 = 81.

Prime / prime number – a number with exactly two **factors**: itself and 1. For example, prime numbers include 3, 5, 7, 11, 13. A number such as 15 is not a prime number as its factors are 1, 3, 5 and 15; 1 is also not a prime number, because it only has one factor: itself.

Probability – a measure of how likely an event is to occur, given on a scale from 0 (impossible) to 1 (certain).

Product – the result of multiplying two or more numbers. The product of 3 and 5 is 15.

Quadrillion – a thousand trillion: 1,000,000,000,000,000.

Radius – the distance from the edge of a circle to the centre. The radius is half of the **diameter**.

Random – having a value that is not pre-determined before the choice is made, and with previous choices having no influence on the choice.

Ratio – the amount of one quantity in proportion to another, often found by dividing one quantity by another. For example, the ratio of women to men in the band Fleetwood Mac is 2:3, or 1:1.5.

Reciprocal – the reciprocal of a number is 1 divided by that number, so the reciprocal of 5 is $\frac{1}{5}$, the reciprocal of 0.5 ($\frac{1}{2}$) is 2, etc.

Sequence – an ordered set of objects, usually numbers, where every value is determined by a given rule.

Series – the sum of values in a **sequence**, usually starting from the first term.

Set – a collection of numbers or objects, either finite or infinite.

Sexagesimal – related to counting in base 60, as originated by the Sumerians.

Significance level – The likelihood, in a statistical test, of a notable outcome occurring by pure chance. More formally, it's the probability of rejecting a null hypothesis, given that it is true.

Sphere – a three-dimensional solid where every point on the surface is equidistant to the centre: in other words, a ball.

Square – to square a number is to multiply it by itself: 'three squared' $= 3^2 = 9$.

Square number – a number that is the **square** of a positive **integer**: 1, 4, 9, 16, …

Standard deviation – a measure of the dispersion of data in a set. A small standard deviation means that data is packed very close to the **mean**; a large standard deviation means that data is very spread out.

Sum – the result of adding two or more numbers or quantities.

Symmetry (reflective) – a type of symmetry in which a shape can be reflected in a line and be mapped exactly to its current shape. For example, a capital letter 'E' has reflective symmetry about a horizontal line through its centre, a letter 'A' has reflective symmetry in a vertical line through its centre.

Symmetry (rotational) – a type of symmetry in which a shape can be rotated by less than 360° and look identical to its starting position. A capital letter 'H' has rotational symmetry of order 2, because there are two times in a full 360° rotation that it looks the same, at a turn of 180° and 360°.

Ternary – related to counting in base 3, using only the digits 0, 1 and 2.

Theorem – a proposed statement that has been proved by a chain of reasoning.

Triangle number – or 'triangular number'; a number that can be made with a triangle of dots; the **sequence** that is formed by starting with 1 and then adding 1 more each time: 1, 3, 6, 10, …

Trillion – a thousand billion: 1,000,000,000,000.

Vertex (plural vertices) – a point where **edges** meet, either on a three-dimensional solid or in a **graph**.

PICTURE CREDITS

teaching | **17 April** – 'Platonic Solids Composition' by David Eric Ffell, licensed under CC BY-SA 4.0 | **19 April** – 'Bandobuocphaidung4mau' by Ntmyhue, licensed under CC BY-SA 3.0 | **21 April** – Peter Lynch, thatsmaths.com | **12 May** – Coxcomb diagram by Florence Nightingale, Public Domain | **18 May** – 'Sphere and circumscribed cylinder' by Emchap4, licensed under CC BY-SA 4.0 | **19 May** – 'ReuleauxTriangle' by Geoff Richards (Qef), Public Domain | **20 May** – Gomboc.eu | **25 May** – Everest photograph by Nirmal Purja | **4 June** – 'Fibonacci lapins 2' by Fschwarzentruber, licensed under CC BY-SA 4.0 | **7 June** – 'SimilarGoldenRectangles' by Ahecht (Original); Pbroks13 (Derivative work), Public Domain | **9 June** – 'Fibonacci Spiral' by Romain, licensed under CC BY-SA 4.0; 'Logarithmic sprial' by Leafnode, Public Domain | **11 June** – 'Gradient sign (imperial) near Downhill' from geograph. org.uk by Albert Bridge, licensed under CC BY-SA 2.0; 'The Struggle Road Sign Bottom' by Pontificalibus, licensed under CC BY-SA 3.0; 'Street sign for Fford Pen Llech' by Jonathan Deamer, licensed under CC BY-SA 4.0 | **21 June** – 'Topology joke' by Keenan Crane and Henry Segerman, licensed under CC BY-SA 3.0 | **2 July** – Still from 'Sieve of Eratosthenes animation' by SKopp, licensed under CC BY-SA 3.0 | **13 July** – 'The problem of the Seven Bridges of Königsberg' by Bogdan Giuşcă, licensed under CC BY-SA 3.0 | **26 July** – 'Ulam-Spirale2', author unknown, licensed under CC BY-SA 3.0 | **4 August** – '4-set Venn diagram in blue with transparent background' by Amousey, Public Domain; '4-way-venn vector' by MidgleyDJ, licensed under CC BY-SA 3.0 | **25 August** – 'Simple pendulum', author unknown, licensed under CC BY-SA 3.0 | **1 September** – 'Prayer hands' by retepwal, licensed under CC BY-SA 3.0 | **16 September** – 'Maze01-01', author unknown, licensed under CC BY-SA 3.0 | **26 September** – 'Anscombe. svg' by Schutz, adapted from Anscombe, Francis J. (1973) Graphs in statistical analysis. American Statistician, 27, 17–21, licensed under

ACKNOWLEDGEMENTS

Writing this book was a colossal exercise in recalling things I had once seen but had only half-remembered. Conversations with my colleagues and brilliant students at Barton Peveril Sixth Form College helped a lot, as did social media or real-life contributions from all of the following: David Bedford, Peter Lynch, Simon Young, Jens Kruse Andersen, Jack West, John Dykes, Kevin Houston, Johann Windt, Paul Harrison, Andy Oldman, Colin Wright, Kjartan Poskitt, Zoe Griffiths, Christian Lawson-Perfect, Kit Yates, Martin Whitworth, David Butler, Matt Fletcher, Katie Mallinson, Chris Smith, Dan Rodriguez-Clark and Tom Briggs. Thank you all. Particular thanks to Colin Beveridge who showed me how to use a transition matrix to solve the four-heads-in-a-row problem, which bothered me for months.

Barry Dolan, Anneli Haimi and Tony Mann read my first draft and made invaluable suggestions – thank you to all three. Hana Ayoob did the wonderful original illustrations – I love her style and I suggest you seek out her other brilliant work.

The following books were particularly useful in jogging my memory at various points in the writing process. I recommend them all wholeheartedly:

A Compendium of Mathematical Methods – Jo Morgan

Four Colours Suffice: How the Map Problem was Solved – Robin Wilson

The Golden Ratio: The Mathematical Language of Beauty – Fernando Corbalán

Introducing Infinity: A Graphic Guide – Brian Clegg and Oliver Pugh

The Joy of x: A Guided Tour of Mathematics, from One to Infinity – Steven Strogatz

Mind-Blowing Maths: Packed with Amazing Facts! – Lisa Regan

Numericon: The Hidden Lives of Numbers – Marianne Freiberger and Rachel Thomas

The Penguin Dictionary of Curious and Interesting Numbers – David Wells

There are some maths writers and communicators whose work has been so influential on me that I daren't read or watch their work back when writing for the fear of copying it wholesale. They are Rob Eastaway, Alex Bellos, Matt Parker, Katie Steckles, James Grime, Simon Singh, Ben Sparks and Professor Ian Stewart. I suppose one could argue that we're all in debt to Martin Gardner, who was himself standing on the shoulders of other giants, but I'm very grateful to the giants upon whose shoulders I stand.

Speaking of giants, the most important thanks go to Jessamine, Edwin and Juno, who support me and are at my side every step of the way.

All of the below worked on the book in some way. I haven't met nearly all of them, but without their work you wouldn't hold this book in your hands. Please keep buying books, and keep supporting independent bookshops and publishers:

Ed Faulkner, Publisher; Kate Ballard, Senior Editor; Emma Heyworth-Dunn, Managing Editor; Mairi Sutherland, copy-editor; Ian Greensill, proofreader; Rich Carr, typesetter; Niccolò De Bianchi, Production Director; Richard Evans, Art Director; Kate Straker, Publicity Campaigns Director; Aimee Oliver-Powell, Senior Marketing Manager; Dave Woodhouse, Sales Director; Rachel Campbell, UK Key Account Manager; Isabel Bogod, Sales, Operations and Contracts Manager; Alice Latham, Rights Director.